"This book focuses on the most important cases and ma[...] of the Convention on Human Rights accessible to b[...] practical legal needs. The book includes cases that esta[...] or clarify the Court's existing case law. The cases are su[...] that the readers' attention is drawn to the essential points, allowing them to [...] on the jurisprudential significance of a particular case. Logical content and a dense use of titles and summaries at the end of the chapters help the reader to quickly find the relevant case law for any practical need, providing an easy-to-use, complete and up-to-date reference book."

Päivi Hirvelä, *Doctor of Laws, Supreme Court Justice and former Judge of the European Court of Human Rights in respect of Finland (2007–2015)*

Fair Trial Rules of Evidence

This book examines how the European Court of Human Rights approaches the matter of evidence, and how its judgments affect domestic law.

The case law of the Court has affected many areas of law in Europe. One of these areas is the law of evidence, and especially criminal evidence. This work examines the key defence rights that may touch upon evidence, such as the right to adduce evidence, the right to disclosure, the privilege against self-incrimination and access to a lawyer, entrapment, and the right to cross-examine prosecution witnesses. It explains the relevant assessment criteria used by the Court and introduces a simple framework for understanding the various assessment models developed by the Court, including "the *Perna* test", "the *Ibrahim* criteria", and "the sole or decisive rule".

The book provides a comprehensive overview on the relevant case law, and will be a valuable asset for students and researchers, as well as practitioners, such as judges, prosecutors, and lawyers, working in the areas of criminal procedure and human rights.

Jurkka Jämsä is a Junior Justice (asessori) in the Vaasa Court of Appeal, Finland.

Routledge Contemporary Issues in Criminal Justice and Procedure

Series Editor **Ed Johnston** is a Senior Lecturer in Law, Bristol Law School, University of the West of England (UWE), UK.

The Law of Disclosure
A Perennial Problem in Criminal Justice
Edited by Ed Johnston and Tom Smith

Challenges in Criminal Justice
Edited by Ed Johnston

Probation, Mental Health and Criminal Justice
Towards Equivalence
Edited by Charlie Brooker and Coral Sirdifield

In Defense of Juveniles Sentenced to Life
Legal Representation and Juvenile Criminal Justice
Stuti S. Kokkalera

Fair Trial Rules of Evidence
The Case Law of the European Court of Human Rights
Jurkka Jämsä

See more at https://www.routledge.com/Routledge-Research-in-Legal-History/book-series/CONTEMPCJP

Fair Trial Rules of Evidence

The Case Law of the European Court of
Human Rights

Jurkka Jämsä

Routledge
Taylor & Francis Group

LONDON AND NEW YORK

First published 2023
by Routledge
4 Park Square, Milton Park, Abingdon, Oxon OX14 4RN

and by Routledge
605 Third Avenue, New York, NY 10158

Routledge is an imprint of the Taylor & Francis Group, an informa business

© 2023 Jurkka Jämsä

The right of Jurkka Jämsä to be identified as author of this work has been asserted in accordance with sections 77 and 78 of the Copyright, Designs and Patents Act 1988.

Trademark notice: Product or corporate names may be trademarks or registered trademarks, and are used only for identification and explanation without intent to infringe.

British Library Cataloguing-in-Publication Data
A catalogue record for this book is available from the British Library

Library of Congress Cataloging-in-Publication Data
A catalog record has been requested for this book

ISBN: 978-1-032-31794-6 (hbk)
ISBN: 978-1-032-31798-4 (pbk)
ISBN: 978-1-003-31141-6 (ebk)

DOI: 10.4324/9781003311416

Typeset in Galliard
by Taylor & Francis Books

Contents

Preface and acknowledgments

This book is partly based on my doctoral dissertation published in 2021. One of the aims of that work was to examine the effects of the Finnish 2016 evidence law reform, which codified several assessment models developed in the case law of the European Court of Human Rights. Going through much of that case law and attempting to understand it kept me busy for several years. Originally, I became interested in admissibility questions because I found the "sole or decisive rule" difficult to grasp.

However, because my dissertation was published in Finnish, it can only reach a very limited audience. This book is intended to be a summary of my dissertation with a more practical and less scientific approach. It is my wish that this book would be useful to anyone who has encountered difficulties, perhaps similar to those I have experienced, in trying to understand the Court's approach to questions of evidence – not only researchers and academics of the field but practitioners as well.

I would like to begin the acknowledgments by mentioning those whose contribution to my thesis has been most significant for this work. I wish to thank my supervisors, Professor Emeritus Risto Koulu and Deputy Parliamentary Ombudsman, docent Pasi Pölönen. I also thank Professor Emeritus Antti Jokela and district judge, docent Antti Tapanila who agreed to act as the preliminary reviewers of my work. Mr Tapanila also took on the duties of the opponent. Vaasa Court of Appeal has provided a stimulating and understanding community throughout my work. My senior colleagues, justice Petteri Korhonen and justice, docent Timo Saranpää have kindly contributed to the work.

Mr Pölönen has also taken the trouble to review the manuscript for this book and again given me important comments. I have also received valuable comments from Professor Jenia I. Turner. Alison Kirk, Hannah Champney and Anna Gallagher from Routledge as well as copy editor Hamish Ironside have helped to make this book a reality. Linus Sandbacka has helped by going through the footnotes.

Lastly, and most importantly, I would like to thank my loving partner, university researcher Mehrnoosh Farzamfar, for not only enduring but encouraging the continuation of a project which has taken so much of my time already.

Cases

European Court of Human Rights

Finland

South Africa

Sweden

The United Kingdom

United Nations Human Rights Committee

The United States

Abbreviations

dec.	decision
GC	grand chamber
ICCPR	The International Covenant on Civil and Political Rights
SCOTUS	The Supreme Court of the United States
The Commission	The European Commission of Human Rights
The Convention	The European Convention on Human Rights
The Court	The European Court of Human Rights
UNCAT	The Convention against Torture and Other Cruel, Inhuman or Degrading Treatment or Punishment

1 Introduction

This is a book about the right to a fair trial – and rules of evidence. The former is a human right protected under Article 6 of the European Convention on Human Rights (hereinafter, the Convention). This is the concept of fair trial we shall be focusing on. The main reason for doing so is that there is a substantial body of case law from the European Court of Human Rights (hereinafter, the Court) on that provision, explaining it and sometimes also expanding it. Fairness of a trial can, of course, be approached from other directions also, but here it is to be understood as the right protected in Article 6 of the Convention. Moreover, we shall focus on its evidentiary aspects only.

Rules of evidence are legal norms governing the process of proof. Here, we will be particularly interested in rule of evidence which may affect the admissibility and use of evidence, having the capacity to restrict it somehow. Parties at a trial may disagree on the law or the facts – or both. Evidence is needed for deciding factual disputes. This evidentiary point of view restricts this book's approach to the right to a fair trial. We are only interested in cases which express rules of evidence or from which rules of evidence can be derived. On the other hand, I will not claim to give an exhaustive account of such rules. Instead, I attempt to show that such rules can be derived in the first place and that they follow a certain logic.

The Court's judgments will have implications on the Member States of the Convention, at least if states are willing to comply with them. This makes it also important for domestic authorities to understand the logic of the Court. When transformed into domestic law, a judgment must be simplified into a norm where the basic mechanism of "if … then" should reflect the logic of the Court's reasoning – a rule of evidence the Court has adopted must be translated into a domestic rule of evidence. This is how Member States can adapt or amend their laws in a way to avoid further violations and respect the right to a fair trial as they are obliged to do under Article 1 of the Convention.

I will state openly that it is not my intention to criticise the Court's judgments so much as try to understand them. After going through many of them from an evidentiary perspective, the sometimes quite confusing phraseology seems to unravel a little bit. For sure, many of the Court's statements can be questioned, but I find it is doing a rather good job at balancing competing rights with the right to a fair trial. Of course, the interpretations I have made may be incorrect – at least in parts.

DOI: 10.4324/9781003311416-1

Perhaps a labyrinth of case law has engulfed me so completely that I am unable to even detect it myself. This will be left for the reader to decide.

My point of view is one of a Finnish researcher and judge. This probably affects my writing and conclusions in ways I do not even notice myself. One of them is that throughout this book, unless the context suggests otherwise, I presume a judge as being the trier of both facts and law. This is because there are no jury trials in Finland in the same sense as, for example, in the United Kingdom. Additionally, courts of appeal in Finland can review both the assessment of evidence and the application of law. I have, however, tried to minimise references to Finnish law and practice.

Some comparative remarks will be made throughout the book. Also, through the Court's case law, some characteristics of domestic legal systems will be discussed. This does not mean using an actual comparative method. Instead, these differences are simply used to present possible problems as well as possible solutions. The most important focus of this work will be on the general principles the Court has developed. Thus, it will not be possible to formulate rules of evidence for individual Member States – only to suggest how those principles could be applied by domestic authorities to avoid violations of Article 6.

The book will begin with an overview of the right to a fair trial, followed by an overview of rules of evidence, or rather how this concept is to be understood for the purposes of the book. These two chapters form the more general part of the book, while the subsequent chapters focus on particular aspects of the right to a fair trial, the Court's case law concerning those aspects and any rules of evidence for the domestic courts that could be formulated based on it. The idea is to try to describe and understand the workings of the assessment models the Court has adopted, often calling them "tests". I consider such tests rules of evidence which may be translated into domestic rules of evidence.

The tests usually consist of several criteria which are used to evaluate the overall fairness of a trial and therefore, whether Article 6 has been violated or whether the trial has been fair in spite of an applicant claiming otherwise. Domestic authorities should, so the Convention system presumes, attempt to avoid and rectify violations although their point of view is somewhat different. Some irregularities or potential violations can be rectified in the course of the domestic proceedings, for example upon appeal. This is why domestic authorities would benefit from understanding the logic behind the Court's assessment and the rules of evidence it has developed based on the right to a fair trial.

I will be quoting the Court extensively. This is because I wish to avoid changing the sentiment and tone of the Court. However, to make the quotes more readable, I have omitted all references to other case law as well as any parts I have considered unnecessary for the purposes of quoting a judgment. Such omissions are marked with "[…]". Additionally, square brackets are used to indicate clarifications not used in the original text. Emphases to quotations have been added in **bold text**. In every chapter, the first reference to literature has been given in full, while the subsequent references include only the author and year of publication.

2 The right to a fair trial

2.1 The elements of the right

Matters of evidence fall under Article 6 of the Convention, which guarantees everyone the right to a fair trial. The crucial question in determining whether Article 6 has been violated is whether the proceedings have been fair *as a whole*. Other Articles of the Convention may, however, play a role in addition to Article 6. The procedures of gathering evidence may violate at least Articles 3 (prohibition of torture) or 8 (right to respect for private and family life). However, if there is a violation of another Article that is relevant for evidence, this does not in itself suffice to find a violation of Article 6, which reads as follows:

Right to a fair trial

1   In the determination of his civil rights and obligations or of any criminal charge against him, everyone is entitled to a fair and public hearing within a reasonable time by an independent and impartial tribunal established by law. Judgment shall be pronounced publicly but the press and public may be excluded from all or part of the trial in the interests of morals, public order or national security in a democratic society, where the interests of juveniles or the protection of the private life of the parties so require, or to the extent strictly necessary in the opinion of the court in special circumstances where publicity would prejudice the interests of justice.

2   Everyone charged with a criminal offence shall be presumed innocent until proved guilty according to law.

3   Everyone charged with a criminal offence has the following minimum rights:

a   to be informed promptly, in a language which he understands and in detail, of the nature and cause of the accusation against him;

b   to have adequate time and facilities for the preparation of his defence;

c   to defend himself in person or through legal assistance of his own choosing or, if he has not sufficient means to pay for legal assistance, to be given it free when the interests of justice so require;

DOI: 10.4324/9781003311416-2

      d   to examine or have examined witnesses against him and to obtain the attendance and examination of witnesses on his behalf under the same conditions as witnesses against him;

      e   to have the free assistance of an interpreter if he cannot understand or speak the language used in court.

As we can see, criminal procedure holds a special place within the Article. Much of what will be said of rules of evidence in criminal trials could be applied with little or no adaptations in civil and administrative procedures, but like majority of the case law, this book will mostly focus on criminal procedure. It should also be noted that of the component rights of Article 6, not all are of great importance from evidence perspective. For example, while the independence of the tribunal and publicity of the trial are cornerstones of a fair trial, they have a more indirect significance for the process of proof and there is little case law concerning these aspects and evidence.

The Court has stated that "the key principle governing the application of Article 6 is fairness" and that "[t]he right to a fair trial under Article 6 § 1 is an unqualified right". In *Ibrahim*, the Court continued:

> However, what constitutes a fair trial cannot be the subject of a single unvarying rule but must depend on the circumstances of the particular case [...]. The Court's primary concern under Article 6 § 1 is to evaluate the overall fairness of the criminal proceedings [...].[1]

Thus, the pivotal question in assessing whether Article 6 has been violated is whether a trial has been fair as a whole. The requirement of **overall fairness** can be understood as the first element of the Article relevant for the process of proof.

The fairness of a trial cannot – and perhaps should not – be defined in absolutely clear terms. Overall assessment of fairness must be based on multiple factors. It may clarify the notion of fair trial to some degree, however, to point out that fairness generally requires that the defendant is given an opportunity to participate effectively in the proceedings against them. Furthermore, there should be a fair balance between the parties, and the defence should not be placed in a disadvantageous position in relation to the prosecution. There seems to be a close connection between these requirements, although the Court has traditionally made a distinction between them.

According to the Court, "the right to an **adversarial trial** means, in a criminal case, that both prosecution and defence must be given the opportunity to have knowledge of and comment on the observations filed and the evidence adduced by the other party".[2] This might be seen as the positive definition of effective participation. On the other hand, "under the principle of **equality of arms**, as one

---

1 Ibrahim and Others v. the United Kingdom [GC], 13.9.2016, § 250.
2 See e.g. Murtazaliyeva v. Russia [GC], 18.12.2018, § 91.

of the features of the wider concept of a fair trial, each party must be afforded a reasonable opportunity to present his case under conditions that do not place him at a disadvantage vis-à-vis his opponent".[3] Here, the concept of fairness is approached negatively, by describing what would *not* allow effective participation.[4]

Article 6 § 2 contains a right known as the **presumption of innocence**. Known to many from American movies, it states the factual starting point in any criminal proceedings. This right

> requires, inter alia, that when carrying out their duties, the members of a court should not start with the preconceived idea that the accused has committed the offence charged; the burden of proof is on the prosecution, and any doubt should benefit the accused. It also follows that it is for the prosecution to inform the accused of the case that will be made against him, so that he may prepare and present his defence accordingly, and to adduce evidence sufficient to convict him.[5]

One possible interpretation is to view the presumption of innocence as an instruction to the authorities to keep an open mind about the suspected guilt of someone until the end of the criminal process. It reminds that even though authorities might believe the accused is guilty, it would be premature to draw any final conclusions until all evidence has been presented and evaluated, allowing the accused to give an explanation of the events. Criminal process, in its early stages, is fairly unpredictable and although the effective functioning of criminal justice requires that the machinery of investigation can be started based on suspicions, it should be remembered that suspicion is far from the truth.[6]

Article 6 § 3 includes a list of **minimum rights** applicable in criminal proceedings just like Article 6 § 2. One might think that a violation of any of these rights would automatically violate the right to a fair trial. The wording "minimum rights" would indeed seem to suggest that Article 6 § 3 lists the absolute minimum requirements for a fair trial, fulfilment of which is essential for a trial to be fair as a whole. However, violating some of those rights might prove meaningless within the wider context of a trial. While their importance should not be underestimated, violating one of the minimum rights will not entail an automatic violation of Article 6.

---

3 See e.g. Öcalan v. Turkey [GC], 12.5.2005, § 140.
4 The principles are sometimes mentioned together, see e.g. Rowe and Davis v. the United Kingdom [GC], 16.2.2000, § 60: "It is a fundamental aspect of the right to a fair trial that criminal proceedings, including the elements of such proceedings which relate to procedure, should be adversarial and that there should be equality of arms between the prosecution and defence."
5 Barberà, Messegué and Jabardo v. Spain [plenary], 6.12.1988, § 77 and, as a more recent example, SA-Capital Oy v. Finland, 14.2.2019, § 107.
6 See R. L. Lippke, *Taming the Presumption of Innocence* (Oxford: Oxford University Press, 2016), 18.

Conversely, it is possible that the overall fairness of a trial is violated although none of the specific aspects listed in Article 6 are. In *Ibrahim*, for example, the Court explained the relationship of paragraphs 1 and 3:

> In evaluating the overall fairness of the proceedings, the Court will take into account, if appropriate, the minimum rights listed in Article 6 § 3, which exemplify the requirements of a fair trial in respect of typical procedural situations which arise in criminal cases. They can be viewed, therefore, as specific aspects of the concept of a fair trial in criminal proceedings in Article 6 § 1 [...]. However, those minimum rights are not aims in themselves: their intrinsic aim is always to contribute to ensuring the fairness of the criminal proceedings as a whole [...].[7]

Goss has criticised this "specific aspects" approach, suggesting that any alleged violation should be primarily investigated under some of the minimum rights under Article 6 §§ 2 and 3. Only if no violation of them are found, should the fairness "as a whole" approach come into play. Rather surprisingly, Goss bases his argument upon a decision from 1961.[8] According to the Court in *Nielsen*,

> [i]n a case where no violation of paragraph 3 is found to have taken place, the question whether the trial conforms to the standard laid down by paragraph 1 must be decided on the basis of a consideration of the trial as a whole, and not on the basis of an isolated consideration of one particular aspect of the trial or one particular incident.[9]

While the passage gives room for interpretation, in my view it seems to clearly support the overall fairness approach. It actually leaves open whether the finding of a violation under §§ 2 or 3 would be the end of analysis or whether overall fairness should also be considered in such situations. Thus, I see no inconsistency between the interpretations in *Nielsen* and *Ibrahim* on the relationship between the general provision and minimum rights. In any case, current case law clearly states that the final question to be answered is whether trial as a whole is fair or not. The minimum requirements or specific aspects of fairness should be assessed in light of that more general requirement.

2.2 The interpretation and application of Article 6

Now, a few words about how the Court interprets the Convention. The starting point can be found from the Vienna Convention of 23 May 1969 on the Law of

---

7 Ibrahim and Others v. the United Kingdom [GC], 13.9.2016, § 251.
8 R. Goss, *Criminal Fair Trial Rights: Article 6 of the European Convention on Human Rights* (Oxford: Hart, 2014), 68–88.
9 Nielsen v. Denmark [plenary], 15.3.1961, § 52.

Treaties, known as "the Vienna Convention". According to Article 31 § 1 of the Vienna Convention, a treaty shall be interpreted in good faith in accordance with the ordinary meaning to be given to the terms of the treaty in their context and in the light of its object and purpose. However, the Court has developed principles of interpretation which go beyond the ordinary meaning given to the terms of the Convention back in the 1950s.[10]

Instead of the original meaning of the Convention text, the Court has given greater emphasis to the object and purpose of the Convention, as they are stated in its preamble and Article 1.[11] In 1968, the Court stated that

> the term "civil rights and obligations" cannot be construed as a mere reference to the domestic law of the High Contracting Party concerned but relates to an autonomous concept which must be interpreted independently, even though the general principles of the domestic law of the High Contracting Parties must necessarily be taken into consideration in any such interpretation.[12]

The doctrine of **autonomous concepts** is also linked with the ordinary meaning of the terms of the Convention. While domestic use of terms is relevant for the determination of that meaning, it is the object and purpose of the Convention which must be given decisive weight. Otherwise, it would be too easy for Member States to water down the protection provided and meant to be provided by the Convention. One important example of autonomous concepts is the term "witness". Article 6 § 3 (d) is to be applied also to a deposition made by a victim or a co-accused and regardless of whether it is given in open court.[13]

The term "criminal charge" may also be subject to autonomous interpretation. This means that the minimum rights may be applicable in proceedings which a Member State has classified as administrative or disciplinary, for example. The concept should be interpreted using the *Engel* criteria, where the domestic classification provides a starting point, but no more. Of greater importance is the very nature of the offence as well as the degree of severity of the penalty that the person concerned risks incurring. It is especially likely that deprivation of liberty would constitute a criminal charge in its autonomous meaning, although even this is no automation.[14]

---

10 See Magyar Helsinki Bizottság v. Hungary [GC], 8.11.2016, § 118 and M. Dahlberg, *Do You Know It When You See It? A Study on the Judicial Legitimacy of the European Court of Human Rights* (Joensuu: University of Eastern Finland, 2015), 26.

11 See Golder v. the United Kingdom [plenary], 12.2.1975, § 34.

12 Twenty-one detained persons v. Germany [dec., plenary], 6.4.1968. See also G. Letsas, *A Theory of Interpretation of the European Convention on Human Rights* (Oxford: Oxford University Press, 2007), 41–43.

13 See S.N. v. Sweden, 2.7.2002, § 45 (concerning a victim whose statement was videotaped) and Kaste and Mathisen v. Norway, 9.11.2006, § 53 (concerning a co-accused).

14 Engel and others [plenary], 8.6.1976, §§ 81 and 82. See also B. Rainey, E. Wicks, and C. Ovey, *Jacobs, White and Ovey: The European Convention on Human Rights*, 7th edn (Oxford: Oxford University Press, 2017), 275–277.

The Court has, on the other hand, accepted that

> [t]here are clearly "criminal charges" of differing weight. What is more, the autonomous interpretation adopted by the Convention institutions of the notion of a "criminal charge" by applying the *Engel* criteria have underpinned a gradual broadening of the criminal head to cases not strictly belonging to the traditional categories of the criminal law, for example administrative penalties [...], prison disciplinary proceedings [...], customs law [...], competition law [...], and penalties imposed by a court with jurisdiction in financial matters [...]. Tax surcharges differ from the hard core of criminal law; consequently, the criminal-head guarantees will not necessarily apply with their full stringency [...].[15]

Because of this autonomous interpretation, Article 6 is applicable in pre-trial proceedings. According to the Court,

> [t]he investigation stage may be of particular importance for the preparation of the criminal proceedings: the evidence obtained during this stage often determines the framework in which the offence charged will be considered at the trial and national laws may attach consequences to the attitude of an accused at the initial stages of police interrogation which are decisive for the prospects of the defence in any subsequent criminal proceedings. An accused may therefore find himself in a particularly vulnerable position at that stage of the proceedings, the effect of which may be amplified by increasingly complex legislation on criminal procedure, notably with respect to the rules governing the gathering and use of evidence [...].[16]

Autonomous concepts, then, are one way to ensure effective protection of the Convention. It is also linked with another doctrine, that of **practical and effective rights**. In *Airey*, the Court – with references to its earlier case law – stated: "The Convention is intended to guarantee not rights that are theoretical or illusory but rights that are practical and effective [...]."[17] This formulation of the requirement of effectiveness has become established in the Court's later case law. Autonomous interpretation of the terms used in the Convention is one way to ensure the effectiveness of rights, whereas the doctrine of practical and effective rights may be seen as a method allowing greater development of the rights via case law.

For the purposes of Article 6 §§ 2 and 3, one must interpret the phrase "charged with a criminal offence". Following the principle of effectiveness, "[a] 'criminal charge' exists from the moment that an individual is **officially notified** by the competent authority of an allegation that he has committed a criminal offence, or from the point at which his situation has been **substantially affected**

---

15 Jussila v. Finland [GC], 23.11.2006, § 43.
16 Ibrahim and Others v. the United Kingdom [GC], 13.9.2016, § 253.
17 Airey v. Ireland, 9.10.1979, § 24.

by actions taken by the authorities as a result of a suspicion against him", which-ever happens first, naturally. For example, as regarded the fourth applicant in *Ibrahim*, he was substantially affected when the police continued to interview him as a witness although there was already a suspicion against him.[18] This determines the moment in time when Article 6 becomes applicable.

In the 1978 *Tyrer* judgment the Court was called upon to assess whether birching as a punishment was in accordance with the Convention. It stated that

> the Convention is a living instrument which, as the Commission rightly stressed, must be interpreted in the light of present-day conditions. In the case now before it the Court cannot but be influenced by the developments and commonly accepted standards in the penal policy of the Member States of the Council of Europe in this field. Indeed, the Attorney-General for the Isle of Man mentioned that, for many years, the provisions of Manx legislation con-cerning judicial corporal punishment had been under review.[19]

This **living instrument** doctrine has also been called the method of dynamic and evolutive interpretation of the Convention. Like the other methods discussed above, it underlines that the starting point for interpretation should not be what the drafters and Member States meant originally. The Court, therefore, openly rejects the idea of originalism as an interpretation method. The Court has, in a way, adopted a unique role which allows it to be the *primus motor* developing the Convention rights and giving them effective interpretation in modern societies. In fact, it allows the Court to impose such obligations on Member States that were not originally meant to be imposed. This may give rise to claims of lacking legiti-macy (see also Section 2.4 below).[20]

While use of the aforementioned doctrines may lead to expansion of the Court's role in relation to national courts as well as legislators, the Court has also adopted principles which give greater weight to national laws. First, the **principle of sub-sidiarity**, which was reinforced by Protocol No. 16 to the Convention. In the preamble of the Convention, Member States affirm

> that the High Contracting Parties, in accordance with the principle of sub-sidiarity, have the primary responsibility to secure the rights and freedoms defined in this Convention and the Protocols thereto, and that in doing so they enjoy a margin of appreciation, subject to the supervisory jurisdiction of the European Court of Human Rights established by this Convention.

18 See Ibrahim and Others v. the United Kingdom [GC], 13.9.2016, §§ 249 and 296; Deweer v. Belgium, 27.2.1980, §§ 42–46.
19 Tyrer v. the United Kingdom, 25.4.1978, § 31.
20 Dahlberg 2015, 28 and 40. Helfer points out that rulings and decisions of bodies such as the Court "have expanded the scope of existing human rights treaties and trans-formed nonbinding norms into legally binding obligations", calling this a form of nonconsensual international lawmaking (L. R. Helfer, "Nonconsensual International Lawmaking" (2008) 2008 *University of Illinois Law Review* 71, 87).

Put simply, the principle means that the Court has a subsidiary role in human rights protection, while national authorities have the primary role. It is for the Member States to secure to everyone within their jurisdiction the rights and freedoms defined in Section I of the Convention, as stated in Article 1. The Court has a secondary and supervisory position within the Convention system. This is reflected in the admissibility criteria of individual complaints. According to Article 34 § 1 of the Convention, non-exhaustion of domestic remedies will result in inadmissibility. The national authorities should have an opportunity to correct any violations of human rights and should do so.

The principle of subsidiarity is, in turn, linked with the doctrine of **margin of appreciation**. Dahlberg even calls it "another element of the subsidiarity principle".[21] It means that there is an area in which national authorities of each Member State have some room to decide how to protect human rights within their jurisdiction. If a decision on national level is made within the boundaries of this margin, the Court is not to intervene by using its supervisory jurisdiction to override the domestic discretion. In other words, the Court's subsidiary role requires it to step in only when Member States transgress the boundaries of their margin of appreciation.

2.3 Waiving rights

It is worth underlining that the right to a fair trial is not absolute. According to the Court's case law,

> neither the letter nor the spirit of Article 6 of the Convention prevents a person from waiving of his own free will, either expressly or tacitly, the entitlement to the guarantees of a fair trial. However, such a waiver must, if it is to be effective for Convention purposes, be established in an **unequivocal** manner; it must not run counter to any important **public interest** [...], and it must be attended by **minimum safeguards** commensurate with its importance [...].[22]

There seems to be only sparse case law on the last two elements, which leads me to conclude that they rarely become key requirements in the context of Article 6.

The minimum safeguards were lacking in *Pfeifer and Plankl*, where according to the Court, the presiding judge, when discussing his own and another judge's disqualification with the first applicant, disregarded three important procedural principles by (1) acting himself although he was in principle disqualified from doing so, (2) failing to inform the president of the court immediately of his disqualification, and (3) inciting the applicant to waive his right to a remedy which

---

21 Dahlberg 2015, 43.
22 Dvorski v. Croatia [GC], 20.10.2015, § 100.

would otherwise been available to him. The waiver was not considered effective because of these shortcomings.[23]

The requirement that waiver does not run counter to any important public interest is often dismissed by the Court with only a phrase.[24] Even in *Håkansson and Sturesson*, a case often referred to in this context, the Court only stated that "it does not appear that the litigation involved any questions of public interest which could have made a public hearing necessary". It seems that under some circumstances waiving a right to a public hearing might not be possible because of an important public interest. The Court chose not to elaborate further what these circumstances might be.[25]

Presumably an important public interest would prohibit anyone from waiving the right to an impartial tribunal or being heard by a tribunal established by law. These are such important features of a fair trial that their relinquishment would not be appropriate even if a defendant was willing to do so. A public hearing might be indispensable if, for example, a high-profile politician stands accused of accepting bribes. In the absence of any specific grounds for secrecy, it would be important for the press to be able to report the progress of such a trial.

More often crucial elements in assessing whether a waiver has been effective are its voluntariness and whether it has been established in an unequivocal manner. The last-mentioned requirement has been elaborated with reference to a standard used by the Supreme Court of the United States (SCOTUS):

A waiver of the right, once invoked, must not only be voluntary, but must also constitute a **knowing and intelligent** relinquishment of a right. Before an accused can be said to have implicitly, through his conduct, waived an important right under Article 6, it must be shown that he could reasonably have foreseen what the consequences of his conduct would be.[26]

This requires, first of all, that a person should be informed of their procedural rights. The Court stated in *Simeonovi* that

the receipt of such information by the accused person is one of the guarantees enabling him to exercise his defence rights and allowing the authorities to ensure, in particular, that any waiver by the accused of the right to legal assistance is voluntary, knowing and intelligent.[27]

23 Pfeifer and Plankl v. Austria, 25.2.1992, §§ 74–79.
24 See e.g. Hermi v. Italy [GC], 18.10.2006, § 79 ("Furthermore, it does not appear that the dispute raised any questions of public interest preventing the aforementioned procedural guarantees from being waived"); Natsvlishvili and Togonidze v. Georgia, 29.4.2014 § 97 *in fine* ("Nor can the Court establish from the available case materials that that waiver ran counter to any major public interest.").
25 Håkansson and Sturesson v. Sweden, 21.2.1990, § 67 *in fine*.
26 Pishchalnikov v. Russia, 24.9.2009, § 77.
27 Simeonovi v. Bulgaria [GC], 12.5.2017, § 128.

In criminal proceedings, the onus is on the authorities to inform those charged with criminal offence of any rights they have. This should also be documented sufficiently for later verification. In *Simeonovi*, for example, the government were unable to show that the applicant had received information of right to legal assistance.

The second requirement of an "intelligent" waiver might not be met if, for example, someone is in a particularly vulnerable state because of their age or health, such as the applicant in *Płonka*:

> During the first police interview the applicant admitted that she had been suffering from an alcohol problem for many years. She further confessed to having drunk a substantial amount of alcohol the day before her arrest [...]. These circumstances clearly suggest that the applicant was in a vulnerable position at the time of interview, and that the authorities should have taken this into account during questioning and in particular when apprising her of her right to be assisted by a lawyer.[28]

For a tacit waiver to be valid, it should be established as an additional safeguard that the person could reasonably have foreseen the consequences of their conduct. This is especially important if someone is particularly vulnerable. The Court elaborated in *Panovits*, for example, that authorities must "ensure that the accused minor has a broad understanding of the nature of the investigation, of what is at stake for him or her, including the significance of any penalty which may be imposed". It then stated that a waiver of an important right under Article 6 by a minor can only be accepted if it is expressed in an unequivocal manner.[29] Of course, an expressly made and properly documented waiver is always the safest option.[30]

In *Natsvlishvili and Togonidze*, the first applicant complained that he was not warned about the waiver of all his procedural rights when entering into a plea bargain. The Court noted, inter alia, that "the first applicant explicitly confirmed on several occasions, both before the prosecuting authority and the judge, that he had fully understood the content of the agreement, had had his procedural rights and the legal consequences of the agreement explained to him, and that his decision to accept it was not the result of any duress or false promises". Furthermore, he had asked for a plea bargain to be arranged and he was also assisted by two lawyers of his own choosing. The terms of the agreement were documented and the agreement itself was subject to judicial review.[31]

The Court has sometimes applied the doctrine of knowing and intelligent waiver in an interesting manner. It stated in *Al-Khawaja*, for example, that

---

28 Płonka v. Poland, 31.3.2009, § 38.

29 Panovits v. Cyprus, 11.12.2008, §§ 67 and 68.

30 In *Zaichenko*, for example, the applicant signed an act of accusation where he stated that he did not require legal assistance and that this was not because of lack of means (Aleksandr Zaichenko v. Russia, 18.2.2010, §§ 13 and 50).

31 Natsvlishvili and Togonidze v. Georgia, 29.4.2014, §§ 92–98. See also Leuska and Others v. Estonia, 7.11.2017, §§ 76 and 77, where the applicants had unequivocally waived their right to be heard.

"[t]o allow the defendant to benefit from the fear he has engendered in witnesses would be incompatible with the rights of victims and witnesses. No court could be expected to allow the integrity of its proceedings to be subverted in this way. Consequently, a defendant who has acted in this manner must be taken to have waived his rights to question such witnesses under Article 6 § 3 (d). The same conclusion must apply when the threats or actions which lead to the witness being afraid to testify come from those who act on behalf of the defendant or with his knowledge and approval".[32]

In *Jones*, the Court noted that it was not clearly established under English law that it was possible to try an accused in his absence throughout. Because of this, it considered that the applicant, as a layman, could not have reasonably foreseen that his failure to attend on the date set for the commencement would result in him being tried and convicted in his absence and in the absence of legal representation. His waiver was not considered valid for the purposes of Article 6.[33]

For our purposes, the concept of waiver is important because if a person has validly waived their right, they normally cannot invoke a violation of that right. The corollary of this is that there is no need to proceed with applying any potentially applicable rule of evidence. For example, after validly waiving the right to a lawyer, one could not logically claim that the subsequent lack of legal assistance would amount to a violation. Naturally, situations may vary quite a lot, but this is the starting point. The validity of a waiver may, therefore, be a decisive preliminary question to be decided before applying rules of evidence derived from Article 6.

2.4 The effects of the Court's case law on evidence

In the field of evidence, the Court's subsidiary role and domestic authorities' margin of appreciation become apparent from the following statement repeated in several judgments: "While Article 6 of the Convention guarantees the right to a fair trial, it does not lay down any rules on the admissibility of evidence as such, which is therefore primarily a matter for regulation under national law."[34] In *Schenk*, the Court continued: "The Court therefore cannot exclude as a matter of principle and in the abstract that unlawfully obtained evidence of the present kind may be admissible. It has only to ascertain whether [the] trial as a whole was fair.[35]

The Court's approach to evidence was explained more in *Moreira Ferreira (No. 2)*:

Normally, issues such as the weight attached by the national courts to particular items of evidence or to findings or assessments submitted to them for

---

32 Al-Khawaja and Tahery v. the United Kingdom [GC], 15.12.2011, § 123.
33 Jones v. the United Kingdom [dec.], 9.9.2003.
34 See e.g. Schenk v. Switzerland [plenary], 12.7.1988, § 46; Moreira Ferreira v. Portugal (No. 2) [GC], 11.7.2017, § 83; and SA-Capital Oy v. Finland, 14.2.2019, § 73.
35 Schenk v. Switzerland [plenary], 12.7.1988, § 46.

consideration are not for the Court to review. The Court should not act as a fourth-instance body and will therefore not question under Article 6 § 1 the national courts' assessment, unless their findings can be regarded as arbitrary or manifestly unreasonable [...].[36]

The paragraph includes a reference to what is known as the **fourth-instance doctrine** – yet another element of the principle of subsidiarity.[37]

In *SA-Capital*, the Court further elaborated:

> The Court notes, however, that there is a distinction between the admissibility of evidence, that is, the question of which elements of proof may be submitted to the competent court for its consideration, and the rights of defence in respect of evidence which in fact has been submitted before the court [...]. There is also a distinction between the latter, that is, whether the rights of defence have been properly ensured in respect of the evidence taken, and the subsequent assessment of that evidence by the court once the proceedings have been concluded. From the perspective of the rights of defence, issues under Article 6 may therefore arise in terms of whether the evidence produced for or against the defendant was presented in such a way as to ensure a fair trial [...].[38]

So, while matters of evidence primarily belong to national authorities' margin of appreciation, situations may arise where the process of proof violates the right to a fair trial. The Court's role (also) in evidence law is, indeed, subsidiary. The objective of this book is to examine the situations where case law regarding evidence is established to a point where one can talk of a rule. For some, the mere suggestion of the Court's case law giving rise to "rules" may be problematic. It might be pointed out that the Court decides only individual cases and thus also any legal arguments are based on the unique facts of such cases, only applicable to factually identical cases.

I see several weaknesses in such thinking. First, the Court expresses legal principles in general terms, nowadays under the heading "general principles" in its judgments. I find it hard to understand the use of such language if the principles explained in such a way are not intended to be used generally. Furthermore, it would amount to arbitrariness if the Court were to come up with new and individual legal argumentation for each individual case. By their very nature, legal norms and concepts must be abstract and generally applicable. This is a basic requirement linked with the Court's legitimacy. The Court, like any other court, has simultaneously the role of a dispute resolver and rule maker. Stone Sweet explains this as follows:

---

36 Moreira Ferreira v. Portugal (No. 2) [GC], 11.7.2017, § 83.
37 Dahlberg 2015, 43.
38 SA-Capital Oy v. Finland, 14.2.2019, § 74.

In adjudicating, the dispute resolver simultaneously resolves a dyadic dispute and enacts elements of the normative structure. Both are forms of rule-making. First, she makes rules that are concrete, particular, and retrospective: that is, she resolves an existing dispute between two specific parties about the terms of one dyadic contract. Second, in justifying her decision – in telling us why, normatively, a given act should or should not be permitted – she makes rules of an abstract, general, and prospective nature. This is so to the extent that her decision clarifies or alters rules comprising the normative structure.[39]

Secondly, the Court usually refers to its previous case law when explaining the general principles to be applied. With time, the number of cases as well as such references may increase, until such an impressive body of case law has formed that the Court itself refers to its established (or even well-established or long-established) case law.[40] While there is no official principle of binding **precedent** or *stare decisis*, "significant rulings by the Court on the interpretation and application of the Convention are generally followed in subsequent cases" – sometimes up to a point where the Court may refuse to admit that it has changed an interpretation and possibly overruled earlier case law.[41]

According to rule 72 § 2 of the Rules of Court, "[w]here the resolution of a question raised in a case before the Chamber might have a result inconsistent with the Court's case law, the Chamber shall relinquish jurisdiction in favour of the Grand Chamber".[42] This also suggests there would be at least some form of *stare decisis*. In *Christine Goodwin*, the Court stated that while it "is not formally bound to follow its previous judgments, it is in the interests of legal certainty, foreseeability and equality before the law that it should not depart, without good reason, from precedents laid down in previous cases".[43]

Thus, at least in practice, the Court does follow its own case law similarly to precedents in national adjudication. With time, case law may even become established, and then an abstract rule is formed which is less tied to a particular case. While certain key cases (and only them) are usually referred to as *de facto* precedents, in situations of established case law the Court may refer to one previous case as an example. An interesting study has been made on how the Court refers to its earlier case law, suggesting that it not only attempts to develop an internally consistent body of law, but also that such references are strategic,

---

39 A. Stone Sweet, "Judicialization and the Construction of Governance", in M. Shapiro and A. Stone Sweet, *On Law, Politics, & Judicialization* (Oxford: Oxford University Press, 2002), 64.
40 See, e.g., Al-Khawaja and Tahery v. the United Kingdom [GC], 15.12.2011, § 107 and Gäfgen v. Germany [GC], 1.6.2010, § 107.
41 A. Mowbray, "An Examination of the European Court of Human Rights' Approach to Overruling Its Previous Case Law" (2009) 9 *Human Rights Law Review*, 179, 183 and 185.
42 *Rules of Court*, The European Court of Human Rights, 1.2.22.
43 Christine Goodwin v. the United Kingdom [GC], 11.7.2002, § 74.

depending on the characteristics of the case as well as the domestic court it communicates with.[44]

Let us now turn to **the relationship between the Court and national legal authorities**, both legislatures and courts. For political (and, hopefully, legal and ethical) reasons, Member States of the Convention hope to avoid judgments where the Court finds they have violated the Convention. To achieve this, they must find ways to translate the authoritative interpretations of the Court into domestic legal framework. Sometimes, a legal reform may be needed to correct systemic errors in legislation. Furthermore, Member States may begin to adapt their behaviour to the expectations based on the Court's case law. This may be called a form of judicialisation.[45]

Member States of the Convention often react to the Court's judgments by amending legislation or changing domestic case law, even when they are not the respondent government of a particular case. Article 46 requires Member States to "abide by the final judgment of the Court in any case to which they are parties", resulting in a binding *res judicata* in that relation. Additionally, judgments may also have a *res interpretata* effect, which reaches beyond that relation. This results from a combination of the Court's authority as the interpreter of the Convention (Article 32) and the Member States' duty to secure the rights and freedoms defined in Section I of the Convention (Article 1).[46]

Domestic authorities have two crucially important functions which make the Convention system work by facilitating compliance. First, they are expected to reflect the Court's case law and adopt domestic rules which respect the conclusions of the Court. By amending the domestic legal framework, which can take place through the domestic supreme courts' case law, domestic actors **diffuse** the Court's rulings and translate the effects of the Court's case law into domestic law. The domestic courts also act as **filters**: they can prevent or at least amend violations before they reach the Court by applying the Court's case law and/or the amended domestic rules correctly.[47] These functions are the flip side of the principle of subsidiarity.

44 Y. Lupu and E. Voeten, *The Role of Precedent at the European Court of Human Rights: A Network Analysis of Case Citations* (2010) 2010 Paper 12 (http://opensiuc. lib.siu.edu/pnconfs_2010/12).

45 A. Stone Sweet, "Constitutional Politics in France and Germany", in M. Shapiro and A. Stone Sweet, *On Law, Politics, & Judicialization* (Oxford: Oxford University Press, 2002), 187: "Policy processes can be described as judicialized to the extent that constitutional jurisprudence, the threat of future constitutional censure, and the pedagogical authority of past jurisprudence alter legislative outcomes."

46 D. Kosař, J. Petrov, K. Šipulová, H. Smekal, L. Vyhnánek and J. Janovský, *Domestic Judicial Treatment of European Court of Human Rights Case Law: Beyond Compliance* (Abingdon: Routledge, 2020), 38–40. See also D. T. Björgvinsson, "The Effect of the Judgments of the ECtHR before the National Courts – A Nordic Approach?" (2016) 85 *Nordic Journal of International Law*, 303 for an overview of the status of both the Convention and the Court's case law in three Nordic countries.

47 Kosař et al. 2020, 41–43.

The essence of the *res interpretata* effect is that domestic authorities can expect the Court to find a violation regarding their legal system if it does not comply with the interpretation given to the Convention in a similar context but regarding another Member State. This applies also in the context of evidence law: If the Court has found a violation of Article 6 as a result of how evidence has been obtained or used by the authorities of one Member State, other Member States can fulfil their obligation to secure the right to a fair trial by amending their rules of evidence accordingly. Exclusion of evidence is a disputed but effective remedy. This is why the Court's finding of a violation under Article 6 can translate into an admissibility rule in domestic law.

In *Khudobin*, the government had expressed the view that because a police operation was documented in the prescribed way, it was lawful and, as a result of this, the ensuing proceedings were fair. The Court expressly rejected this argument and made a rare statement in the context of admissibility of evidence and Article 6:

> Domestic law should not tolerate the use of evidence obtained as a result of incitement by State agents. If it does, domestic law does not in this respect comply with the 'fair-trial' principle, as interpreted in the *Teixeira* and follow-up cases.[48]

However, the Court's role and legitimacy are now, perhaps more than ever, under a political threat. For decades, the Council of Europe was a regime of like-minded democratic states of Western Europe. Nowadays, "populist attacks have swept through both Western and Eastern European countries, challenging the core principles of the Convention as well as the authority of the Strasbourg Court, and resisting both its existence and the direction of its case law".[49] Kosař et al. have identified three major factors challenging the effectiveness and the authority of the Court. First, although a democratic political regime is a precondition for entry into the Council of Europe, regimes and societies are dynamic and may change. The Member States include not only established democracies but also weaker ones, where the development might be reversing. This can create problems such as lacking human rights awareness or even serious human rights violations. Second, sometimes implementation of the Court's judgment might require substantial changes to domestic legislation. This can lead to criticism of overreaching and stepping into the sphere of state sovereignty. The recent strengthening of the principle of subsidiarity may be seen as a response to such claims. Third, although compliance of the Court's rulings is monitored carefully, the Court must still rely heavily on domestic actors. Usually, domestic courts are best placed to translate the Court's judgments into reality. They also have a crucial role in adding or reducing the legitimacy of the Court.[50]

48 Khudobin v. Russia, 26.10.2006, §§ 132 and 133.
49 Kosař et al. 2020, 22.
50 Kosař et al. 2020, 22–23.

While Helfer similarly acknowledges the Court as "the globe's compliance bright spot", he also points out that "where [international] tribunals expand obligations into areas that states have identified as falling within their exclusive domestic jurisdiction, backlashes in the form of rule violations and norm denials have occurred, even among states whose human rights practices are reasonably advanced". He concludes that "[b]ecause the international law lacks the coercive enforcement authority of its domestic counterparts, nonconsensual legal obligations may produce a perverse result. They may reduce international law's participation deficit, but only at the expense of increasing its compliance deficit".[51]

2.5 Public interest considerations

One key argument against exclusion of evidence, perhaps the heaviest in weight and easiest to understand, is that exclusion of reliable evidence may lead to guilty defendants escaping conviction. This would, obviously, be an outcome violating the very purpose of criminal law. This point of view, valid as it may be, is not without its problems either. It reduces the values and rights protected by procedural norms into words, suggesting at least indirectly that substantive criminal law offers the only yardstick of the rule of law. Fairness of a trial could, accordingly, be sacrificed and the correct outcome is an end which justifies any means.

The public interest in effective investigation of crimes can also be derived from human rights. The Court has considered that "the duty of High Contracting Parties to deter or punish crime extends to other Convention provisions involving the active protection of individuals' rights against harm caused by others".[52] Indeed, many acts are criminalised because they would violate such profound values as the right to life, the right to liberty and security of person, the right to respect for private and family life, and the protection of property. In fact, it would be difficult to imagine the proper functioning of a modern state without such rights being effectively protected against the violations of others.

The very point in having procedural norms, though, is that ends do not justify means and a system under rule of law requires that people's values and rights are protected also when they are subjected to criminal procedure. It should also be remembered that often there is only a relatively vague suspicion against someone when the procedure is set in motion. It is assumed that more information can be obtained during the proceedings and such information may be proof of guilt or innocence. Even if a suspect is factually guilty of a crime, rule of law is built upon the idea that authorities are bound by law even though individuals sometimes break it.

As was already explained, one of the cornerstones of criminal procedure is the presumption of innocence. Although such presumption may appear useless in situations where a criminal is caught "red-handed", such cases are rare. The protection of society from crime requires that investigations can be initiated at a

---

51 Helfer 2008, 87 and 124–125.
52 Van der Heijden v. the Netherlands [GC], 3.4.2012, § 62 *in fine*.

relatively low factual threshold, accepting uncertainty, and thus accepting that factually innocent sometimes become the subject of criminal investigations. It is also worth reminding that even for the guilty suspects, the procedure itself is not intended to be an additional punishment.

Rawls's famous concept, *the veil of ignorance*,[53] has been used in an empirical study on the fairness of procedural justice. The study concluded that "the fundamental adversary model corresponds generally with the conception of fairness held by subjects behind the veil". Behind the veil, people were willing to give weight to the interests of the disadvantaged party.[54] The study design itself suggests fair procedural legislation creates a procedure we could trust ourselves to, especially considering we might be innocent. Having such procedures must be accepted as a price we pay for protection in a state under rule of law, but they should not interfere with people's rights more than is necessary nor for any other than investigative purposes.

Zuckerman manages to explain this conflict in an elegant manner:

> There is an uncanny symmetry between the consequences of an admissibility and an inadmissibility rule. If applied consistently, each of these rules will undermine public confidence in the criminal process. If the court always admits illegally obtained evidence, it will be seen to condone the malpractice of the law-enforcement agencies. If it always excludes it, it will be seen to abandon its duty to protect us from crime. The first thing that we must therefore accept is that the criminal trial presents a dilemma which cannot be solved by an inflexible rule.[55]

In *Gäfgen*, the Court addressed this tension:

> On the one hand, the exclusion of – often reliable and compelling – real evidence at a criminal trial will hamper the effective prosecution of crime. There is no doubt that the victims of crime and their families as well as the public have an interest in the prosecution and punishment of criminals, and in the present case that interest was of high importance. Moreover, the instant case is particular also in that the impugned real evidence was derived from an illegal method of interrogation which was not in itself aimed at furthering a criminal investigation, but was applied for preventive purposes, namely in order to save a child's life, and thus in order to safeguard another core right guaranteed by the Convention, namely Article 2.[56]

---

53 J. Rawls, *A theory of justice*, rev. edn (Cambridge, MA: Harvard University Press, 1999), 10–15.
54 J. Thibaut, L. Walker, S. LaTour and P. Houlden, "Procedural Justice as Fairness" (1974) 26 *Stanford Law Review*, 1271, 1273 and 1288–1289.
55 A. A. S. Zuckerman, *The Principles of Criminal Evidence* (Oxford: Clarendon Press, 1989), 345.
56 Gäfgen v. Germany [GC], 1.6.2010, § 175.

It then proceeded to point out that

> on the other hand, a defendant in criminal proceedings has the right to a fair trial, which may be called into question if domestic courts use evidence obtained as a result of a violation of the prohibition of inhuman treatment under Article 3, one of the core and absolute rights guaranteed by the Convention. Indeed, there is also a vital public interest in preserving the integrity of the judicial process and thus the values of civilised societies founded upon the rule of law.[57]

This argument that public interest does not only require punishing the guilty, to which the Court seems to give greater emphasis, is explained well by Turner:

> [W]hen government agents are not held accountable for violations of the law, this opens the door to the exercise of arbitrary discretion by the executive, not constrained by reasons, precedent, or pre-existing rules. Executive discretion – when unconstrained by law – is easily subject to abuse, often on a grander scale than violations of the law by private individuals. It is therefore more injurious to the rule of law than an exclusionary rule that hinders the state's inability to convict guilty defendants only in cases where a court concludes, in a reasoned decision bound by precedent, that key evidence was obtained unlawfully.[58]

There are unquestionably situations where weight should be given to public interest considerations, but the aim of punishing the (supposedly) guilty cannot overrule the rule of law and render procedural norms meaningless automatically. Indeed, the Court has stated that

> when determining whether the proceedings as a whole have been fair the weight of the public interest in the investigation and punishment of the particular offence in issue may be taken into consideration and be weighed against the individual interest that the evidence against him be gathered lawfully.[59]

The dilemma explained by Zuckerman and the Court must be resolved by discretion.

Resorting to another famous legal concept one might argue that "taking rights seriously" requires room for exclusionary discretion in cases where rights are violated to an extent incompatible with rule of law, even when free proof remains the starting point in evidence law. According to Dworkin's theory we might allow

---

57 Gäfgen v. Germany [GC], 1.6.2010, § 175.
58 J. I. Turner, "The Exclusionary Rule as a Symbol of the Rule of Law" (2014) 67 *SMU Law Review*, 821, 831.
59 Jalloh v. Germany [GC], 11.7.2006, § 97.

people's rights to be restricted in three situations: (1) if the values protected by the right are not at stake or are at stake only in some attenuated form, (2) if there is a competing right at stake, or (3) if the cost to society would be of a degree far beyond the cost paid to grant the original right.[60]

To sum up, public interest need not be put aside when assessing the overall fairness of a trial. What is important, though, is that a court has discretion to exclude evidence in a situation where the overall fairness would be compromised if such evidence were used. In such situations, the public interest of punishing the guilty or even protecting the society or a potential victim's rights must be balanced against the importance of a fair trial. Thus, when doing such a balancing act, it should not be forgotten that "it is in the face of the heaviest penalties that respect for the right to a fair trial is to be ensured to the highest possible degree by democratic societies".[61]

60 R. Dworkin, *Taking Rights Seriously* (Cambridge, MA: Harvard University Press, 1978), 200.
61 Salduz v. Turkey [GC], 27.11.2008, § 54 *in fine*.

3 Rules of evidence

3.1 The importance of evidence

Evidence has been defined as "the information with which the matters requiring proof in a trial are proved" and the study of evidence as "the study of the process by which such matters are proved in court".[1] Fair enough. Evidence, then, seems to have something to do with *information*. Indeed, as stated by Jeremy Bentham, "the field of evidence is no other than the field of knowledge".[2] It has also been pointed out that "[t]he trial is fundamentally an epistemological event".[3] I have no doubt that the reader is at least broadly aware of what evidence law is, but we shall begin with some interesting aspects of this subject.

First, evidence is not only a legal but also an epistemological concept. **Epistemology** is the study (or philosophy) of knowledge, a concept classically defined as justified, true belief. Evidence is linked with the first condition of knowledge, justification. In fact, it can justify a proposition, making a belief true and, thus, knowledge. Both the evidence and the proposition are information, but evidence has the capacity to support a belief, give us reason to consider it knowledge. People have various beliefs, of course, but what makes them knowledge is justification through evidence.[4] I believe this is a point worth making in what has been called "a post-truth world".[5]

According to Goldman:

> One approach to justification says (roughly) that a belief is justified if the believed proposition better explains what it purports to explain than any rival position. Furthermore, this "best-explanation" approach may be presented as a theory of *evidence*. That is, it may claim that evidential support for a

1 A. L-T Choo, *Evidence*, 4th edn (Oxford: Oxford University Press, 2015), 1.
2 J. Bentham, "An Introductory View of the Rationale of Evidence" in J. Bowring (ed.), *The works of Jeremy Bentham*, vol. VI (Edinburgh: William Tait, 1843), 5.
3 M. S. Pardo, "The Field of Evidence and the Field of Knowledge" (2005) 24 *Law and Philosophy*, 321.
4 See, for brief introduction, entries "Epistemology" and "Evidence" in *Stanford Encyclopedia of Philosophy* (online sources accessed 12.11.2021).
5 J. Baggini, *A Short History of Truth. Consolations for a Post-Truth World* (London: Quercus, 2017).

DOI: 10.4324/9781003311416-3

proposition is to be understood in terms of the position of that proposition in an explanatory network.[6]

This sounds reminiscent of what evidence theorists call story models. Indeed, it is Pennington and Hastie's conclusion that "the juror is a sense-making information processor who strives to create a meaningful summary of the evidence available that explains what happened in the events depicted through witnesses, exhibits, and arguments at trial".[7]

Fear not, I will soon return to law. There is, however, a second point to be made about epistemology and the method attributed to the seventeenth-century French scholar René Descartes. His philosophy is profoundly sceptical towards knowledge: "Using sceptical doubts, the meditator shows how to find 'some reason for doubt' in all his preexisting claims to knowledge."[8] To simplify, the method of doubt would require us to remain sceptical towards our beliefs. The connection between this idea and evidence law is fairly obvious. Because in criminal procedure proof of guilt is required "beyond reasonable doubt", we apply – *knowingly* or not – the method of doubt in trials every day.

Goldman adds that

> epistemology should be concerned with not only whether there are reliable processes, or methods, but which ones these are. Epistemology should be interested in *specifying* the good procedures, not simply ensuring that there are such. [...] Even if there are not any *sufficiently* reliable cognitive processes to qualify a person for either knowledge or justified belief, there might still be differences among processes in degrees of reliability. A worthy epistemological task is to identify the *comparatively* reliable processes, to discriminate the better from the worse.[9]

The same applies to process of proof in my opinion.

Another way to approach the definition and importance of evidence might be the separation of **law and facts**. The term law refers, here, to various types of norms often structured "if X, then Y", where X is a description of phenomena which may occur in real life (facts) and Y a normative outcome, be it punishment or affirming that a person has a right to something. This normative outcome indicates how the judge shall judge.[10] For example, according to the Criminal

---

6 A. I. Goldman, *Epistemology and Cognition* (Cambridge, MA: Harvard University Press, 1986), 37.

7 N. Pennington and R. Hastie, "A Cognitive Theory of Juror Decision Making: The Story Model" (1991) 13 *Cardozo Law Review*, 519. See also F. Bex and B. Verheij, "Legal Stories and the Process of Proof" (2013) 21 *Artificial Intelligence and Law*, 253.

8 "Descartes' Epistemology" in *Stanford Encyclopedia of Philosophy* (online source accessed 12.11.2021).

9 Goldman 1986, 39–40.

10 See A. Ross, *On law and justice* (Berkeley, CA: University of California Press, 1959), 214.

Code of Finland, chapter 21, section 1: "A person who kills another shall be sentenced for manslaughter to imprisonment for a fixed period of at least eight years."

The norm is structurally very simple. The facts are stated simply as "a person who kills another". Next, the normative outcome, "shall be sentenced for manslaughter to imprisonment for a fixed period of at least eight years". Notice that the normative outcome includes the directive to a judge ("shall be sentenced"). In other words, this structural element, one that Finnish legal theorist Aulis Aarnio has termed "the must-element",[11] offers the judge no discretionary power. If the operational fact "a person who kills another" has been proven, the judge *must* sentence the guilty party to the punishment described.

Put bluntly, triers of fact in the criminal procedure are not interested in just any facts, but only such facts which may be relevant to determine whether someone is guilty of a crime. According to Ho, "[t]ruth is pursued for the sake of justice, where justice is primarily understood as the correct application of law to true findings of fact".[12] Because norms include descriptions of facts, knowledge of facts is actually essential for applying them. In other words: "The truth needs to be found not for its own sake but to apply the rules and principles to the dispute correctly."[13]

Yet a third point of view to the subject of this book, broadly speaking, might be what I have suggested in my dissertation: that the legal process of proof could be understood more generally as a **process** with inputs and outputs. Inputs are claims of facts and evidence that parties offer to support their legal claims. The court, acting as a sort of machine or computer in this analogy, evaluates the evidence offered to it and compares its factual findings to the claims of the parties and to the norms valid in that particular legal system. The outcome is a judgment in which the parties' claims are either accepted or rejected.

Questions of fact and, therefore, proof and evidence, may be the only disputed questions in trials. The parties may well agree that "if X, then Y", but disagree "whether X". While people's rights are at stake in trials, because they seek or attempt to avoid a certain normative outcome, they are at stake with regard to evidence, too. The ways in which evidence is gathered, presented and assessed may have an effect on people's rights. These rights may, in turn, be of either substantive or procedural nature. Both human rights and national legislation provide normative limits to the process of proof.

3.2 Basic concepts of evidence law

There are several excellent textbooks on evidence law which explain the basic concepts of this field. Perhaps it is worth briefly reminding the reader of some of

---

11 A. Aarnio, *Mitä lainoppi on?* (Helsinki: Tammi, 1978), 65–66.
12 H. L. Ho, *A Philosophy of Evidence Law* (Oxford: Oxford University Press, 2008), 48.
13 M. D. Bayles, *Principles of Law: A Normative Analysis* (Dordrecht: D. Reidel Publishing Company, 1987), 20.

the most important ones. First, **relevance**, a term which might be used in relation to both facts and evidence. When deciding a case, a court is not interested in just any facts, but those that are directly (*factum probandum*) or indirectly (*factum probans*) relevant to the claims of the parties.[14] Using the example of manslaughter, the fact "the defendant struck the victim with a knife causing the victim's death" is directly relevant. Notice, however, that whether this fact can be proved or not is another matter.

Of indirect relevance may be the fact that the defendant was present at the scene of the crime. This fact does not, in isolation, lead us to conclude that the defendant is guilty of a crime. It may prove significant if it is suggested that the fact is relevant for such a conclusion with other indirect facts, such as motive. Such evidence is called **circumstantial** as opposed to **direct** evidence. Even less important, at first glance, is a fact such as "it was a rainy evening". This sort of information may also become relevant as collateral facts, if for example an eyewitness claims it was sunny or that they were able to see the perpetrator's facial features from a distance of 50 metres. In such situations, seemingly unimportant details may gain importance for the assessment of the witness's credibility.[15]

Another possible meaning for relevance is whether a piece of evidence has any probative value at all (i.e. whether any relevant conclusions can be drawn from it). As Choo explains:

> an item of evidence is considered relevant if it renders the fact to be proved *more probable than it would be without that evidence*. Thus, an item of evidence is relevant so long as it has probative value or probative force, however little.[16]

Irrelevant evidence, then, has no probative value. Here it should be noticed that irrelevant evidence may be offered to prove relevant facts or, in the worst case, irrelevant facts. In either case, such evidence should not be admitted. Similarly, evidence should not be admitted if it can only be used to prove an irrelevant fact.

The concept of **admissibility** is of great importance to the subject of this book. According to Choo's definition, "[i]f it is relevant and does not infringe any exclusionary rule, [evidence] will be *admissible*. Admissible evidence can, however, be excluded in the exercise of *judicial discretion*."[17] In other words, admissibility concerns the question of whether evidence can be allowed to be assessed as such or whether there are norms restricting the use of evidence in some ways. Even if evidence is admitted, there may be rules of use that the trier of fact must obey.

---

14 A. L.-T. Choo, *Evidence*, 2nd edn (Oxford: Oxford University Press, 2015), 2.
15 Choo 2015, 2 and 5.
16 Choo 2015, 3. The American Federal Rule of Evidence 401 distinguishes between the relevance of evidence and facts as follows: "Evidence is relevant if: (a) it has any tendency to make a fact more or less probable than it would be without the evidence; and (b) the fact is of consequence in determining the action."
17 Choo 2015, 2.

Such rules may also have a restrictive effect on the freedom of proof, which is the subject of the following subchapter.

As explained in *Kilbourne*, "'[w]eight' of evidence is the degree of probability (both intrinsically and inferentially) which is attached to it by the tribunal of fact once it is established to be relevant and admissible in law".[18] A better term for this feature is, in my opinion, **probative value**. It depends, first of all, on the reliability of the evidence, which may require proof of collateral facts. I believe this is what is meant by intrinsic degree of probability in *Kilbourne*. Secondly, and especially if the fact is an only indirectly relevant *factum probans*, the probative value is dependent on what (if any) meaningful inferences can be drawn from the existence of that fact. Of course, the existence of the fact must be proven first.

Next, evidence may be classified into testimonial and real evidence. Testimonial evidence is usually an oral statement made in open court. However, I would not consider a written or recorded statement of what a person has said as real evidence. Rather, I think real evidence is best defined as objects and documents. Perhaps, then, a better dichotomy for the purposes of this book is to separate **real evidence** from **statements**, be they made by the parties, witnesses or experts and presented orally or through other means. My point here is that statements are different from real evidence not only because of the medium of evidence but also because of the content. Real evidence can only rarely be as comprehensive as statements and the evaluation of statements includes similar problems regardless of how they are presented.[19]

Finally, the burden and standard of proof. The former refers to the party bearing the "duty" to present sufficient evidence. A failure to do so will lead to the issue being decided in favour of their counterparty. In criminal trials it follows from the presumption of innocence that the prosecution bears the **burden of proof**. There are, however, certain situations where the defendant's inactivity may have adverse effects for their case. **Standard of proof**, on the other hand, describes how convinced the trier of fact must be of the existence of the facts in issue. In criminal proceedings, many countries (Finland included) have adopted the common law standard of proof "beyond reasonable doubt".[20]

What constitutes a "reasonable" doubt is a perennial question in evidence law and cannot be explored in detail here. An often-quoted definition in *Miller* reads:

> That degree is well settled. It need not reach certainty, but it must carry a high degree of probability. Proof beyond reasonable doubt does not mean proof beyond the shadow of a doubt. [...] If the evidence is so strong against a man as to leave only a remote possibility in his favour which can be dismissed with the sentence "of course it is possible, but no in the least probable," the case is proved beyond reasonable doubt, but nothing short of that will suffice.[21]

18 DPP v. Kilbourne [1973] A.C. 729, 756.
19 Choo 2015, 8.
20 Choo 2015, 29 and 47.
21 Miller v. Minister of Pensions [1947] 2 All E.R. 2, 372.

This means that instead of certainty of guilt we must accept a high probability of guilt.

Interestingly, in The Crown Court Compendium it is pointed out that "[i]t is unwise to elaborate on the standard of proof".[22] This may be so with regard to a jury, but it doesn't offer much help to professional judges. Of course, a precise definition of "reasonable doubt" probably cannot be presented. Although the question is an important one, I will simply repeat that the standard of proof requires us to adopt a method of scepticism. If, after a fair and proper assessment of all the evidence, we are satisfied that the case against the accused is convincing and the hypotheses favourable to the defence can be dismissed as mere claims without any valid factual support, then the standard has been reached. Otherwise, there is a reasonable doubt at hand.

3.3 Free proof

One key function of evidence and proof is to ensure that the factfinder may reach a correct verdict. In a criminal procedure, rectitude of decision simply requires that the innocent go free and the guilty are convicted. The starting point in evidence law is freedom of proof as opposed to a rigid system of legal proofs. For example, according to the 1734 Swedish Code of Procedure similar testimonies of two disinterested witnesses were required for "full proof", whereas the statement of a single witness was only "half proof". There was also a rather intricate system of norms on the competence of witnesses, clearly to make sure that they are disinterested. Such a system, although fairly advanced in its time, was later deemed a hindrance to the administration of justice and was far too easy to abuse.

The rationale behind the freedom of proof is to allow correct decision-making by freeing factfinders from the constraints of legal norms and "legal proof". It is important to understand that free proof is often, if not usually, defined in relation to legal proof, namely that free proof is *not* legal proof. Such a definition leaves open what it actually *is*, then. One definition might be that "all facts having rational probative value are admissible, unless some specific rule forbids".[23] Without normative restrictions, it is believed that the parties can bring the best available evidence to the trial and the court can evaluate it properly based on only epistemological rules. Freedom of proof does not mean, however, freedom from the requirement that factual findings are the result of a sound and proper factual assessment.

As already noted, freedom of proof does not mean that the factfinder would be free not to reason why they have arrived at certain findings or not. The process of factfinding and reasoning, although free from normative boundaries, must follow

---

22 *Crown Court Compendium. Part I: Jury and Trial Management and Summing Up* (Judicial College, 2021) § 5.3.
23 J. H. Wigmore, *A Treatise on the Anglo-American System of Evidence in Trials at Common Law*, 2nd edn (Boston, MA: Little, Brown and Company, 1923), vol. I, 152.

valid epistemological and empirical rules. In other words, the judge is not allowed to simply follow their intuition. This is a rule I think is embedded in the high standard of proof: one cannot draw final factual conclusions based on the first glance of claims or evidence. A defendant can only be found guilty after all possible doubts of their guilt have been properly investigated. It may well be that the initial hypothesis introduced by the prosecution is correct, but it must be tested rigorously.

Unfortunately, the human mind is prone to making shortcuts in thinking. Intuition and rules of thumb have developed to help our ancestors deal with tricky situations quickly. However, sometimes "individuals draw inferences or adopt beliefs where the evidence for doing so in a logically sound manner is either insufficient or absent". In such situations, our cognition is biased.[24] It has also been suggested that "people rely on a limited number of heuristic principles which reduce the complex tasks of assessing probabilities and predicting values to simpler judgmental operations. In general, these heuristics are quite useful, but sometimes they lead to severe and systematic errors."[25]

A recent study has found that wrongful convictions are often the result of confirmation bias, defined as "a type of selective thinking. Once a hypothesis has been formed, our inclination is to confirm rather than refute it. We tend to look for supporting information, interpret ambiguous information as consistent with our beliefs, and minimize any inconsistent evidence."[26] The effects of confirmation bias were supported by faulty assumptions, probability errors, and groupthink. Usually, such cognitive errors are the result of premature judgment, which may result from pressure to solve a crime. In such situations, our best intentions may act against sound empirical rules.

Freedom of proof, then, can be said to require that although the basic system of rules to be applied is epistemological (empirical, logical, scientifically valid), those rules must be taken seriously and followed carefully. Normative rules have been rejected as the basic framework because they have not been capable to ensure an epistemologically sound process or, in Goldman's words cited above, taking freedom of proof as a starting point seems to be the comparatively reliable process, even though it is not sufficiently reliable to guarantee a completely certain outcome.

To allow freedom to the extent of basing judgments on intuition would mean allowing arbitrariness. According to the Court in *Moreira Ferreira (No. 2)*:

> a domestic judicial decision cannot be qualified as arbitrary to the point of prejudicing the fairness of proceedings unless no reasons are provided for it or

---

24 M. G. Haselton, D. Nettle and P. W. Andrews, "The Evolution of Cognitive Bias" in D. M. Buss (ed.), *Handbook of Evolutionary Psychology* (Hoboken, NJ: Wiley, 2005), 724.

25 A. Tversky and D. Kahneman, "Judgment under Uncertainty: Heuristics and Biases" (1974) 185 *Science*, 1124.

26 D. K. Rossmo and J. M. Pollock, "Confirmation Bias and Other Systemic Causes of Wrongful Convictions: A Sentinel Events Perspective" (2019) 11 *Northeastern University Law Review*, 970, 810–816.

if the reasons given are based on a manifest factual or legal error committed by the domestic court, resulting in a "denial of justice".[27]

Conversely, a manifest factual error or lacking reasoning could amount to a denial of justice and violate Article 6. The requirement that judgments are **reasoned** is, of course, applicable to questions of fact. This requirement is considered, here, to be a sort of meta-level rule of evidence.

The general requirement of reasoning is explained well in the previous section of *Moreira Ferreira (No. 2)*:

> The Court also reiterates that according to its established case-law reflecting a principle linked to the proper administration of justice, judgments of courts and tribunals should adequately state the reasons on which they are based. The extent to which this duty to give reasons applies may vary according to the nature of the decision and must be determined in the light of the circumstances of the case [...]. Without requiring a detailed answer to every argument advanced by the complainant, this obligation presupposes that parties to judicial proceedings can expect to receive a specific and explicit reply to the arguments which are decisive for the outcome of those proceedings [...].[28]

In other words, a general requirement is that courts explain to the parties and the society as a whole, through the reasoning of their judgments, why disputed facts have been established or not. Reasoning a judgment is, in my opinion, a form of art which requires understanding the needs of various stakeholders and balancing them to create a sufficiently concise, yet properly reasoned judgment. The episte-mological process should not be hidden behind meaningless phrases or empty words, because such practices give rise to suspicions towards the validity of such process and the whole judgment. Freedom of proof, then, does not free judges from the requirement of giving a reasoned judgment.

3.4 Rules of evidence

Another concept which may prove difficult to define is **rules of evidence**. As already noted, such rules govern the process of proof (i.e. how courts admit and assess evidence). For our purposes, rules of evidence are models which the Court has developed and uses to determine whether the use of evidence violates Article 6 or not. The domestic authorities can translate such models into domestic rules of evidence, including admissibility rules, when performing their diffusing function and translating the Court's interpretations into domestic law. This is based on the effects of the Court's case law on domestic law discussed above.

Freedom of proof applies in all three main stages of the process of proof. Parties and authorities are free to gather, present, and evaluate evidence. These freedoms

27 Moreira Ferreira v. Portugal (No. 2) [GC], 11.7.2017, § 85.
28 Moreira Ferreira v. Portugal (No. 2) [GC], 11.7.2017, § 84.

can be restricted, but freedom is the general rule and restrictions are the exception. The mere concept of (normative) rules of evidence might be problematic for a "hardcore" proponent of freedom of proof. Ultimate freedom would require that only empirical rules should be relevant in the process of proof. It might appear a little paradoxical that the rationale – or a rationale – behind some rules of evidence is ensuring the **reliability** or reliable assessment of evidence.

How can it serve as a rationale for both freedom of evidence and rules possibly restricting evidence? It must be understood that freedom of proof should not be seen as an end, but as means to ensure the correctness of the outcome by not restraining the process of proof. As a starting point, freedom of proof allows a more reliable process of proof. Empirical rules are usually too complex to be stated as normative rules, at least in such a way that they could form the starting point. However, normative rules may be well-founded if it can be empirically proved that human cognition is likely to lead to erroneous outcomes when assessing certain evidence. In such situations, freedom of proof would no longer be able to guarantee the most reliable process of proof.

Sometimes, then, rules of evidence may be needed to supplement the freedom of proof and to make sure that intuition cannot take over the process of proof instead of the sound epistemological rules that should be employed. Tversky and Kahneman have shown, for example, that our intuitive heuristics are not in line with the theories of probability mathematics.[29] Rules of evidence could counteract any tendencies to over- or undervalue the reliability of evidence and to remind the factfinder that the matter may be more complex than rules of thumb might suggest at first glance. This is also in line with the method of doubt.

Rules of evidence can be classified in many ways. One famous classification is that explained by Wigmore:

> [R]ules of admissibility may be grouped under three heads, the first dealing with the probative value of specific facts [rules of relevance], the second including artificial rules which do not profess to define probative value but yet aim at increasing or safeguarding it [rules of auxiliary probative policy], and the third covering all those rules which rest on extrinsic policies irrespective of probative value.[30]

The first two groups of rules, which Wigmore called *rules of probative policy*, are designed to protect the accuracy of fact-finding and rectitude of decision.

A point worth making here already is that rules of evidence are not necessarily rigid or absolute. They may be flexible in several ways. For example, a rule of evidence may require corroboration in cases where there is a risk of erroneous assessment of the reliability of evidence. If such rules were very rigid, requiring the

29 Tversky and Kahneman 1974.
30 Wigmore 1923, vol. I, 154–155. See also J. D. Jackson and S. J. Summers, *The Internationalisation of Criminal Evidence: Beyond the Common Law and Civil Law Traditions* (Cambridge: Cambridge: University Press, 2012), 70–71.

automatic exclusion of evidence, they would be very close to the rigid rules of evidence known in times of legal proofs. On the other hand, even empirical rules allow rigidity in situations where a piece of evidence lacks relevance (i.e. cannot be used to prove or disprove any meaningful facts). Such evidence should be excluded even in a system of free proof for epistemological reasons.

Wigmore continues:

> The third group of rules invokes, for the exclusion of certain kinds of facts, extrinsic policies which override the policy of ascertaining the truth by all available means. These rules concede that the evidence in question has all the probative value that can be required, and yet exclude it because its admission would injure some other cause more than it would help the cause of truth, and because the avoidance of that injury is considered of more consequence than the possible harm to the cause of truth. Most of these rules consist in giving certain kinds of persons an option – i.e. a Privilege – to withhold the evidential fact.[31]

These, by contrast, are *rules of extrinsic policy*.

Substantive legislation, such as criminal law, exists fundamentally to protect certain **rights and values**. This is also true of procedural legislation. Such legislation may be needed to ensure that the process of proof does not lead to violations of the rights and values which should enjoy protection and are, indeed, protected by substantive legislation as well. One way to classify extrinsic policies further is to divide them into secrecies and human rights, such as the right to privacy and prohibition of torture. Perhaps needless to say, the right to a fair trial is an important extrinsic policy. Other classifications than the ones suggested here are possible, too.

Rules of extrinsic policy may, by definition, lead to the exclusion of reliable evidence. I would underline, though, that it is not their purpose to exclude such evidence nor to suppress the search for truth.[32] The public interest of punishing the guilty cannot be set, as a rule, above the extrinsic policies protected by procedural legislation. While extrinsic policies may lead to seemingly unjust outcomes in certain situations, it should be common ground in any democratic society under the rule of law that evidence cannot be obtained without any normative limits. And when normative limits are imposed, allowing them to be ignored would mean a deviation from the very principle of rule of law. Procedural safeguards must, like any legislation, be taken seriously.

The term "rules of evidence" seems also fitting in the context of the Court's case law because of the formulation of Alexy's Law of Competing Principles: "The circumstances under which one principle takes precedence over another constitute the conditions of a rule which has the same legal consequences as the principle taking precedence."[33] This, in my view, can be interpreted as follows: if we can

---

31 Wigmore 1923, vol. I, 155.
32 Compare Wigmore 1923, vol. IV, 623.
33 R. Alexy, *A Theory of Constitutional Rights* (Oxford: Oxford University Press, 2002), 53–54.

point out circumstances under which the Court would find that the use of evidence violates Article 6 or not, we can formulate a rule of evidence in which those circumstances become conditions for using evidence in a domestic trial.

Nowadays there is a clear trend in the Court's case law towards explaining in more detail the criteria they use to assess potential violations. This will become clear from the judgments we shall examine in the following chapters. Such criteria and their weight in relation to one another form normative mechanisms which can be, at least in principle, applied by domestic courts just as well as the Court in Strasbourg. Thus, for the purposes of this book, the concept of "rules of evidence" must be understood as a synonym to the assessment models or tests the Court employs. Such rules consist of various criteria with various importance.

It is also useful to examine what rights and values rules of evidence seek to promote (i.e. what is their rationale). Understanding the rationale may be necessary to understand the logic of the test and why the test includes the components it does. It may also help interpret the criteria. While the Court often expresses the rationale(s) of a test, sometimes the criteria themselves reveal something about the rationale as well. This is because the mechanism of a rule of evidence reflects its rationale, which is why I shall also make an attempt to find out what interests each rule is intended to protect in the Court's thinking. I will not, however, attempt to discuss theories of exclusion of evidence in general.[34]

As a result of the Court's role and the need to adopt a flexible approach to exclusion of evidence, the rules that can be derived from the Court's case law are rarely strict in nature. Sometimes, the tests the Court has adopted should be viewed as requirements that should be met instead of admissibility rules. They are, to use an analogy, hurdles to be cleared instead of solid walls. Such rules could better be termed as "rules of use".[35] However, there are also situations where the Court requires exclusion of evidence or a similar outcome. This is another reason for me using the term "rules of evidence" while understanding that it can be used in a broader meaning as well.

Another classification worth mentioning here is the distinction made between three types of admissibility rules based on their scope (i.e. what is restricted). The first type would be *Beweisthemenverbote*, which forbid presenting evidence of certain facts, such as state secrets. Secondly, *Beweismittelverbote* are rules forbidding the use of certain means of evidence, such as a family member of the accused. And thirdly, *Beweismethodenverbote* forbid a certain method of obtaining evidence.[36] The scope could, in my opinion, be expanded to include other uses of evidence as well. Furthermore, these types can overlap.

---

34 See Jackson and Summers 2012, 153–158, and M. Madden, "A Model Rule for Excluding Improperly or Unconstitutionally Obtained Evidence" (2015) 33 *Berkeley Journal of International Law*, 442 for overviews of the various theories suggested both for and against exclusion of evidence.

35 P. McNamara, "The Canons of Evidence – Rules of Exclusion or Rules of Use?" (1986) 10 *The Adelaide Law Review*, 341; 343 and 364.

36 F. Eder, *Beweisverbote und Beweislast im Strafprozess* (Munich: Herbert Utz Verlag, 2015), 31–32.

3.5 Seriousness, impact, and counterbalancing

I have developed a simple framework or model to describe the basic mechanism the Court seems to employ when assessing whether the use of evidence has violated the fairness of a trial as a whole. As the formulation already implies, various factors for or against finding a violation should be taken into account. The main factors can be classified under three broader concepts, namely the seriousness, impact, and counterbalancing (SIC) of the interference in question. Whether an interference with defence rights amounts to a violation of Article 6 can be decided based on these factors.

First, there may be violations of different degrees when it comes to their **seriousness**. For example, getting a confession through torture would be more serious a breach than getting it by way of planting an informant in the same cell as a suspect with instructions to push the suspect for information. Likewise, denying a suspect the right to choose their lawyer seems less serious a breach than denying access to any lawyer. Refusal to arrange possibility to cross-examine a witness while knowing they will soon be out of reach of the authorities would seem more serious than if cross-examination becomes impossible due to the witness's surprising illness. And so on.

Second, the **impact** of an interference may also vary. If the impugned evidence is sole or decisive proof of the defendant's guilt, a breach in retrieving it would have a greater impact than if it was only a small piece of a vast body of evidence. The impact of a breach would also be greater if it leads the authorities to discover new evidence or a new crime of which they were not aware and would not even have become aware had the breach not occurred. If, on the other hand, the impugned evidence is not used against the defendant at all, the impact of a breach would be removed altogether. In the context of Article 6, the point of comparison must always be the outcome of the trial and the material relied on by the court.

Third, the assessment of fairness "as a whole" allows certain breaches to be **counterbalanced**. Even if an initial or primary breach may have happened in the evidence procedure, some procedural safeguards may suffice to counteract the impact of the breach later on. For example, the use of video recording of a hearing may counterbalance the fact that opportunity to cross-examine a witness was restricted. In the context of illegally gathered evidence, it is considered a counterbalancing factor if the reliability of the impugned evidence has not suffered as a result of how it was obtained.

The three types of arguments are linked to each other. The more serious the breach is and the more impact it has on the procedure, the more counterbalancing factors should weigh for the overall fairness to be restored. Mathematically this can be formulated as $S \times I = C$. This illustrates that the seriousness and impact of the breach must be assessed together. Even if a serious breach has taken place but it has had no impact on the outcome of the procedure, no counterbalance is required in principle. A breach which may not appear very serious may, on the other hand, have serious impact on the procedure. If there aren't sufficient procedural safeguards in place to counterbalance that impact, the overall fairness cannot be restored, and the Court must find that Article 6 has been violated.

Any domestic exclusionary rule is aimed at removing the impact of a violation of some interest the rule seeks to protect by breaking the causal link between a piece of evidence and the violation of a right it has resulted from. For example, information about what a doctor has heard from a patient may have to be excluded to protect the confidential nature of their communication. If evidence is excluded, it would place the parties in a position similar to that in which the information was never presented – it should not affect the outcome of the trial. This is why the Court's case law easily transforms into rules of admissibility on the domestic level. Exclusion is an appropriate means to remove the impact of a violation against the right to a fair trial even if the violation is very serious.

In *Gäfgen*, when assessing whether the applicant had lost his victim status as the result of partial exclusion of evidence, the Court did not "exclude the possibility that in cases in which the deployment of a method of investigation prohibited by Article 3 led to disadvantages for an applicant in criminal proceedings against him, appropriate and sufficient redress for that breach may have to entail, in addition to the above-mentioned requirements, measures of restitution addressing the issue of the continuing impact of that prohibited method of investigation on the trial, in particular the exclusion of evidence obtained by breaching Article 3". It later continued that "both a criminal trial's fairness and the effective protection of the absolute prohibition under Article 3 in that context are only at stake if it has been shown that the breach of Article 3 had a bearing on the outcome of the proceedings against the defendant, that is, had an impact on his or her conviction or sentence".[37]

In *Martin*, the domestic court of appeal has excluded the applicant's pre-trial statements made in breach of his defence rights. However, the court of appeal had considered that the making of a confession could be used as "general knowledge". This ineffectiveness of the exclusion of evidence was noticed by the Court: "Although tainted evidence as such can be left aside in the subsequent proceedings, in the present case the Court of Appeal's decision nevertheless demonstrated that the consequences of the breach of defence rights had not been totally undone."[38]

Of course, similar effects could be reached if the impugned evidence is never presented. Nothing would prevent the prosecutor from anticipating that the use of some particular information would violate the right to a fair trial (or some other relevant interest) and choose not to present it. Exclusion, on the other hand, might take place during a hearing, where the trial judge could immediately reject evidence and make it clear that it will not be relied upon when deciding the case. It would also be possible to apply exclusionary rules after a trial but before delivering the judgment. Finally, a court of appeal would often be well placed to assess the fairness of a trial as a whole and exclude evidence if needs be.

37 Gäfgen v. Germany [GC], 1.6.2010, §§ 128 and 178.
38 Martin v. Estonia, 30.5.2013, §§ 94–96.

As will become apparent when we go through the various rules of evidence, the Court has developed its own models for the assessment of overall fairness under different circumstances. Nowadays there is an apparent trend towards explaining these models and making them more understandable. Often, the Court itself calls such models "tests", such as "the test set out in *Salduz*". It seems clear to me that these tests, especially since they are explained under the heading "general principles", are just that: meant to be applied generally to assess the overall fairness of certain types of breaches. That is why I choose to call them rules of evidence. Naturally, the unique facts of each case determine the outcome of such assessment.

The framework proposed here, abbreviated hereinafter as **SIC**, is not meant to replace those tests. It is meant to serve as a meta-level theory helping to understand the mechanisms of the tests and rules of evidence derived from them. While the importance and application of the three criteria may change between tests, the framework is also intended to help understand such variations. Of course, the rationale of a rule of evidence explains, in turn, why the mechanism is what it is. For example, why torture evidence should be assessed applying a different rule than untested evidence. We shall now proceed with these rules and examine their mechanisms more closely.

4   Basic evidentiary rights

4.1 Introduction

In this first chapter discussing rules of evidence, we shall take a look at three separate evidentiary rights. Although they differ from each other greatly, what they have in common is that they form the basics of the process of proof in criminal trials, which is why I have grouped them together. They include, first, the presumption of innocence protected under Article 6 § 2, second, the right to adduce evidence, and third, the right to full disclosure of evidence. These rights, in a way, open the space for the other evidentiary rights and provide the settings for the presentation and evaluation of evidence.

A central element of the right to a fair trial is to allow the defence to participate effectively in the proceedings. Sometimes the defence may adopt a purely defensive strategy, questioning the reliability of prosecution evidence without adducing any evidence to the contrary, save perhaps a statement from the defendant. However, the defence may also choose a more active strategy and wish to adduce evidence of its own. Indeed, Article 6 § 3 (d) includes the minimum right for an accused to obtain the attendance and examination of witnesses on their behalf under the same conditions as witnesses against them.

In *Perna*, a landmark case on the right to adduce evidence, the Court considered the right to adduce evidence under that provision as well as Article 6 § 1, the right to a fair trial. Without elaborating the reasons to do so, the Court also considered whether the applicant's rights were violated because the national courts refused his requests to add two press articles to the file. While the Convention only expressly mentions the right to adduce evidence in the context of oral evidence, the Court applied similar principles to real evidence as well. This approach is well-founded since there is no reason to distinguish between the types of evidence.

Furthermore, it seems obvious that the right to adduce real evidence could be seen as an inherent part of not only the right to a fair trial generally, but another specific minimum right, namely the right to have adequate time and facilities for the preparation of one's defence. According to the Court, "[t]he right to an adversarial trial means, in a criminal case, that both prosecution and defence must be given the opportunity to have knowledge of and comment on the observations

DOI: 10.4324/9781003311416-4

filed and the evidence adduced by the other party [...]". This also requires that "the prosecution authorities disclose to the defence all material evidence in their possession for or against the accused [...]".[1]

In *Rowe and Davis*, for example, the Court stated that it would be unnecessary to examine the adequacy of the facilities for the preparation of the applicants' defence, because they amount to a complaint that they did not receive a fair trial. An assessment of the overall fairness under Article 6 § 1 was, therefore, sufficient.[2] This is in line with the Court's approach to the minimum rights specified under Article 6 § 3, which has been explained in Chapter 2. Because they are to be considered specific aspects rather than absolute requirements, assessment of the overall fairness is decisive.

Of course, we are now discussing two separate questions already: after having started with the defence's right to adduce evidence, the citation from *Rowe and Davis* takes us to the so-called "**knowledge of – comment on**" doctrine, which has to do with prosecution evidence and other material in their possession. What evidence may be adduced by the defence and whether they can gain knowledge of the evidence adduced by the defence are, while separate, also very basic questions in any criminal trial. They are, in a way, the two sides of a coin. Hopefully this makes sense to the reader as well.

4.2 The presumption of innocence

As mentioned already, the presumption of innocence expresses the factual starting point of a criminal trial. Because the accused is presumed innocent until proved guilty, a prosecutor seeking to convict them must present sufficient proof of guilt. Moreover, this should take place according to law. It should be noted right away that we shall not be dealing with matters of publicity or public expressions of guilt, because such aspects of the presumption of innocence are not primarily evidentiary in nature.[3] Instead, we shall focus on the burden of proof and legal presumptions.

Perhaps the easiest way to prove the worth and fundamental role of the principle is to think, for a moment, a criminal procedure based on the assumption that every accused is guilty until proven innocent. This would certainly affect how the authorities would investigate any suspected crime and result in a number of innocent convicts as well as, of course, guilty ones. Even if prosecutors tried their best to act as gatekeepers and only press charges against those they really believe to be guilty, such a system would not sound fair. The better alternative – although sometimes theoretical – would be to increase the resources aimed at investigating crime instead of watering down defence rights.[4]

---

1 Rowe and Davis v. the United Kingdom [GC], 16.2.2000, § 60.
2 Rowe and Davis v. the United Kingdom [GC], 16.2.2000, § 58.
3 For these aspects and the relevant case law see *Guide on Article 6 of the European Convention on Human Rights: Right to a Fair Trial (Criminal Limb)*, The European Court of Human Rights, 1.2.2022, 31 December 2021, 68–71.
4 R. L. Lippke, *Taming the Presumption of Innocence* (Oxford: Oxford University Press, 2016), 121.

In *Barberà, Messegué and Jabardo* the Court declared that "any doubt should benefit the accused".[5] Of course, as discussed already, guilt need not be proven beyond *any* doubt. Many European countries have adopted the common law standard "beyond reasonable doubt", as indeed has the Court itself. However, such a standard also reflects the presumption of innocence and the idea that a high degree of certainty must be reached before convicting an accused. But because criminal procedure is imperfect in that absolute certainty of events cannot be reached, a remote possibility of just any doubt would lead to an acquittal.

The presumption is linked with the privilege against self-incrimination, which will be discussed in Chapter 5, as well as the right to adduce evidence, which we shall discuss next. This becomes apparent from the following passage: "It also follows that it is for the prosecution to inform the accused of the case that will be made against him, so that he may prepare and present his defence accordingly, and to adduce evidence sufficient to convict him."[6] Additionally, the presumption sets requirements for the reasoning of a conviction. The right to a fair trial pre-supposes, in this regard, that the arguments of the defence are considered, and a finding of guilt reasoned sufficiently to show that any reasonable doubt can be precluded.

The Court assessed **legal presumptions** in *Salabiaku*, stating first that because presumptions of fact or of law operate in every legal system, they are not pro-hibited by the Convention in principle, but their application in criminal law should be limited. It added that "the national legislature would be free to strip the trial court of any genuine power of assessment and deprive the presumption of inno-cence of its substance, if the words 'according to law' were construed exclusively with reference to domestic law."[7] The point of the Court would seem to be that if such presumptions are used too freely, they might turn into presumptions of guilt and deprive domestic courts from the powers and independent discretion they must have in deciding criminal cases.

The applicant had gone to an airport to pick up a parcel which he was expecting to arrive on a specific flight. Unable to find it first, he picked up a trunk without recipient information left uncollected and took it through the customs. The applicant was detained, and the trunk investigated. It contained 10 kg of cannabis, of which the applicant claimed to have no knowledge, having expected foodstuff. Two days later, a parcel with the applicant's name and address was found in Brussels. When the authorities opened it, they found manioc flour, palm oil, pimento, and peanut butter.

The applicant was convicted in the first instance of both a narcotics crime and a customs offence. The court of appeal quashed the former conviction but upheld the second, because according to the domestic legislation the mere possession of prohibited goods when passing through customs was sufficient for liability, unless the accused showed "force majeure beyond his control". The applicant had not

5 Barberà, Messegué and Jabardo v. Spain [plenary], 6.12.1988, § 77.
6 Barberà, Messegué and Jabardo v. Spain [plenary], 6.12.1988, § 77.
7 Salabiaku v. France, 7.10.1988, § 28.

only gone through but also declared to the customs officers that the trunk was his property, although he had been warned by an airline official before picking up the anonymous parcel that it might contain illegal material. His failure to do so, together with the lower instance's finding of "bad faith" since he expressed no surprise upon discovering the real contents of the trunk, were sufficient to convict him of a customs offence. The Court noted that this was not the result of an automatic application of the presumption and found no violation of the presumption of innocence.[8]

Additionally, the presumption of innocence does not prevent the drawing of inferences from the accused's silence (see Section 5.8). The general principle is that prosecution must first adduce enough evidence to establish a prima facie case calling for an explanation from the defendant. If no explanation is given, the silence can be taken into consideration when evaluating the evidence against the accused. But to reverse the burden of proof in this way prior to the prosecution having established a sufficiently strong case against the accused would violate the presumption of innocence.

The Court found a violation of the presumption of innocence in *Telfner*. The applicant was convicted of causing injury by negligence. The victim had been hit by a car. He was able to identify the car but not the driver. The car was registered to the applicant's mother, who stated that she had not been driving it. She also told the police that the applicant was not home yet and that several family members used the car. The police had observed, however, that the applicant was its main user. The Court found that "[i]n requiring the applicant to provide an explanation although they had not been able to establish a convincing prima facie case against him, the courts shifted the burden of proof from the prosecution to the defence". Additionally, the domestic courts had speculated about the unsupported possibility of drunk driving, which added to "the impression that the courts had a preconceived view of the applicant's guilt".[9]

4.3 The *Perna* test

Very briefly put, the Court's case law on the **right to adduce evidence** underlines the national courts' duty to assess the relevance of any evidence the defence seeks to adduce and to give proper reasons if such evidence is rejected. It seems clear that the defendant does not have an absolute right to adduce any evidence they wish, for such a right could be easily abused. On the other hand, refusal to accept irrelevant evidence does not violate the rights of the defence, for such evidence would not have any affect – neither in favour of the defence or against them.

While recapitulating the general principles as they have appeared in its previous case law in *Perna*, the Court noted in particular that as a general rule, it is for the national courts to assess the evidence before them as well as the relevance of the

---

8 Salabiaku v. France, 7.10.1988, § 30.
9 Telfner v. Austria, 20.3.2001, §§ 17–20, compare John Murray v. the United Kingdom [GC], 8.2.1996, discussed below in chapter 5.8.

evidence which defendants seek to adduce. Thus, Article 6 § 3 (d) leaves it to the national courts, again as a general rule, to assess whether it is appropriate to call witnesses. It is accordingly not sufficient for a defendant to complain that he has not been allowed to question certain witnesses; he must, in addition, support his request by explaining why it is important for the witnesses concerned to be heard and their evidence must be **necessary for the establishment of the truth**. The Court added that these principles were applicable in examining defamation cases.[10]

The applicant in *Perna* was a journalist who was accused of defamation through the medium of the press after publishing an article about the principal public prosecutor in Palermo. In the article he claimed that the Italian communist party and its follower intended to gain control of the public prosecutors' offices of every city in Italy in order to gain power by non-electoral means. This was to happen by opening groundless investigations to destroy their political opponents' careers. The latest example of such practice, claimed the journalist, was an investigation concerning a well-known Italian statesman, which was based in part on information given by an informer.

At the trial, the defence requested that two press articles concerning the prosecutor's professional relations with the informer to be added to the file of the case. Additionally, the defence requested that the complainant should give evidence. The district court, however, refused the requests stating that the documents were not relevant to the object of the proceedings and that there was no point taking evidence from the complainant in view of the tenor of the article written by the applicant. The applicant was convicted.

The court of appeal dismissed the applicant's appeal, ruling inter alia that certain facts mentioned in the article as well as the trial were not defamatory. They included the prosecutor's political leanings, his friendship with a left-wing politician, and that as prosecutor he had used the statements of the informer who had been paid by the state. It was therefore not relevant, explained the court of appeal, to try to ascertain what political beliefs the prosecutor holds and whether or not he expressed them in specific circumstances. It was, on the other hand, defamatory to claim that the prosecutor acted for political reasons and with political interests.

Siding with the national courts, the Court agreed that the evidence the defence attempted to adduce would not have been capable of establishing that he had failed to observe the principles of impartiality, independence and objectivity inherent in his duties, that being the gist of the prosecution case. The applicant's defence was that these were critical judgments which there was no need to prove. Thus, he had not established that his requests to produce evidence would have been helpful in proving the alleged misconduct. There was no violation of Article 6.

The seemingly high threshold of "necessity" was interpreted slightly less strictly in practice. The Court went through its case law in great extent in *Murtazaliyeva*, noting that according to it,

---

10 Perna v. Italy [GC], 6.5.2003, § 29 (with further references).

[a]n applicant satisfies Article 6 § 3 (d) requirements if he or she submits a request which is sufficiently reasoned, relevant to the subject matter of the accusation and can arguably strengthen the position of the defence or lead to his or her acquittal". Such a request should include a sufficiently clear explanation as to "why the examination of a particular witness is necessary.[11]

Of course, the necessity is mentioned here, too, but in the company of a seemingly lower threshold of "sufficiency".

Examining its post-*Perna* case law in *Murtazaliyeva*, the Court also noted that it had repeatedly clarified that "when a defence witness' testimony is capable of reasonably establishing an accused's alibi, such a witness is considered *prima facie* relevant". On the other hand, the absence of a witness will not compromise fairness if the defence seeks to adduce evidence "in order to establish an issue beyond the scope of a charge" or the testimony would be incapable of proving the accused's innocence. Furthermore, the Court "has also stressed that a domestic court is not required to answer clearly vexatious requests to call defence witnesses".[12]

A further, important point is that the significance of a defence witness's testimony needs to be weighed against its ability to influence the outcome of a trial. The same principle would seem applicable to real evidence as well. In other words, the greater the significance of the evidence the defence is seeking to adduce, the more is expected of the reasoning of the court if it rejects it. What makes this more difficult is the fact that significance and relevance must be assessed before the evidence is actually presented and properly evaluated. This would call for healthy caution from the court before rejecting evidence. As an example, the Court mentioned that evidence of ill-treatment "might not be necessary if the impugned confession did not play a crucial role in establishing the applicant's guilt".[13]

The Court has also expressed a threshold for rejecting the defence's requests, stating that when the defence requests the examination of a witness who could have arguably strengthened the position of the defence or whose testimony could even have given rise to an acquittal, the domestic authorities must provide relevant reasons for dismissing such a request. In this context a reference by the courts to other facts of the case, which indicate why a witness could not have supplied new or important information, might be sufficient.[14] It seems obvious that the relevance and sufficiency of the reasoning, when rejecting evidence, should be assessed in relation the defendant's request and its reasoning.

The second step of the *Perna* test is whether the domestic courts' refusal to call a witness would undermine the **overall fairness** of the proceedings. According to the Court:

11 Murtazaliyeva v. Russia [GC], 18.12.2018, § 144 (with further references).
12 Murtazaliyeva v. Russia [GC], 18.12.2018, § 143 (with further references).
13 Murtazaliyeva v. Russia [GC], 18.12.2018, § 145 (with a further reference).
14 Murtazaliyeva v. Russia [GC], 18.12.2018, § 146.

It is only in exceptional circumstances that the Court will be led to conclude that the failure to hear a witness was incompatible with Article 6 of the Convention [...]. The dismissal of a request without giving reasons or the "silence" of the domestic courts in respect of a sufficiently reasoned and relevant request to call a defence witness does not necessarily lead to a finding of a violation of Article 6 [...].

Additionally, an applicant has to demonstrate that the examination of that witness was necessary and that the refusal to call the witness prejudiced the rights of the defence.[15]

4.4 Clarifications in Murtazaliyeva

After an exceptionally comprehensive recapitulation of its earlier case law, the Court proceeded in *Murtazaliyeva* to clarify the principles stated in *Perna*. The applicant had invited the Court to do precisely that, claiming that the *Perna* test was mechanical and placed an unduly high burden on the defence. According to the applicant, the standard of necessity should be fulfilled by not only witnesses whose testimony could lead to an acquittal, but also "generally witnesses of fact". The applicant contended that the witness in question was of great importance, because his activities had led to the creation of the body of evidence against her. Accordingly, his activities could be likened to those of an *agent provocateur*.

The Court started by rejecting the suggestion that the rules of international law concerning the examination of witnesses had evolved considerably beyond the *Perna* standard. However, it noted that while the *Perna* test consisted of two questions, namely whether the applicant has substantiated his or her request to call a particular witness by referring to the relevance of that individual's testimony for "the establishment of the truth" and, secondly, whether the domestic courts' refusal to call that witness undermined the overall fairness of the proceedings, the Court had also consistently examined the manner in which the domestic courts decided on a request to call a certain witness.[16]

The main clarification was that the reasoning offered by national courts was the "missing link" the Court wanted to make explicit, combining the two elements of the *Perna* test. This, the Court explained, is also in line with its role and the principle of subsidiarity concerning matters of evidence. As a summary, the Court concluded that "the question whether the domestic courts considered the **relevance** of an individual's testimony and provided **sufficient reasons** for their decision not to examine a witness at trial must be recognised as an independent and integral component of the test under Article 6 § 3 (d) of the Convention".[17]

In this context, the Court also underlined "the decisive importance of the domestic courts' duty to engage in a careful scrutiny of the relevant issues if the

15 Murtazaliyeva v. Russia [GC], 18.12.2018, § 148.
16 Murtazaliyeva v. Russia [GC], 18.12.2018, §§ 103–104 and 150–151.
17 Murtazaliyeva v. Russia [GC], 18.12.2018, §§ 154–156.

defence advances a sufficiently reasoned claim", in other words, the requirement that national courts must give sufficient reasons to their decisions. The Court reminded that "when the domestic authorities are presented with a legal challenge which might influence the overall fairness of the proceedings they must engage in a careful scrutiny of the issues, take steps to establish the relevant circumstances, and provide reasons adequate for their decisions".[18]

Because it is not the Court's role to decide questions of fact as a fourth instance but is limited to assessing the overall fairness of proceedings, it is in practice very much dependant on how national courts reason their judgments. If they fail to address reasonable issues raised by the parties which might affect the overall fairness of a trial, the Court will have great difficulty in approving their decision (let alone lack of one). On the other hand, if a national court does address such claims properly and in relation to their importance and also within the margin of appreciation, the principle of sub-sidiarity would require that the Court should not replace the national court's reasoning with its own.

As a summary of its approach to evidence the defendant seeks to adduce, including the now explicitly stated "logical link" between the two steps, the Court concluded in *Murtazaliyeva*:

> Where a request for the examination of a witness on behalf of the accused has been made in accordance with domestic law, the Court, having regard to the above considerations, formulates the following three-pronged test:
>
> 1 Whether the request to examine a witness was sufficiently reasoned and relevant to the subject matter of the accusation?
> 2 Whether the domestic courts considered the relevance of that testimony and provided sufficient reasons for their decision not to examine a witness at trial?
> 3 Whether the domestic courts' decision not to examine a witness under-mined the overall fairness of the proceedings?[19]

Thus, a detailed and sufficiently reasoned request to adduce evidence should still be regarded as the starting point. Instead of necessity, though, it will be enough that the evidence in question would be **relevant** to the subject matter. What should perhaps be highlighted is that it is enough for such evidence to be poten-tially relevant for the case (i.e. that it would help the prosecution case if it was credible and believed). Note also that evidence in some way favourable to the defendant should be admissible in principle, not only evidence capable of leading to an acquittal. This dually lower threshold was explained by the Court by giving examples from case law:

18 Murtazaliyeva v. Russia [GC], 18.12.2018, § 157 (with further references).
19 Murtazaliyeva v. Russia [GC], 18.12.2018, § 158.

While certain post-*Perna* cases examined whether a witness' testimony was relevant for the "establishment of the truth", others relied on its ability to influence the outcome of a trial [...], reasonably establish an accused's alibi [...], arguably lead to an acquittal [...] or arguably strengthen the position of the defence or even lead to the applicant's acquittal [...]. What appears to unite all of the above standards is the relevance of a witness's testimony to the subject matter of the accusation and its ability to influence the outcome of the proceedings. In the light of the evolution of its case law under Article 6 of the Convention the Court considers it necessary to clarify the standard by bringing within its scope not only motions of the defence to call witnesses capable of influencing the outcome of a trial, but also other witnesses who can reasonably be expected to strengthen the position of the defence.[20]

The relevance of the evidence should normally be explained by the defence. But the sufficiency of the reasoning also depends on the circumstances of a single case. In this connection the Court only referred to *Pello*, apparently as a warning example. It added that no abstract rule could be formulated, but listed the applicable provisions of the domestic law, the stage and progress of the proceedings, the lines of reasoning and strategies pursued by the parties and their procedural conduct as possible criteria, adding that the relevance of defence evidence might be so obvious in some situations that even scant reasoning given by the defence would suffice.[21]

The second question focuses on the reasoning of the national court if it rejects the request. The sufficiency of the reasoning is, in turn, proportional to the reasoning of the accused's request:

Any such assessment would necessarily entail consideration of the circumstances of a given case and the reasoning of the courts must be commensurate, i.e., adequate in terms of scope and level of detail, with the reasons advanced by the defence. [...] Accordingly, the stronger and weightier the arguments advanced by the defence, the closer must be the scrutiny and the more convincing must be the reasoning of the domestic courts if they refuse the defence's request to examine a witness.[22]

While clearly irrelevant or vexatious requests by the defence can be scantily dismissed by the court, it should be remembered that evidence may also be clearly relevant (such as evidence of an alibi) and, in such situations, scant reasoning from the defence should be accepted. National courts should always consider the defence's request to adduce evidence carefully, but how such a request needs to be

20 Murtazaliyeva v. Russia [GC], 18.12.2018, § 160.
21 Murtazaliyeva v. Russia [GC], 18.12.2018, § 161. See also Pello v. Estonia, 12.4.2007, §§ 28–35, where the Court concluded that "the domestic courts failed to make every reasonable effort to obtain the attendance and examination of the witnesses initially named by the prosecution and then called by the defence".
22 Murtazaliyeva v. Russia [GC], 18.12.2018, §§ 164–166.

answered depends on the circumstances of the case as well as the reasoning for the request. Courts should, in a way, give such requests the answer they deserve, whether it be more or less detailed.

Finally, the Court provided clarification to how it examines whether the **overall fairness** of a trial has suffered as a result of a domestic court's refusal to allow the suggested evidence. Again, the unique circumstances of each case must be considered. It is the development of the proceedings as a whole and not any particular aspect or incident which will be decisive in determining overall fairness. This approach also allows a more flexible assessment, as the Court pointed out. While the Court did refer to its judgment in *Ibrahim*, it did not specifically refer to the paragraph including the criteria for overall assessment.[23] Thus, it is unclear which factors might be relevant for the overall assessment.

The assessment of overall fairness seems, however, not to carry a decisive weight within the *Perna* test, even in its clarified form. Instead, it should perhaps be seen as a kind of safety valve. According to the Court, "[w]hile the conclusions under the first two steps of that test would generally be strongly indicative as to whether the proceedings were fair, it cannot be excluded that in certain, admittedly exceptional, cases considerations of fairness might warrant the opposite conclusion".[24] This seems to amount to a presumption of a violation of Article 6 in situations where a national court has dismissed a properly reasoned request to adduce evidence without giving sufficient reasons to it dismissal.

In the case of *Murtazaliyeva*, the defence did not provide strong arguments supporting the relevance and importance of two witnesses. As a result, the domestic court's decision to refuse the evidence was sufficiently reasoned. When assessing the overall fairness, the Court noted that the applicant had been assisted by two professional lawyers as well as able to conduct her defence effectively, confront and examine witnesses testifying against her, comment without hindrance on the incriminating evidence, adduce evidence she considered relevant, and to present her account of the events to the domestic courts. Her conviction was based on a considerable body of evidence against her including the statements of several prosecution witnesses, the material seized from her flat, forensic examination reports and the transcripts of the police surveillance videotapes. The Court found no violation of Article 6.[25]

The applicant argued in *Topić*, a pre-*Murtazaliyeva* case, that the trial court only relied on prosecution evidence and failed to allow the evidence he was seeking to adduce, including witnesses and a fingerprint analysis. He claimed to have thrown a beer can into a rubbish bin instead of the package of drugs which was the basis of the accusation against him. One of the prosecution witnesses had testified that there were beer cans in the bin, making this claim possible ("not fully vexatious or improbable"). No fingerprints or DNA were retrieved in spite of the applicant's request. What was more, "the trial court dismissed the applicant's

---

23 Murtazaliyeva v. Russia [GC], 18.12.2018, § 167.
24 Murtazaliyeva v. Russia [GC], 18.12.2018, § 168.
25 Murtazaliyeva v. Russia [GC], 18.12.2018, §§ 175 and 176.

request by merely noting that all the relevant facts had been sufficiently established [...], which cannot be considered a reasoned decision in itself [...], and could suggest that the witness statements heard by the domestic court were one-sided [...]".[26]

Just like the prosecution, the defence might inform a court in advance that they wish to hear certain witnesses. That a court does not reject the evidence does not automatically mean that the authorities would secure the **attendance** of any witnesses the defence is seeking to examine. In other words, there is a grey area between admitting evidence on paper and the right to obtain the attendance and examination of witnesses on the accused's behalf under the same conditions as witnesses against them. The effectiveness of this element of Article 6 § 3 (d) would require that witnesses can, if necessary, be compelled to attend.

There is a considerable body of case law describing the use of untested evidence against an accused and it includes the requirement that the authorities should make every reasonable effort to secure the attendance of prosecution witnesses for the purposes of cross-examination (see Chapter 9). However, the Court stated in *Sigurður Einarsson* that those considerations were not directly relevant when the applicants complained they would have wanted to examine. Instead, the Court applied the *Murtazaliyeva* test, indicating that the compellability of witnesses could be relevant as regards the domestic court's reasoning.[27]

The applicants had failed to submit a sufficiently reasoned request to hear the witnesses both in the domestic proceedings and before the Court. Their reasoning remained on a very general, if not speculative level. At the next stage of the test, the Court noted that the domestic supreme court had ruled that there was no reason to quash the district court judgment because it was not shown that the absence of the two witnesses might have had a significant impact on the outcome. Additionally, the prosecution would have suffered any adverse consequences of the lack of evidence. The Court also pointed out that both witnesses were outside Icelandic jurisdiction and not compellable to witness. They had also refused to give evidence by telephone upon the prosecution's request. At the third stage (overall assessment), the Court noted that there was a considerable volume of evidence and the testimonies of the two witnesses "did not go to the core of the charges against the applicants". Lastly, the domestic courts had not relied on the statements of the two witnesses. The had been no violation of the right to a fair trial.[28]

Nonetheless, the Court did refer to its earlier case law under the general principles it reiterated in *Murtazaliyeva* and stated that

> once the domestic courts have accepted, at least in principle, that the examination of a witness for the defence was relevant, they have an obligation to take "effective" measures to ensure the witness' presence at the hearing by

26 Topić v. Croatia, 10.10.2013, §§ 43–48.
27 Sigurður Einarsson and Others v. Iceland, 4.6.2019, § 107.
28 Sigurður Einarsson and Others v. Iceland, 4.6.2019, § 108–117.

way of, at the very least, issuing a summons [...] or by ordering the police to compel a witness to appear in court [...].

Failures to do so led to violations in both *Polufakin and Chernyshev* and *Pello*, respectively.[29]

4.5 Non-disclosure of information

If the defence is not allowed to adduce evidence, its position may be undermined in a way which would be incompatible with Article 6. A rather similar problem may arise if prosecution is in possession of material it does not disclose to the defence. In such a situation, the defence is left unaware of the nature and content of the material and may at least claim it includes information favourable to the defence case. Obviously, an even greater restriction of adversarial proceedings would be at hand if the prosecution could adduce evidence which would not be revealed to the defence but to the judges who would be able take it into account.

Normally, as already discussed, the right to an **adversarial procedure** – an element of the right to a fair trial – requires that "both prosecution and defence must be given the opportunity to have knowledge of and comment on the observations filed and the evidence adduced by the other party". Furthermore, "[t]he **facilities** which should be enjoyed by everyone charged with a criminal offence include the opportunity to acquaint himself, for the purposes of preparing his defence, with the results of investigations carried out throughout the proceedings".[30] The latter refers to the minimum requirement in Article 6 § 3 (b). Both can be seen as rationales of the rule requiring disclosure.

But the right to disclosure is not absolute:

In any criminal proceedings there may be competing interests, such as national security or the need to protect witnesses at risk of reprisals or keep secret police methods of investigation of crime, which must be weighed against the rights of the accused [...]. In some cases it may be necessary to withhold certain evidence from the defence so as to preserve the fundamental rights of another individual or to safeguard an important public interest. However, only such measures restricting the rights of the defence which are strictly necessary are permissible under Article 6 § 1 [...]. Moreover, in order to ensure that the accused receives a fair trial, any difficulties caused to the

29 Murtazaliyeva v. Russia [GC], 18.12.2018, § 147, Polufakin and Chernyshev v. Russia, 25.9.2008, §§ 207 and 208; Pello v. Estonia, 12.4.2007, §§ 34 and 35.
30 Murtazaliyeva v. Russia [GC], 18.12.2018, § 91. See also Edwards v. the United Kingdom, 16.12.1992, § 36: "The Court considers that it is a requirement of fairness under paragraph 1 of Article 6 [...], indeed one which is recognised under English law, that the prosecution authorities disclose to the defence all material evidence for or against the accused and that the failure to do so in the present case gave rise to a defect in the trial proceedings."

defence by a limitation on its rights must be sufficiently counterbalanced by the procedures followed by the judicial authorities [...].[31]

As in many other situations, the Court cannot usually assess the relevance or importance of the material in question but is limited to making an assessment the disclosure procedure and its fairness. Such an assessment would be impossible if the material is never revealed. The citation above includes three key elements which together form a rule of evidence. First, there must be a **competing interest** at hand. Second, it must be **strictly necessary** for the protection of that competing interest that information is not disclosed. And third, to preserve equality of arms as far as possible, the procedures must include sufficient **counterbalancing factors** capable of alleviating the possible disadvantage created by non-disclosure.

In this context it is necessary in my opinion to draw a distinction between evidence (i.e. information tendered to judges in order to affect the outcome of the trial) and potential evidence (i.e. information gathered during the investigation which may be of significance but is not tendered as evidence). An extremely malevolent prosecutor might, for example, have in their possession exonerating information obtained through surveillance of the defendant without their knowledge, but decide to keep such material secret to secure a conviction of an innocent defendant. Then again, any defendant might claim, without any factual support, that such exonerating material might exist. Obviously, it would be quite difficult to prove the opposite.

The landmark grand chamber judgments *Jasper* and *Rowe and Davis* concerned potential evidence. In *Jasper*, the applicant had been convicted after having been arrested in a garage where his meat lorry was parked, containing a large amount of cannabis resin. He had been under surveillance of customs officers and later investigation revealed other circumstantial evidence such as a safety deposit box of which the applicant was an authorised signatory under a false name, and which contained a large amount of cash and passport under the same false name. He was convicted of drug trafficking.

Before the applicant's trial the prosecution made an application to keep certain material in its possession secret on the basis of public interest immunity. While the defence were notified that such an application was to be made, they were not informed of the category of material which the prosecution sought to withhold. They were, however, given the opportunity to outline the defence case to the trial judge and request that any evidence relating to its claims would be disclosed. The trial judge examined the material and ruled that it should not be disclosed. The reasons of this decision were not disclosed to the defence either.

After reiterating the general principles, the Court noted that the defence were kept informed of the disclosure procedure and were allowed to participate in it as far as was possible without revealing the material the prosecution sought to not disclose. It also noted that the secret material formed no part of the prosecution

31 Jasper v. the United Kingdom [GC], 16.2.2000, § 52.

case and was never put to the jury which, of course, decided the question of facts in a jury trial. Furthermore, the trial judge had seen the material and was able to monitor throughout the proceedings whether the information would assist the defence. There was no violation of Article 6 § 1.[32]

By contrast, in *Rowe and Davis*, the decision to withhold material was not under judicial supervision in the first instance. Instead, the prosecution had decided, without notifying the judge, to withhold certain relevant evidence on grounds of public interest. The Court stated at the outset that such a procedure did not comply with the requirements of adversarial procedure, equality of arms and sufficient facilities for the preparation of a defence. It was only revealed in the appeal procedure that information had been withheld. The court of appeal reviewed the information *ex parte*, but this did not suffice to remedy the non-disclosure in first instance. The Court speculated that the court of appeal "may even, to a certain extent, have unconsciously been influenced by the jury's verdict of guilty into underestimating the significance of the undisclosed evidence".[33] There had been a violation of Article 6 § 1.

We shall soon take a closer look at the counterbalancing factors. Attempting to proceed step by step, we find that there is very little to be said about the Court's assessment of a competing interest and strict necessity required to withhold information from the defence. This is precisely because the Court is usually unable to assess the relevance of such material at all. How, then, can it ever ascertain that there is a competing interest at hand or that protecting this interest makes non-disclosure strictly necessary? There is an understandable yet noticeable absence of a substantive test of non-disclosure in the Court's approach.

Of course, some examples of what the competing interests might be are given. The short and non-exhaustive ("such as") list includes national security concerns, the need to protect witnesses at risk of reprisals and the interest of keeping secret police methods of investigation of crime. Protecting witnesses by non-disclosure of information would usually take the form of anonymous witness statements, a subject which will also be considered separately (see Chapter 9). However, identifying an interest which might be affected is not enough. For a trial to remain fair, non-disclosure must be practically the only way to protect that interest in a particular case. The decision must be based on a balancing exercise.

After repeating the principle of subsidiarity, the Court proceeded in both *Jasper* and *Rowe and Davis* to give what appears to me a slightly expansive interpretation of its *Edwards* judgment from 1992, stating that "[i]n cases where evidence has been withheld from the defence on public interest grounds, it is not the role of this Court to decide whether or not such non-disclosure was strictly necessary since, as a general rule, it is for the national courts to assess the evidence before them".[34] Thus, the Court will not control the substantive elements of the test,

---

32 Jasper v. the United Kingdom [GC], 16.2.2000, see especially §§ 54–56.
33 Rowe and Davis v. the United Kingdom [GC], 16.2.2000, § 65 *in fine*.
34 Jasper v. the United Kingdom [GC], 16.2.2000, § 53; Rowe and Davis v. the United Kingdom [GC], 16.2.2000, § 62. In Edwards v. the United Kingdom, 16.12.1992,

namely whether a competing interest strictly requires some material in possession of the prosecution to be withheld.

What makes this even more problematic is that often at the heart of a disclosure procedure is information concerning methods of police investigation. If potential evidence of entrapment is withheld from the defence and even the factfinders, there is a serious risk of miscarriage of justice. As we shall see later, the Court does require that a strict substantive test is used in assessing whether entrapment has taken place or whether the police have remained passive enough in an undercover role (see Section 7.3). Such a test will be impossible to apply or control if the relevant information is kept secret. In theory, the malevolent authorities might also want to keep secret other information which could lead to the exclusion of prosecution evidence.

In the assessment of a competing interest and necessity, then, the principle of subsidiarity gains great weight as does the integrity of national judges. It would be practically impossible to prove the negative, namely that the police would definitely not have secret information which might assist the defence. In the final analysis, the question boils down to one of trust. National authorities must scrutinise carefully whether there is a competing interest and whether it necessarily requires a deviation from the core values of a fair trial. Judicial supervision is indispensable precisely because the decision-making is otherwise completely shrouded in secrecy. Judges must exercise caution and take a critical approach instead of acting as rubber stamps.

In the recent case of *M v. the Netherlands* the applicant claimed that the domestic intelligence service had controlled the evidence by not disclosing all the relevant information. This, according to the applicant, also prevented him from an effective cross-examination of witnesses (see Chapter 9). The Court found that there was nothing to suggest that a report the accused wanted to access even existed and, in any event, it formed no part of the prosecution case and the domestic courts did not have the report either. The Court added: "In so far as the applicant wishes to imply that the investigation might have yielded information capable of disculpating him, the Court dismisses such a suggestion as entirely hypothetical."[35]

Some documents which did form a part of the evidence were redacted. According to the Court, "the information blacked out could in itself be of no assistance to the defence. Since the applicant was charged with having supplied State secret information to persons not entitled to take cognisance of it, the only question in relation to these documents was whether or not they were State secret". The last-mentioned fact in issue was proved with statements from the intelligence service and it was not disputed that the copies were genuine. Those measures did not violate Article 6.[36]

§ 34 referenced in both, no explicit mention is made of non-disclosure. Instead, only the more general subsidiary approach to evidentiary matters is mentioned.

35 M v. the Netherlands, 25.7.2017, § 68.
36 M v. the Netherlands, 25.7.2017, §§ 69–71.

On the other hand, the fact that the applicant was required to keep some potentially relevant information secret even from his own lawyer did violate the right to a fair trial because such communication should normally be free. Moreover, this effectively deprived him the assistance of a lawyer as regards the issue of disclosure. The Court stated that "it cannot be expected of a defendant to serious criminal charges to be able, without professional advice, to weigh up the benefits of full disclosure of his case to his lawyer against the risk of prosecution for so doing".[37]

Finally, as regards the cross-examination, an investigating judge had heard 13 witnesses whose names were revealed and seven unnamed witnesses. The unnamed witnesses were heard at a secret location and their voice and appearance were disguised. The hearing was attended by a representative of the intelligence service who, according to the applicant, had the power to prevent questions by the defence being answered. The Court found that in light of vast prosecution evidence against the applicant and that his defence relied on the possibility that someone else had leaked the secret information, these measures were not unreasonable and did not materially impair his defence.[38]

4.6 Counterbalancing non-disclosure

Let us now focus on the various possible procedures to counterbalance non-disclosure of (potential) evidence. First, an obvious way to allow some form of effective participation is to allow the defence to take part in the **disclosure procedure** itself. A rather ingenious way to do this is to allow the defence to outline their case. Should the material the prosecution seeks to keep secret contain any information which would assist this case, it should be revealed. Of course, it might be possible that no such information exists, but in principle, such a procedure provides the defence with an incentive to make truthful claims.

Defence participation should be as extensive as possible to be most effective. This might require that, if possible, something is revealed about the nature or content of the information in question. Naturally, it would not be possible to reveal the information completely if it is claimed that important competing interests require its secrecy. Revealing nothing as a rule would seem inconsistent with the principle of an adversarial procedure. Instead, it should perhaps be seen as a minimum. In *Jasper*, for example, the Court mentioned several times the importance of the decision-making procedure ensuring "as far as possible" the requirements of adversarial proceedings and equality.[39]

The second counterbalancing factor considered by the Court in *Jasper* was the fact that the information in question did not form any part of the prosecution case and was not put to the jury.[40] In other words, it was **not used to establish any**

---

37 M v. the Netherlands, 25.7.2017, §§ 93–97.
38 M v. the Netherlands, 25.7.2017, §§ 111–113.
39 Jasper v. the United Kingdom [GC], 16.2.2000, §§ 53, 55, and 58.
40 Jasper v. the United Kingdom [GC], 16.2.2000, § 55.

facts of the case. Because such information was only potential evidence, it would seem too hasty to say that this would have completely removed any impact of non-disclosure. However, it could be said that equality of the proceedings suffered less in a situation where neither the defence nor the prosecution relied on the information. What should be remembered also is that prosecution bears the burden of proof.

The third safeguard was that the trial judge, who had seen the withheld material and made the decision of non-disclosure, was in a position to continuously **monitor** whether the material would, after all, prove capable of assisting the defence case. Thus, he could review his decision during the trial if something new would have come up during the proceedings. The Court also pointed out, in this connection, that there was no reason to question the impartiality and independence of the judge. Thus, there was no reason to suspect that he would not have reversed his earlier decision, should the information prove in some way relevant for the defence.[41] Again, because the judge's discretion cannot be actually controlled, his monitorship could only be regarded as a counterbalance.

It must also be heavily underlined that such monitorship has been approved in the context of jury trial, where one of the judge's primary functions is to screen the evidence procedure but not to assess the evidence. This means the trial judge is well-placed to perform a monitoring function in situations where they are aware of the secret information, but this information cannot have a bearing on the outcome of the case in the sense that it could assist the prosecution case. This separation of functions was underlined in *Edwards and Lewis*. It seems that a similar approach cannot be accepted in situations where the judge also decides questions of fact.

Although the chamber judgment in *Edwards and Lewis* was first referred to the grand chamber, the government dropped this request, which led to the approval of the chamber decision. This has not – and, indeed, should not have – kept the Court from referring to the judgment in subsequent cases. *Edwards and Lewis*, as many others, concerned alleged police entrapment. Under English law, entrapment cannot be relied upon as a substantive defence against the charges but, instead, as a sort of procedural defence, requiring a stay of proceedings or exclusion of any evidence so obtained. Such a decision rests with the trial judge.

Information in both applicants' cases was not disclosed on public interest grounds and the judge was aware of the contents after having decided on non-disclosure. The Court concluded that because of non-disclosure, the applicants were unable to argue their case, and "[m]oreover, in each case the judge, who subsequently rejected the defence submissions on entrapment, had already seen prosecution evidence which may have been relevant to the issue".[42] In other words, the secret information could have affected a question of fact which the trial judge decided. Here, the Court set a seemingly low threshold of (potential) relevance.

41 Jasper v. the United Kingdom [GC], 16.2.2000, § 56.
42 Edwards and Lewis v. the United Kingdom [GC], 27.10.2004, § 46.

The authorities revealed, for the first time, during proceedings at the Court that the material had included information suggesting that the other applicant had been involved in the supply of heroin before the start of the undercover operation. Unaware of this, his defence were unable to even attempt to counter this allegation. The Court concluded that although no such revelation was made concerning the other applicant, there was a possibility that the judge was aware of material which would have damaged the submission of entrapment. Article 6 § 1 had been violated.[43]

In *McKeown*, the Court summarised the development of its case law at some length, underlining the importance of the trial judge being aware of the non-disclosed material in jury trials. The applicant submitted that his trial had been unfair because the trial judge had not decided on non-disclosure and was unaware of the secret material. Consequently, the judge could not have monitored the proceedings similarly to *Jasper* and decide to disclose some of the material based on the development of the defence arguments and the case. Crucially, though, there was no jury in that case. The trial judge was sitting alone as tribunal of fact as well as law.[44]

In Northern Ireland, a specialised disclosure procedure had been introduced where a professional judge decided whether to issue an order preventing disclosure. The "disclosure judge" would not sit later as the trial judge, preventing the possibility deemed rightfully problematic in *Edwards and Lewis* where relevant but secret information might affect the decision making without allowing adequate defence participation. At the outset of its analysis, the Court stated clearly that "subject to appropriate appellate review, the appointment of a disclosure judge would, in principle, meet the requirements of Article 6 § 1 of the Convention".[45]

The role of the disclosure judge was partly similar to the trial judge in *Jasper*. An *inter partes* hearing was held where the defence could outline their case. The disclosure judge noted that the material included only information which was either adverse to the defence or irrelevant. Furthermore, the disclosure judge concluded that "he did not anticipate any circumstances which would result in the material becoming of value to the defence". As the Court pointed out, the defence case remained unchanged, which meant that there was no need to re-evaluate the validity of the non-disclosure decision where that same defence had already been factored in. In fact, the Court agreed with the domestic court of appeal that there was "a purely speculative possibility of a change in the situation".[46]

In summary, a continuous monitoring of the grounds of non-disclosure is not necessary if the defence remains substantially the same as that explained to a disclosure judge. Such a monitoring function can be fulfilled by the trial judge, but

43 Edwards and Lewis v. the United Kingdom [GC], 27.10.2004, § 46.
44 McKeown v. the United Kingdom, 11.1.2011, see especially §§ 44–47.
45 McKeown v. the United Kingdom, 11.1.2011, § 48.
46 McKeown v. the United Kingdom, 11.1.2011, §§ 52 and 53.

only when sitting with a jury. If the trial judge is meant to also decide questions of fact, they should not be aware of any secret material which might prejudice the defence. In such situations, the balancing might be best left to a disclosure judge, a system expressly accepted by the Court as one which would satisfy the requirements of a fair trial, when accompanied with an adequate appellate review.

Finally, it would be possible to use a special counsel for the monitoring function. Such a counsel would be an independent agent, aware of the undisclosed material and able to follow the trial. In *Jasper*, the Court took notice of the United Kingdom having introduced the possibility of appointing one but deemed it unnecessary.[47] I would be very careful to generalise this statement, as the cases concerned a jury trial where the trial judge was able to carry out continuous monitoring, which was considered an important safeguard. Thus, the appointment of a special counsel need not be an exception in cases where some information is not provided to the defence.

4.7 The basic rules of evidence

I shall begin with the rule on adducing evidence for the defence. A domestic judge, especially in the first instance, may find it difficult to exclude evidence as irrelevant. But such an attitude is generally safer, although there is a limit to how much evidence can be presented without allowing the defence to "flood" the trial with useless evidence in a vexatious manner. Naturally, if a crime is exceedingly complex, more defence evidence can be admitted than if a petty crime and small amount of prosecution evidence are in question. Some guidance for such situations can be derived from the *Perna* test.

The admission of evidence should, in principle, reflect the adversarial nature of a trial. In other words, the accused should be allowed to present favourable evidence in order to prove their case. An arbitrary or unfounded restriction of this opportunity would give the prosecution (and prosecution evidence) an advantage at the cost of the defence or, as the Court might say, place the defendant at a substantial disadvantage vis-à-vis their opponents. At the same time, though, the balance would be tipped in the other direction if vexatious defence evidence were allowed.

As a starting point, the onus is on the defence to show that the evidence they seek to adduce is relevant. This rule would, in principle, apply similarly to any other party adducing evidence. The relevant threshold is not that the defence evidence would have to be necessary for the establishment of the truth – instead, it will suffice that it could reasonably be expected to strengthen the defendant's position in the trial. Put another way, the evidence should be in some way favourable for the defence and thus potentially relevant for the outcome. Whether the evidence will prove reliable or not is a question to be usually determined after it has been admitted.

The evidence may prove irrelevant even before it is admitted on two grounds, both of which were discussed in Section 3.2. First, evidence offered as proof of an

47 Jasper v. the United Kingdom [GC], 16.2.2000, § 55.

irrelevant fact would, as a consequence, be irrelevant. We might call this "factual irrelevance" to separate it from the second situation, where the evidence is offered as proof of a relevant fact, but that evidence is incapable of proving the fact. This sort of "evidentiary irrelevance" may also be difficult to assess beforehand. Indeed, the case of *Perna* was an example of factual, not evidentiary irrelevance.

If evidence is not admitted, a domestic court should provide sufficient reasons for a rejection. There is a correlation between the grounds of the motion to adduce evidence and the requirement of sufficient reasoning. The stronger the defence claims of relevance are, the more is required to dismiss their motion, and *vice versa* – keeping in mind, though, that sometimes factual or evidentiary relevance is fairly obvious. So, for example, proof offered of the defendant's alibi would be difficult to reject, unless there is an abundance of it offered already. I see no unfairness in principle if a domestic court informs both the prosecution and the defence that, for example, two witnesses are allowed from both sides on the issue of alibi.

In any case, it would not be sufficient to conclude after hearing the case for the prosecution that all the relevant facts would have been sufficiently established. Such a blatant disregard of the equality of arms would, in my mind, render a trial automatically unfair as long as the evidence would have been potentially relevant, and the rejection would lead to there being little or no evidence from the defence on a particular issue. In domestic trials, it would be usually for the court of appeal to review both the relevance of the proposed evidence and the sufficiency of the lower court's reasoning for rejecting it. Overall fairness could be maintained only under exceptional circumstances if potentially relevant defence evidence were rejected.

Turning to the rule of non-disclosure, the starting point in domestic procedures should be granting the defence access to all the material which has been gathered during the pre-trial investigation, regardless of whether the police or prosecution consider it relevant. This is to minimise the possibility that they overlook material which would be relevant but only the defendant would understand the relevance (i.e. what links a certain piece of information with the defence case). The material in question need not be evidence as such. It would be enough if the piece of information could lead to a piece of evidence.

The right to disclosure, although an important element of an adversarial process, is not absolute. Sometimes it must be weighed against other interests, such as national security or secrecy investigation methods. Non-disclosure would be permissible only if it is strictly necessary to protect some competing interest. Even if that is the case, the interests mentioned now are problematic if the defendant claims to have been incited into committing a crime. In such situations, non-disclosure might prevent any substantive evaluation of the claim.

In jury trials, the Court has approved a constant monitoring and balancing of the competing interests by the trial judge. While being aware of the undisclosed material and the defence case, the judge could reconsider the need to disclose information, but would not rule on the applicant's guilt. Even in jury trials, though, a judge might have to assess a claim of police incitement, which has the potential to affect the defence case substantially. Under such circumstances, the Court has not considered it permissible that the trial judge would be aware of any undisclosed material which might affect the outcome of their decision.

So, the point of the rule of non-disclosure is that a trier of fact should be unaware of any material the defence is unaware of. On the other hand, there should be sufficient judicial review to examine the validity of non-disclosure. For example, the prosecution or the police should not decide the matter on their own. Apparently, the best way to organise such review would be the use of a disclosure judge, who would rule on disclosure only, while being aware of the defence case. Such a procedure could also include a special advocate, whose role would be to argue in favour of the defence. Additionally, a special advocate could be allowed to follow the trial and make submissions to review the non-disclosure decision.

These rights of the defence can also be linked with the presumption of innocence. An accused must have an effective opportunity to prove wrong the prosecution case. This requires not only an opportunity to challenge the credibility of the prosecution evidence or claim that it is inadmissible but also an opportunity to present evidence in their favour. Such opportunities are undermined if evidence is rejected or if the defence is not aware of all the potentially relevant material the authorities have gathered. Denying either right might also indicate a preconceived view of guilt.

From a domestic court's point of view, the presumption of innocence requires that the trier of fact keeps an open mind and approaches the prosecution evidence with a healthy scepticism. For the very reason that there must be some evidence to support the defendant's guilt (why would the charges be brought otherwise), it is essential that someone counterbalances the machinery intended to prove guilt by simply asking whether there are any other reasonable alternatives. The reasoning of a judgment, especially if the defendant is convicted, should reflect this attitude. It should be explained how any reasonable doubt of the defendant's guilt has been ruled out.

The presumption of innocence does not forbid presumptions of fact and law, but their application in criminal law must be limited and there must be an effective judicial control of the facts. This means, essentially, that such presumptions cannot be used in a mechanical or uncritical manner by the domestic courts. Additionally, the presumption does not forbid drawing inferences from the accused's silence under circumstances proven by the prosecution which call from an explanation from the accused. If such *prima facie* case is not established, requiring an explanation would amount to shifting the burden of proof to the defence and violate the presumption of innocence.

5 The privilege against self-incrimination

5.1 Introduction

The privilege against self-incrimination can be seen by some as a form of "non-consensual lawmaking" because it is not explicitly mentioned in Article 6 unlike, for instance, in Article 14 § 3 (g) of the International Covenant on Civil and Political Rights (ICCPR). It grants everyone "in the determination of any criminal charge against him" the right "not to be compelled to testify against himself or to confess guilt". In *Funke*, the Court acknowledged such a right for the first time, ruling that an attempt to compel the applicant to provide evidence against him violated "the right of anyone 'charged with a criminal offence', within the autonomous meaning of this expression in Article 6, to remain silent and not to contribute to incriminating himself".[1]

The privilege is perhaps one of the most widely known features of a fair trial. This is in no small part thanks to American movies, where the police would read suspects their "*Miranda* rights" (i.e. that "he has a right to remain silent, that any statement he does make may be used as evidence against him, and that he has a right to the presence of an attorney, either retained or appointed"). In its landmark *Miranda* judgment from 1966, SCOTUS ruled that prior to any questioning, the person must be warned of these rights. The right to be informed was deemed a necessary procedural safeguard protecting an effective privilege against self-incrimination and a prerequisite for any valid waiver of those rights.[2]

However, the privilege remains a controversial issue. Some may think that it provides too much protection in relation to effective criminal investigation. It might seem perfectly acceptable to let someone confess to a crime while unaware of the right not to do so, if this happens without any coercion. One might also think that an innocent suspect would have nothing to hide and that the privilege would only protect the guilty.[3] We will shortly proceed to the rationale of the rule as it has been expressed in the Court's case law. I would already like to stress that

---

1 Funke v. France, 25.2.1993, § 44.
2 Miranda v. Arizona, 384 U.S. 436 (1966).
3 J. Bentham, *A Treatise on Judicial Evidence* (London: J. W. Paget, 1825), 241 and A. A. S. Zuckerman, *The Principles of Criminal Evidence* (Oxford: Clarendon Press, 1989), 314–317.

DOI: 10.4324/9781003311416-5

no comprehensive account of the arguments for and against the privilege is possible in the confines of this work.

Before any such account, though, I would like to discuss the nature of self-incrimination and self-incriminatory evidence. The essence of the right would seem to be that nobody can be compelled to provide evidence against themselves in an active manner. For example, the applicant in *Funke* complained not that he was compelled to make a statement, instead he was compelled to produce documents. The key to understand the privilege in this context is that this would have required active participation from the applicant. This is why the privilege is sometimes referred to as a **passive right**. It is also important to note that the privilege covers not only statements but other forms of evidence as well.

However, as the Court explained in *Saunders*, the privilege "does not extend to the use in criminal proceedings of material which may be obtained from the accused through the use of compulsory powers but which has an existence independent of the will of the suspect such as, *inter alia*, documents acquired pursuant to a warrant, breath, blood and urine samples and bodily tissue for the purpose of DNA testing".[4] Such material can be obtained without the suspect's active co-operation. If the authorities had discovered the bank statements in *Funke* from the applicant's desk, they could have been used as evidence against him.

The grand chamber also clarified that in order to determine whether material was of an incriminating nature, it is essential to examine "the use to which evidence obtained under compulsion is put in the course of the criminal trial". The government had argued that "nothing said by the applicant in the course of the interviews was self-incriminating and that he had merely given exculpatory answers or answers which, if true, would serve to confirm his defence". The Court did not agree, because "some of the applicant's answers were in fact of an incriminating nature in the sense that they contained admissions to knowledge of information which tended to incriminate him".[5]

It had already noted that

> the right not to incriminate oneself cannot reasonably be confined to statements of admission of wrongdoing or to remarks which are directly incriminating. Testimony obtained under compulsion which appears on its face to be of a non-incriminating nature – such as exculpatory remarks or mere information on questions of fact – may later be deployed in criminal proceedings **in support of the prosecution case**, for example to contradict or cast doubt upon other statements of the accused or evidence given by him during the trial or to otherwise undermine his credibility.[6]

Thus, the use to which evidence was put in that case was incriminating, although indirectly.

---

4 Saunders v. United Kingdom [GC], 17.12.1996, § 69.
5 Saunders v. United Kingdom [GC], 17.12.1996, §§ 70 and 71.
6 Saunders v. United Kingdom [GC], 17.12.1996, § 71.

As the last introductory remarks, I would like to add, first, that the privilege is often used as a synonym to the right to remain silent.[7] Trechsel points out that they are different in theory, for the right to remain silent would also cover exculpatory statements and, on the other hand, would only cover oral evidence.[8] Secondly, the privilege does not prevent domestic courts from drawing, under certain circumstances, the appropriate inferences from the accused having remained passive. As with the right to be heard, the right not to take part in the criminal trial is distinct from an imaginary right to secure a particular outcome.[9] Put briefly, invoking the privilege may lead to adverse consequences.

5.2 Rationale and development of the rule

In *Funke*, the first judgment where the privilege appears, there is no mention of its rationale. It is simply considered it as one of the rights of someone charged with a criminal offence and as a result of it being violated, the Court found a violation of Article 6 § 1. The Court essentially fails to explain why it introduced a new right not explicitly mentioned by the Convention. Goss points out that the judgment poorly explains not only the introduction of a right not expressly mentioned in Article 6, but also the whole doctrine of "implied rights".[10] Paradoxically, the Court's own reasoning is not always beyond reproach.

In the subsequent case law, the Court has mentioned two possible rationales. In *John Murray*, the Court reasoned as follows: "By providing the accused with protection against improper compulsion by the authorities these immunities contribute to **avoiding miscarriages of justice** and to securing the aims of Article 6."[11] This is perhaps a reference to the most widely accepted rationale of any exclusionary rule, the need to exclude unreliable evidence. The privilege against self-incrimination can be violated through compulsion which obviously might have an effect on the reliability of any statement made as a result. The mere possibility of this would entail a risk of unreliability.

---

7 See, for example, Bykov v. Russia [GC], 10.3.2009, § 92: "the privilege against self-incrimination or the right to remain silent".

8 S. Trechsel, *Human Rights in Criminal Proceedings* (Oxford: Oxford University Press, 2005), 342. See also Jalloh v. Germany [GC], 11.7.2006, §§ 110 and 111: "[The Court] notes that the privilege against self-incrimination is commonly understood in the Contracting States and elsewhere to be primarily concerned with respecting the will of the defendant to remain silent in the face of questioning and not to be compelled to provide a statement. However, the Court has on occasion given the principle of self-incrimination as protected under Article 6 § 1 a broader meaning so as to encompass cases in which coercion to hand over real evidence to the authorities was in issue."

9 L. H. Tribe, *American Constitutional Law*, 2nd edn (New York: The Foundation Press, 1988), 666.

10 R. Goss, *Criminal Fair Trial Rights: Article 6 of the European Convention on Human Rights* (Oxford: Hart, 2014), 92–94.

11 John Murray v. the United Kingdom [GC], 8.2.1996, § 45.

Furthermore, even in the absence of any direct compulsion, a person who would think they are under an obligation to give a statement might lie about their involvement in a crime. The privilege would serve to remove any incentive to give false statements. "The aims of Article 6" might also refer to the more general notion of fairness in the sense that if someone were required to provide self-incriminating information, they would be put in a disadvantaged position and, to some extent at least, reduced from an equal party to a subject of investigation. But this is open to interpretation, as Trechsel has pointed out.[12]

Later that year, in *Saunders*, the Court elaborated some more, stating that the "rationale lies, inter alia, in the protection of the accused against improper compulsion by the authorities thereby contributing to the avoidance of miscarriages of justice and to the fulfilment of the aims of Article 6". Additionally:

> The right not to incriminate oneself, in particular, presupposes that the prosecution in a criminal case seek to prove their case against the accused without resort to evidence obtained through methods of coercion or oppression in defiance of **the will of the accused**. In this sense the right is closely linked to the presumption of innocence contained in [Article 6 § 2].[13]

So, within a year the Court seems to have, at least to some extent, diluted its earlier statement in *John Murray* regarding the rationale behind a right it has derived from Article 6 § 1. As subsequent case law confirms, avoiding miscarriages of justice became a secondary rationale, which can be inferred from the wording "inter alia" and "in particular". In *Saunders*, the primary rationale is expressly what perhaps was meant in *John Murray* already, that fairness would require respecting the will of someone to use the right to remain silent. Any other conclusion would lead to that right becoming ineffective and illusory. The Court also expressly linked the right with the presumption of innocence. Indeed, to compel someone into giving self-incriminating evidence would often have to be a consequence of presuming someone guilty.

The two rationales are sometimes presented in a different order. In *Bykov*, the grand chamber first quoted *John Murray* (avoiding miscarriages of justice) without the words "inter alia", and then *Saunders* (respecting the will of the accused). However, instead of quoting *Saunders* to the letter, the Court has switched the words "in particular" to "primarily". In *Ibrahim*, these rationales are the other way around, beginning with the primary rationale of respecting the will of the accused. Of course, the order in which they are written is not decisive and I take it to be established that avoiding miscarriages of justice is "only" a secondary rationale of the privilege.

It has already been mentioned that the privilege can be criticised. In light of the Convention and the Court's case law, I find no reason to join the critics. However, I wish to underline two features of the privilege. First:

12 Trechsel 2005, 347–348.
13 Saunders v. United Kingdom [GC], 17.12.1996, § 68.

decisive evidence and there was no room for exclusionary discretion. The privilege had been violated.[26]

Finally, let us take look at the rather special circumstances in *Allan*, the prime example of what the Court called subterfuge in *Ibrahim*. For subterfuge to amount to compulsion, some level of psychological pressure is required. Moreover, that pressure must be, at least to some degree, the result of active involvement of the authorities. That is, the psychological pressure of one's guilt is not a type of compulsion attributable to the authorities and amounting to a violation. In effect, the rule against subterfuge sets limits to police tactics in the investigation of crimes. While some degree of deception is perfectly legitimate, the right to a fair trial would be violated it deception is taken too far.[27]

The police had arrested the applicant and another person on suspicion of having robbed a shop near Manchester. The other person arrested with the applicant admitted to the offence as well as several other late-night shop robberies, while the applicant denied any involvement. When arrested, the men were in possession of a handgun. About a fortnight earlier a store manager of another shop, also near Manchester, had been shot dead. Soon after their arrest, the police were tipped by an anonymous informant that the applicant had been involved in the shooting. The applicant remained silent during questioning, but the police had secretly installed devices to monitor his cell and other detainment facilities. After a period of not being able to obtain any useful information, the police placed a long-time informant in the applicant's cell, instructing him to "push the applicant for what he can" to obtain information. The informant was also carrying recording devices. In his witness statement later, the informant asserted that the applicant had admitted to him having been present at the murder scene. This admission, however, was not part of any recorded interview, and the applicant disputed it.

The Court stated in general terms that

> the freedom of a suspected person to choose whether to speak or to remain silent when questioned by the police [...] is effectively undermined in a case in which, the suspect having elected to remain silent during questioning, the authorities use subterfuge to elicit, from the suspect, confessions or other statements of an incriminatory nature, which they were unable to obtain during such questioning and where the confessions or statements thereby obtained are adduced in evidence at trial. Whether the right to silence is undermined to such an extent as to give rise to a violation of Article 6 of the Convention depends on all the circumstances of the individual case.[28]

26 Jalloh v. Germany [GC], 11.7.2006, §§ 117–122.
27 J. D. Jackson and S. J. Summers, *The Internationalisation of Criminal Evidence: Beyond the Common Law and Civil Law Traditions* (Cambridge: Cambridge University Press, 2012), 169–170.
28 Allan v. the United Kingdom, 5.11.2002, §§ 50 and 51.

Those relevant circumstances, derived from a Canadian supreme court case, included the relationship between the informer and the State on the one hand and the relationship between the informer and the accused on the other. As regards the former relationship, it was to be determined whether an exchange between the accused and the informer would have taken place, and in the form and manner in which it did, but for the intervention of the authorities. As regards the latter, a crucial factor would be whether the informer caused the accused to make a statement. A key concept, which the Court adopted, was the possibility that using informants could amount to *a functional equivalent of an interrogation*.

The Court applied these principles in *Allan* by noting, first, that the applicant had consistently remained silent. The informant was put in his cell for the very purpose of eliciting incriminating information from him and even coached to put pressure on him. The statements made to the informant were not spontaneous, but a result of the informant's persistent questioning and guiding the conversation. This was regarded a functional equivalent of an interrogation but without any safeguards of a formal interview by the police. It is also relevant in this regard that the applicant had an attorney who, of course, was not present in the cell. Although there was no sign of any direct coercion, the Court noted that "the applicant would have been subjected to psychological pressures which impinged on the 'voluntariness' of the disclosures allegedly made by the applicant". Additionally, the informant's statement of an alleged admission was the main or decisive evidence against the applicant, whose privilege against self-incrimination (or, rather, its very essence) was violated.[29]

The types of improper compulsion addressed above are not the only possible infringements of the privilege against self-incrimination. Additionally, there is significant case law about two other potential violations or their combination: The right to be informed of the privilege against self-incrimination and/or the right to a lawyer. Furthermore, they are perhaps even more controversial owing to the nature of the violation (i.e. that they are not, on the face of it, as serious as direct compulsion to give evidence). Before proceeding to the assessment criteria which is also applicable to improper compulsion, we shall examine these other violation types.

5.4 The right to notification and the right to a lawyer

It has been mentioned already that the knowledge of having a right is a prerequisite for an effective use of any right as well as a valid waiver. Referring to the effectiveness principle, it considered in *Aleksandr Zaichenko* that "in the circumstances of the case it was incumbent on the police to inform the applicant of the privilege against self-incrimination and the right to remain silent".[30] This approach was confirmed by the grand chamber in *Ibrahim*, where the Court stated that "it is inherent in the privilege against self-incrimination, the right to silence and the

---

29 Allan v. the United Kingdom, 5.11.2002, § 52.
30 Aleksandr Zaichenko v. Russia, 18.2.2010, § 52.

right to legal assistance that a person 'charged with a criminal offence' for the purposes of Article 6 has **the right to be notified** of these rights".[31]

The corollary, if not the actual essence of the right to notification is the corresponding *duty* of the authorities *to inform* a suspect of their rights. As the Court stated, it becomes incumbent to notify a suspect of their rights when Article 6 becomes applicable (i.e. when they become "charged with a criminal offence"). As the reader might remember from Section 2.2, this can happen either through official notification or when a person is substantially affected by an investigation, which makes matters difficult sometimes. The crucial point in time is when a suspicion against someone "crystallises". While no exact threshold can be given, if there is a reasonable suspicion of someone having committed a crime and they are investigated, they would be substantially affected.

In *Aleksandr Zaichenko*, the relevant circumstances were that the applicant had been working as a driver for a company which suspected its employees of stealing fuel from their service vehicles and had requested the local authorities to investigate. The police had stopped and inspected the applicant's car and discovered two cans of diesel in his car. He was then questioned and confessed having poured the fuel from the tank of his service vehicle. Prior to being interviewed, the police did not inform the applicant of his rights. The Court concluded that "[g]iven the context of the road check and the applicant's inability to produce any proof of the diesel purchase at the moment of his questioning by the police, [...] there should have been a suspicion of theft against the applicant at that moment".[32]

In 2005, the first three applicants of the *Ibrahim* case and a fourth man, Mr Osman, detonated four bombs in central London. For the purposes of interpreting the time when someone becomes "charged with a criminal offence", I find the fourth applicant's case most interesting. He was convicted of assisting Mr Osman by letting him stay at his apartment and failing to disclose information. The fourth applicant was first interviewed by the police as a witness. He then disclosed information of a self-incriminating nature, at which point the officers suspended the interview and consulted their superiors. The officers were told to continue interviewing him as a witness. At that point, however, a suspicion had "crystallised", and the applicant's situation was substantially affected by the actions of the police, who should have informed him of his rights.[33]

Instead of the investigative authorities, the suspect's lawyer can also appraise them of their rights. Although the privilege against self-incrimination and the **right to a lawyer** protected by Article 6 § 3 (c) are often assessed together, it should be underlined right away that these are separate rights. This is something

---

31 Ibrahim and Others v. the United Kingdom [GC], 13.9.2016, § 272.
32 Aleksandr Zaichenko v. Russia, 18.2.2010, §§ 41 and 42.
33 Ibrahim and Others v. the United Kingdom [GC], 13.9.2016, § 296. Compare, for example, Severini v. San Marino [dec.], 30.5.2017, § 19, where there was no doubt that the authorities had manipulated the applicant's role when questioned as a witness and where his role did not change during that questioning.

the Court seems not to mention very often, but it was stated unequivocally in *Navone*.[34] It also becomes apparent from the fact that a defendant may waive one but retain the other, as the applicant in *Aleksandr Zaichenko* had done.[35] Naturally, a violation may be limited to only one of them. Crucially, though, the right to a lawyer is a right which, in a way, is subordinate to the privilege against self-incrimination.

One of the most influential landmark judgments of the Court has been *Salduz*. The Court stated that Article 6 would normally require that the accused be allowed to benefit from the assistance of a lawyer already at the initial stages of police interrogation. This is because the evidence obtained during this stage determines the framework in which the offence charged will be considered at the trial. On the other hand, an accused often finds himself in a particularly vulnerable position at the early stage of the proceedings. A lawyer is meant to compensate this particular vulnerability and help to ensure respect of the privilege against self-incrimination.[36]

In a passage which can be easily overlooked, the Court explains the connection between the right to a lawyer and the privilege against self-incrimination: "Early access to a lawyer is part of the procedural safeguards to which the Court will have particular regard when examining whether a procedure has extinguished the very essence of the privilege against self-incrimination [...]."[37] That one sentence seems to explain why the privilege and access to a lawyer are often considered together: The latter is an important factor when assessing whether the very essence of the privilege has been extinguished.

Let us remember that the privilege is not absolute and only destroying its very essence is contrary to Article 6. The Court referred to the three-part test formulated in *Jalloh*, according to which the factors used to determine whether the essence of the privilege is destroyed are the nature and degree of the compulsion, the existence of any relevant safeguards in the procedures and the use to which any material so obtained is put.[38] Access to lawyer, then, is to be considered an important procedural safeguard. Having early access to a lawyer would mitigate the impact of any possible breach against a suspect during the first stages of an investigation.

Additionally, the Court summarised in *Ibrahim*:

> Prompt access to a lawyer constitutes an important counterweight to the vulnerability of suspects in police custody, provides a fundamental safeguard against coercion and ill-treatment of suspects by the police, and contributes to

34 Navone et autres c. Monaco, 24.10.2013, § 74.
35 Aleksandr Zaichenko v. Russia, 18.2.2010, §§ 50 and 55.
36 Salduz v. Turkey [GC], 27.11.2008, § 54.
37 Salduz v. Turkey [GC], 27.11.2008, § 54.
38 Salduz v. Turkey [GC], 27.11.2008, § 55 and Jalloh v. Germany [GC], 11.7.2006, § 101. As also pointed out, when applying those principles in § 117, the Court adds another factor without much explanation: the weight of the public interest in the investigation and punishment of the offence in issue.

the prevention of miscarriages of justice and the fulfilment of the aims of Article 6, notably equality of arms between the investigating or prosecuting authorities and the accused [...].[39]

Indeed, it is understandably less likely that the police will violate the suspect's rights if they have a lawyer. So, the rationale of the right to a lawyer is multi-faceted but they all boil down to equality of arms and compensating for the suspect's vulnerable position.

5.5 The *Salduz* test

The Court ruled in *Salduz* that

> in order for the right to a fair trial to remain sufficiently "practical and effec-tive" [...], Article 6 § 1 requires that, as a rule, access to a lawyer should be provided as from the first interrogation of a suspect by the police, unless it is demonstrated in the light of the particular circumstances of each case that there are **compelling reasons** to restrict this right. Even where compelling reasons may exceptionally justify denial of access to a lawyer, such restriction – whatever its justification – must not **unduly prejudice** the rights of the accused under Article 6 [...].[40]

These two stages form what was in *Ibrahim* called "the *Salduz* test". The para-graph cited just now continued with the following sentence: "The rights of the defence will in principle be irretrievably prejudiced when incriminating statements made during police interrogation without access to a lawyer are used for a con-viction." The first three applicants in *Ibrahim* claimed that *Salduz* intended to lay down a clear rule precluding any use at trial of statements made during pre-trial questioning without legal advice. Although such an interpretation seems possible because of the last sentence, the Court made it clear that this was not the case. But let us proceed in the order of the stages.

The concept of compelling reasons was not explained in *Salduz*. That is why the Court set out to clarify it in *Ibrahim*. It begun by stating that

> the criterion of compelling reasons is a stringent one: having regard to the fundamental nature and importance of early access to legal advice, in parti-cular at the first interrogation of the suspect, restrictions on access to legal advice are permitted only in **exceptional circumstances**, must be of a **tem-porary nature** and must be based on an **individual assessment** of the parti-cular circumstances of the case [...].[41]

---

39 Ibrahim and Others v. the United Kingdom [GC], 13.9.2016, § 255.
40 Salduz v. Turkey [GC], 27.11.2008, § 55.
41 Ibrahim and Others v. the United Kingdom [GC], 13.9.2016, § 277.

Thus, at least any systemic restrictions of domestic legislation would fail to fulfil this criterion.[42]

On the other hand, any restriction of the right to legal assistance should have a basis in domestic law. Such legislation should offer guidance to operational decision-making of the authorities by setting clear boundaries to the scope and content of possible restrictions. *Ibrahim* also makes it clear that the onus is on the respondent government to justify the compelling nature of any restriction of the right to legal assistance during pre-trial investigation and the Court will examine such claims case by case using the above-mentioned criteria.[43] Article 3 § 6 of directive 2013/48/EU,[44] for example, provides the following basis for restrictions:

> In exceptional circumstances and only at the pre-trial stage, Member States may temporarily derogate from the application of the rights provided for in paragraph 3 [including the right to consult a lawyer prior to and having him present during questioning] to the extent justified in the light of the particular circumstances of the case, on the basis of one of the following compelling reasons:
>
> (a)   where there is an urgent need to avert serious adverse consequences for the life, liberty or physical integrity of a person;
> (b)   where immediate action by the investigating authorities is imperative to prevent substantial jeopardy to criminal proceedings.

Recitals 31 and 32 of the directive provide further guidance to how the restriction clause should be applied. For example, according to them suspects may be questioned only if they have been informed of their right to remain silent. Thus, it would be incumbent on the authorities to fulfil some of the functions of a lawyer. Furthermore, the suspect should only be questioned to the extent necessary to obtain information relevant for one of the derogation grounds. Questioning in the absence of a lawyer should only focus on the compelling reasons at hand. Both recitals end with a quote from *Salduz*: any abuse of this derogation would in principle irretrievably prejudice the rights of the defence.

The directive and its exception clause are mentioned and, effectively, approved in *Ibrahim*. The Court accepted that

> where a respondent Government have convincingly demonstrated the existence of an urgent need to avert serious adverse consequences for life, liberty

42 Salduz v. Turkey [GC], 27.11.2008, § 56. See also Beuze v. Belgium [GC], 9.11.2018, § 142 and Sarar v. Turkey, 15.6.2021, § 30.
43 Ibrahim and Others v. the United Kingdom [GC], 13.9.2016, § 258.
44 Directive 2013/48/EU of the European Parliament and of the Council of 22 October 2013 on the right of access to a lawyer in criminal proceedings and in European arrest warrant proceedings, and on the right to have a third party informed upon deprivation of liberty and to communicate with third persons and with consular authorities while deprived of liberty.

or physical integrity in a given case, this can amount to compelling reasons to restrict access to legal advice for the purposes of Article 6 of the Convention. In such circumstances, there is a pressing duty on the authorities to protect the rights of potential or actual victims under Articles 2, 3 and 5 § 1 of the Convention in particular.

On the other hand, "a non-specific claim of a risk of leaks cannot constitute compelling reasons".[45]

Interpreting *Salduz* the Court clarified that the words "in principle" meant that although the rule against the use of incriminating statements made in the absence of a lawyer was strict, it was not absolute. Conveniently for the SIC framework, it described the second stage as an examination of the impact of the restriction on the overall fairness of the proceedings. The final question, as ever, is whether the proceedings as a whole were fair. This is why even "[t]he absence of compelling reasons does not, therefore, lead in itself to a finding of a violation of Article 6 of the Convention".[46] However, such a finding will trigger an interesting presumption mechanism.

In the absence of compelling reasons, the Court stated it should apply a very strict scrutiny to its fairness assessment. The approach is similar to the lack of a good reason for the non-attendance of a witness in the context of the so-called sole or decisive rule (see Chapter 9). The failure to show compelling reasons weighs heavily, perhaps decisively, in favour of finding a violation of Article 6 §§ 1 and 3 (c): "The onus will be on the Government to demonstrate convincingly why, exceptionally and in the specific circumstances of the case, the overall fairness of the trial was not irretrievably prejudiced by the restriction on access to legal advice."[47] A violation could be presumed in the absence of compelling reasons.

Additionally:

Immediate access to a lawyer able to provide information about procedural rights is likely to prevent unfairness arising from the absence of any official notification of these rights. However, where access to a lawyer is delayed, the need for the investigative authorities to notify the suspect of his right to a lawyer and his right to silence and privilege against self-incrimination takes on a particular importance [...]. In such cases, a failure to notify will make it even more difficult for the Government to rebut the presumption of unfairness that arises where there are no compelling reasons for delaying access to legal advice or to show, even where there are compelling reasons for the delay, that the proceedings as a whole were fair.[48]

45 Ibrahim and Others v. the United Kingdom [GC], 13.9.2016, § 259.
46 Ibrahim and Others v. the United Kingdom [GC], 13.9.2016, § 262.
47 Ibrahim and Others v. the United Kingdom [GC], 13.9.2016, § 265.
48 Ibrahim and Others v. the United Kingdom [GC], 13.9.2016, § 273.

The above paragraph seems to uncouple the two rights. It becomes clear that a combined violation of both access to lawyer and right to notification would, quite logically, strengthen the presumption of irretrievable prejudice being done. The same logic would require that a failure to notify of the right to silence would, even alone, trigger the presumption of unfairness:

> In the light of the nature of the privilege against self-incrimination and the right to silence, the Court considers that in principle there can be no justification for a failure to notify a suspect of these rights. Where a suspect has not, however, been so notified, the Court must examine whether, notwithstanding this failure, the proceedings as a whole were fair [...].[49]

It should also be remembered that access to a lawyer is a sort of auxiliary right in relation to the privilege against self-incrimination. It would, therefore, be highly inconsistent to not apply the presumption of unfairness if only the right to be informed of the privilege is violated. That being said, overall fairness should also be assessed if compelling reasons for restricting right to legal assistance are found to have been established. But under such circumstances, if the accused has been properly notified, there would be no presumption of unfairness.

The mechanism of the *Salduz* test is being complicated further by the fact that instead of "compelling reasons", a lower threshold is apparently applied if a complaint focuses only on the right to choose one's lawyer, also guaranteed in Article 6 § 3 (c). In *Dvorski*, the Court reiterated that the right is not absolute and added that "[i]t is necessarily subject to certain limitations where free legal aid is concerned and also where it is for the courts to decide whether the interests of justice require that the accused be defended by counsel appointed by them".[50]

Next, the relevant test was explained:

> The Court has consistently held that the national authorities must have regard to the defendant's wishes as to his or her choice of legal representation, but may override those wishes when there are **relevant and sufficient grounds** for holding that this is necessary in the interests of justice [...]. Where such grounds are lacking, a restriction on the free choice of defence counsel would entail a violation of Article 6 § 1 together with paragraph 3 (c) if it adversely affected the applicant's defence, regard being had to the proceedings as a whole.[51]

The applicant was questioned as a suspect in the presence of lawyer M.R., who the applicant had chosen from a list of lawyers. The applicant's mother had contacted another lawyer, G.M. He had agreed to represent the applicant, but the police

49 Ibrahim and Others v. the United Kingdom [GC], 13.9.2016, § 273.
50 Dvorski v. Croatia [GC], 20.10.2015, § 79.
51 Dvorski v. Croatia [GC], 20.10.2015, § 79.

denied him access on more than one occasion, claiming that he had no power of attorney. This happened in spite of the applicant's father having signed a power of attorney in favour of G.M. Furthermore, the applicant had not been informed of G.M. having attempted to meet him at the police station and to represent him. His choice of lawyer was, according to the Court, not an informed one, because he had no knowledge of his parents having arranged another lawyer for him. There were no relevant and sufficient reasons for the restriction and the applicant had not waived his right to be represented by a lawyer of his own choosing although he had signed a power of attorney in favour of M.R. There was a violation of Article 6.

Thus, this test – perhaps we can call it "the *Dvorski* test" – is clearly less stringent than the *Salduz* test. Instead of compelling reasons, the defendant's choice of lawyer could, *e contrario*, be overridden if there are relevant and sufficient grounds, such as limitations of legal aid. Such a difference in standards is also understandable, because a suspect would obviously be better off with a lawyer chosen against their will than without any lawyer at all. Although *Dvorski* preceded *Ibrahim*, I would submit that the overall fairness assessment should follow the *Ibrahim* criteria. But it seems the lack of relevant and sufficient grounds as regards the choice of a lawyer would not trigger a presumption of irretrievable prejudice similar to the *Salduz* test.

5.6 The *Ibrahim* criteria

One important part of the *Ibrahim* judgment is confined into one paragraph, where the Court begins by stating that because "a criminal trial generally involves a complex interplay of different aspects of criminal procedure, it is often artificial to try and categorise a case as one which should be viewed from the perspective of one particular Article 6 right or another". The Court then gives a non-exhaustive list of possibly relevant factors for the assessment of "the impact of procedural failings at the pre-trial stage on the overall fairness of the criminal proceedings".[52] The impact assessment forms the second stage of the *Salduz* test. We shall proceed following the order of the list.

(a) **Whether the applicant was particularly vulnerable, for example, by reason of his age or mental capacity.** It seems clear that particular vulnerability would increase the impact of a violation. For example, improper compulsion would usually have a far greater impact on a child than an adult. By comparison, though, the lack of it would not reduce the impact significantly. This explains why the Court in its post-*Ibrahim* case law might simply mention "the applicant was not particularly vulnerable" as a factor which would argue in favour of considering the proceedings fair.[53] It was already pointed out in Section 2.3 that particular

---

52 Ibrahim and Others v. the United Kingdom [GC], 13.9.2016, § 274.
53 See, for example, Dudka v. Ukraine, 4.12.2018, § 112; Fefilov v. Russia, 17.7.2018, § 64; and Bajić v. North Macedonia, 10.6.2021, § 72.

vulnerability also raises the threshold for a valid waiver. This applies to the privilege as well.

The Court stressed in *Płonka* that the applicant's alcoholism of several years was one of the specific features of that case. She had told the police about her condition during the first interview. She had also mentioned having drunk a substantial amount of alcohol the day before her arrest. These circumstances "clearly suggested" that she had been in a vulnerable state when confessing to have killed the victim.[54]

In *Panovits*, the applicant was considered vulnerable because he was 17 years old during the police investigation. According to the Court, an accused minor should be dealt with taking into consideration his vulnerability and capacities. This should happen from the very first stages of investigation and especially during any questioning. Steps should be taken to reduce feelings of intimidation and inhibition. Additionally, authorities should ensure that minor accuseds have a broad understanding of the nature of the investigation and of their rights.[55]

Perhaps surprisingly, the Court ruled in *Beuze* that the applicant was not in a greater state of vulnerability than any other person when questioned by the police. The applicant had claimed the contrary, based on his detention, low IQ, and extremely poor verbal skills, of which a medical statement had been presented. The Court noted that while the applicant had limited intellectual capabilities, his reasoning was within the norm. He could not indicate any concrete examples of difficulties in expressing himself and the interviews were not unusual or excessively long.[56]

Beuze seems to have underlined that the threshold of being *particularly* vulnerable is higher than being "just" vulnerable. To meet the criterion, vulnerability should have an impact on the proceedings. Because there was nothing suggesting the opposite, the Court could conclude that he could at least broadly understand the investigation or, as it was put in *S.C.*, "the general thrust of what is said".[57] To speculate a little further, it may be that this attitude also reflects a shift towards a stricter interpretation of vulnerability.[58]

(b) The legal framework governing the pre-trial proceedings and the admissibility of evidence at trial, and whether it was complied with; where an exclusionary rule applied, it is particularly unlikely that the proceedings as a whole would be considered unfair. This criterion can be divided into at least three elements: The domestic legal framework as such, compliance with it, and the application of an exclusionary rule. The key question is whether the domestic law is capable of mitigating the impact of a restriction of the privilege.

---

54 Płonka v. Poland, 31.3.2009, § 38.
55 Panovits v. Cyprus, 11.12.2008, especially § 67.
56 Beuze v. Belgium [GC], 9.11.2018, §§ 142 and 143.
57 S.C. v. the United Kingdom, 15.6.2004, § 29.
58 For example, "a rather stressful situation" and "relatively quick sequence of the events" have been sufficient grounds to conclude that the applicant's waiver was not valid (Aleksandr Zaichenko v. Russia, 18.2.2010, § 55). The Court did not state in that case, however, that the applicant would have been particularly vulnerable or, indeed, vulnerable at all.

The first stage under this criterion is to assess the quality of the domestic legal framework and whether it is in line with Article 6 and the Court's case law. Otherwise, compliance with it will not reduce the impact of a potential violation. For example, Turkish legal framework governing the pre-trial proceedings does not grant the right to a lawyer to persons accused of offences falling within the jurisdiction of the State Security Courts. This has been found to violate Article 6 in *Salduz* and several subsequent cases.[59] If the legislation does not provide sufficient guarantees of fairness, this would naturally increase the impact of any restriction.

Secondly, the decisive weight is if and how the domestic legal framework is applied in the concrete case. Put simply, even if the quality of the domestic legal framework is beyond reproach *in abstracto*, but that framework is not complied with *in concreto*, the mere existence of appropriate norms cannot compensate a restriction of defence rights. Furthermore, the impact of a potential violation would in principle be greater if authorities have violated the relevant legislation. Although there would not seem to be a mechanism similar to the good faith exception known in the United States, an intentional violation could be considered more harmful.[60]

The third element of the criterion, "where an exclusionary rule applied", leaves open whether it refers to applicability *in abstracto* or application *in concreto*. If an exclusionary rule is applied (i.e. the impugned evidence is excluded), this would usually remove any impact of a potential violation. Going through the whole *Ibrahim* criteria would seem unnecessary in such situations. In *Loboda*, for example, the impugned evidence was excluded by the domestic first instance. The Court did not agree with the applicant that the statements made by him were, in fact, "used for his conviction or that they had otherwise affected the conclusions ultimately reached by the domestic judicial authorities concerning his guilt".[61] The application was dismissed as manifestly ill-founded.

The mere potential applicability of an exclusionary rule would seem like a poor means to reduce the impact of improper compulsion. But, on the other hand, it could be considered that lack of exclusionary discretion would increase the impact of a breach. In *Jalloh*, the domestic courts had simply considered the use of emetics legal and thus no discretion to exclude evidence was possible. The lack of such discretion meant that the impact of the breach could not be removed. But this element also takes us to the domain of the following *Ibrahim* criterion, the opportunity to challenge the use of evidence.

(c) **Whether the applicant had the opportunity to challenge the authenticity of the evidence and oppose its use.** Like the previous criterion, criterion (c) is composed of multiple elements. In this case there are two: the opportunity to

59 See, for example, Bayram Koç v. Turkey, 5.9.2017; Güneş v. Turkey, 28.11.2017; and Sarar v. Turkey, 15.6.2021. On the other hand, a systemic restriction will not lead to an automatic finding of Article 6 violation according to the current case law (see Dayanan v. Turkey, 13.10.2009 § 33, and Beuze v. Belgium [GC], 9.11.2018, §§ 140 and 144).
60 Beuze v. Belgium [GC], 9.11.2018, § 171.
61 Loboda v. Ukraine, 17.11.2016, §§ 40 and 43.

challenge the authenticity of the evidence and the opportunity to oppose its use. The first element refers to the reliability of a statement obtained through compulsion, while the second element refers to its admissibility. The accused may challenge both the reliability and admissibility, or only the one or the other, or neither. What is essential is whether he has an effective opportunity to do so in the domestic process.

Of course, one might say that the accused must have these opportunities in an adversarial trial anyway.[62] Indeed, they must, but the point is to scrutinise if and how domestic courts take a stand on the issues raised by the defence. If they challenge the authenticity or admissibility of evidence, domestic courts should provide adequate and proper reasons for rejecting such claims. It is especially important to provide an answer to any particular factors the defence have relied upon. Any failures in this regard would increase the impact of the violation. However, domestic courts are not under any obligation to undervalue the reliability of evidence or exclude it.

It should be noted already that the first element of criterion (c) is also linked with criterion (d), because they have to do with the reliability of the impugned evidence. I would also underline that neither the proper assessment of reliability nor the fact that it has not suffered as a result of the violation of the privilege do not, on their own, lead to the conclusion that the overall fairness of a trial would not have been irretrievably prejudiced. So, rather like criterion (a), this criterion seems to have greater potential of tipping the balance in favour of finding a violation rather than not finding a violation of Article 6.

This means that even if the defence has a proper opportunity to challenge the authenticity of evidence and a domestic court gives a well-reasoned decision rejecting such claims, this does not suffice to mitigate the impact of a violation by itself. Should a domestic court provide insufficient reasoning even if an arguable complaint has been made, this would indicate that the court is favouring the prosecution which, in turn, would increase the impact of a violation. The defendant would be deprived of an effective opportunity to challenge the authenticity of evidence in the latter situation.

As mentioned, the opportunity to oppose the use of evidence was not effective in *Jalloh*, where the domestic courts considered the impugned method legal. In *Beuze*, the Court assessed the criteria (b) and (c) together and concluded that although the domestic assize court were requested to rule on the nullity of the accused's statements, there was "no indication that the court engaged in the requisite analysis of the consequences of the lawyer's absence at crucial points in the proceedings". This was not remedied by the court of cassation either.[63] Apparently, the Court would have required a more substantial analysis as to whether the restriction has caused irretrievable damage to the essence of the privilege.

The similarity between the two elements of criterion (c) lies in that the defendant should also have an effective opportunity to challenge the admissibility of

---

62 Goss 2014, 146.
63 Beuze v. Belgium [GC], 9.11.2018, § 174.

evidence if they wish to use it. Instead of summarily declaring the impugned evidence admissible, they should perform an adequate assessment of the submissions of the defence and give a reasoned decision. An appropriate balancing act by the domestic courts would probably mitigate the impact of a violation more than appropriate determination of evidentiary value. But I consider it unlikely that such a decision would be determinative for the outcome.

If evidence is excluded, the criterion would seem to link with criterion (b), more precisely, it's final sentence "where an exclusionary rule applied, it is particularly unlikely that the proceedings as a whole would be considered unfair". Indeed, already after going through the first three, the criteria seem to be overlapping even to the point of redundancy. Perhaps this is why even the Court itself decided to bundle some of them together in *Beuze*. Although the list is non-exhaustive and was apparently intended to be applied in the overall assessment of any alleged violation in the pre-trial phase, so far it seems to bring little added value to the four-part test used in *Jalloh*.

(d) **The quality of the evidence and whether the circumstances in which it was obtained cast doubt on its reliability or accuracy, taking into account the degree and nature of any compulsion.** The only real difference between criterion (d) and the first part of criterion (c) seems to be that while criterion (c) is more procedural in nature, criterion (d) is more substantive. In any case, to me they seem as the two sides of one coin: when assessing the authenticity of evidence, domestic courts should assess whether its reliability or accuracy have suffered as a result of the circumstances in which it was obtained.

Obviously, the impact of a restriction of the privilege would be increased if it also casts doubt on the reliability of the evidence obtained. I maintain, however, that securing the reliability or reliable assessment of evidence is far from being the decisive factor in play because it is not the essence of the privilege against self-incrimination. For sure, it can serve as an additional factor in the overall assessment, but rather like the procedural aspects discussed before, criterion (d) would seem to have a "one-way" effect: if reliability has suffered as a result of the way in which evidence was obtained, this would increase the impact of a violation, but not *vice versa*.

Although some think that reliability should be the only factor affecting the admissibility of evidence, this is not the standing of the Court. In *Jalloh*, for example, no mention is made of the reliability of the evidence obtained through inhuman and degrading treatment. There is little room for doubt that the authenticity of the real evidence in that case would have been affected in any way as a result of the coercion. The words "reliability" and "accuracy" are completely absent from *Salduz* and no mention is made of whether the circumstances in which the impugned statement were obtained cast doubt on that. In *Beuze*, this criterion is dismissed by one (!) paragraph,[64] and in *Simeonovi* no substantive assessment of reliability is made.[65]

---

64 Beuze v. Belgium [GC], 9.11.2018, § 169.
65 Simeonovi v. Bulgaria [GC], 12.5.2017, see §§ 132–144.

In *Ibrahim*, the assessment of this criterion focused on how the applicants were cautioned before interviews and whether those cautions would have amounted to compulsion which would have had an adverse effect on the reliability of the statements they gave. The Court rejected such claims, concluding that in spite of a technically wrong caution, the applicants "were well aware that any possible prejudice averted by choosing not to remain silent had to be weighed against the inevitable prejudice to their defence which would be caused by the admission of their lies at trial".[66]

It is worth noting that the domestic courts had applied sections 76 and 78 of PACE and according to the first provision a confession would be inadmissible if it was obtained "in consequence of anything said or done which was likely, in the circumstances existing at the time, to render unreliable any confession which might be made by [an accused person] in consequence thereof". Thus, reliability was a relevant factor under the domestic legal framework, and this may at least partially explain why the Court also addressed the question of reliability. The Finnish supreme court, by contrast, has stated that the use of evidence obtained in violation of the privilege is not primarily linked with the reliability of such a statement but the defence rights.[67]

(e) Where evidence was obtained unlawfully, the unlawfulness in question and, where it stems from a violation of another Convention Article, the nature of the violation found. I also find it difficult to draw a line between criteria (d) and (e), both of which require examining the "nature" of a violation. Apparently, while both of them could be considered substantive, the current criterion focuses more on the violation than the impugned evidence. "Unlawfulness" would also link the criterion with criterion (b). Supposedly, the core of this criterion would be that the more serious the violation is, the more this would point towards irretrievable prejudice.

Criterion (e) has also the potential of being a watershed between rules of evidence. A violation of Article 3 would be assessed following different criteria, as would a violation of Article 8. Both of these will be discussed later (Chapters 6 and 8). As we have already discovered, a violation of Article 3 may lead to the conclusion that the privilege is applicable to real evidence. As will become clear later, statements obtained by way of violating Article 3 should be automatically excluded, as well as any torture evidence (both statements and real evidence). On the other hand, violations of Article 8 do not lead to such conclusions.

(f) In the case of a statement, the nature of the statement and whether it was promptly retracted or modified. The first part of this criterion refers to whether a statement is self-incriminating or not. In this regard it is important to remember that "the privilege against self-incrimination is not confined to actual confessions or to remarks which are directly incriminating; for statements to be regarded as self-incriminating it is sufficient for them to have substantially affected

---

66 Ibrahim and Others v. the United Kingdom [GC], 13.9.2016, § 286.
67 KKO 2012:45, § 46.

the accused's position [...]".[68] As long as a statement can be used against the defendant, its nature is self-incriminating. A rule of thumb could perhaps be that if the prosecutor invokes a statement, it could be considered incriminating.

Secondly, if a statement is promptly retracted or modified, this could be an indication of a violation. But such conclusion should not be an automation. By contrast, if a statement is not retracted, this might indicate that any potential violation has not led to the accused having given a statement they would not have given anyway. Then, of course, the impact of a violation would be small. One might ask if a violation has had any impact, if the accused repeats the statement after being informed of their rights or having consulted a lawyer. In the last-mentioned situation, it seems unlikely that overall fairness of a trial would have suffered.

Both elements of the criterion were addressed in *Kalēja*, where the applicant's statements remained unchanged during the proceedings against her:

> She did not confess to the crime in question at any stage of the proceedings. The applicant admitted only to three instances of her taking cash and annulling the relevant cash transactions. She denied having misappropriated those funds. Her submission was that she had handed them over to the deputy head of the company [...].[69]

In *Zherdev*, "the applicant consistently repeated his initial confessions throughout the investigation and at his first trial, even though he did not allege that he was subjected to continuing intimidation or feared reprisals during that later period".[70] And in *Komarov*, the applicant made no self-incriminating statements at any stage of the proceedings. Instead, he consistently maintained that he was not guilty.[71]

Based on the heading before the relevant paragraphs, the Court only assessed the nature of the statement in *Beuze*, but did so at some length, noting inter alia: "[W]hile it is true the applicant never confessed to the charges and therefore did not incriminate himself *stricto sensu*, he nevertheless gave detailed statements to the investigators which influenced the line of questioning." These statements included admitting having been present at the scene of a murder and having threatened a witness. He had also effectively confessed another crime. Later on, the applicant changed his story several times, which undermined his general credibility. The Court found that the nature of the statements was a significant factor in the overall assessment.[72]

In *Ogorodnik*, the police were aware of the applicant's involvement in a number of crimes. He was apprehended but faced nominally a penalty for the administrative offence of disobedience to police orders. During his detention, the

---

68 Beuze v. Belgium [GC], 9.11.2018, § 178.
69 Kalēja v. Latvia, 5.10.2017, § 67.
70 Zherdev v. Ukraine, 27.4.2017, § 155.
71 Komarov v. Ukraine, 19.1.2017, § 142.
72 Beuze v. Belgium [GC], 9.11.2018, §§ 177–181.

applicant gave numerous confessions and waivers of legal assistance. He claimed, in addition, to have been ill-treated during his custody. The Court found a violation of Article 3 on the basis that this claim was not investigated properly. Under such dubious circumstances, the Court did not consider his waivers or confessions voluntary. Although the applicant never retracted most of his confessions, even after receiving legal assistance, he could not be reproached for this under the circumstances.[73]

It might be added that the application of an admissibility rule (b) might be relevant for any subsequent confessions a suspect makes during the course of an investigation. Mirfield explains the problem in the context of English law: "Even if the later interview has been conducted entirely properly, things said or done in the earlier one may still be operative on the accused's mind." Indeed, some English case law would suggest that a suspect must have "a safe and confident opportunity of withdrawing the admissions" if they have been obtained by way of violating the privilege against self-incrimination.[74] A similar rule is known in Germany as *Fortwirkung* (see Section 6.6).

(g) The use to which the evidence was put, and in particular whether the evidence formed an integral or significant part of the probative evidence upon which the conviction was based, and the strength of the other evidence in the case. Finally, we come across a criterion which is clearly a relative of the simpler *Jalloh* test, albeit with some elaboration. The criterion means basically making an assessment of the importance of the impugned evidence in relation to the outcome of the case. The more important the impugned evidence is, the greater the impact of any violation in obtaining it. Unlike some of the criteria discussed above, (g) would seem to be a factor weighing quite heavily in the assessment.

The Court seems to have taken a more dynamic and effective approach to this criterion in *Ibrahim*. Basically, the importance of evidence should be determined not only by how much other incriminating evidence there is in relation to the impugned evidence but also by how the impugned evidence has affected the course of the investigation. If the statement reveals to the authorities a completely different crime or a participant they would not have suspected, it should be considered significant even though the authorities may obtain plenty of evidence to corroborate such a statement. Of course, if the impugned evidence is not used at all, this would considerably mitigate any impact of a potential violation.

In *Ibrahim*, for example, the fourth applicant's statement

> provided a narrative of what had occurred during the critical period, and it was the content of the statement itself which first provided the grounds upon which the police suspected the fourth applicant of involvement in a criminal offence. The statement thus provided the police with the framework around

---

73　Ogorodnik v. Ukraine, 5.2.2015, §§ 88–91 and 105–111.
74　P. Mirfield, *Silence, Confessions and Improperly Obtained Evidence* (Oxford: Clarendon Press, 1997), 146–148.

which they subsequently built their case and the focus for their search for other corroborating evidence.

The Court concluded that the statement formed "an integral and significant part of the probative evidence upon which the conviction was based", in spite of there being other, strong evidence.[75]

By contrast, it was stated in *Artur Parkhomenko* that the impugned statement

> was not made at the initial stage of the investigation but was rather a confirmation of the statements made by the applicant previously. It cannot be said, therefore, that the impugned statement provided the authorities with the narrative of what happened or framed the process of evidence-gathering [...].[76]

Thus, it was not considered to have been an integral or significant part of the evidence against him. In *Fefilov*, referring to both *Ibrahim* and *Artur Parkhomenko*, the Court concluded that the impugned evidence was integral and significant, because "the applicant's confession [...] provided the domestic investigating authorities with the framework around which they subsequently built their case and the focus for their search for other corroborating evidence".[77]

In the United States, such derivative evidence might be treated as a "fruit of the poisonous tree", which means that it, too, is considered to be tainted by the initial violation of defence rights because of the causal link between that violation and the evidence. SCOTUS explained in *Chavez v. Martinez* that "those subjected to coercive police interrogations have an automatic protection from the use of their involuntary statements (or evidence derived from their statements) in any subsequent criminal trial".[78] In German procedural law, a similar rule barring derivative evidence is known as *Fernwirkung*.[79]

In another Ukrainian case, the applicant had stated in his first police interview that the crime had been committed by someone else. This statement, which the applicant repeated at his trial, was used as part of the evidence supporting his and his co-defendants' conviction. The Court concluded:

> Those early admissions likely framed the way the authorities approached the investigation and therefore likely formed a significant part of the evidence against him. Despite the limited role that each of them played in the applicant's conviction for each of the three episodes taken separately, it is probable

75 Ibrahim and Others v. the United Kingdom [GC], 13.9.2016, § 309.
76 Artur Parkhomenko v. Ukraine, 16.2.2017, § 87.
77 Fefilov v. Russia, 17.7.2018, § 63.
78 Chavez v. Martinez, 538 U.S. 760 (2003). See also J. J. Tomkovicz, *Constitutional Exclusion* (Oxford: Oxford University Press, 2011), 89–91.
79 F. Eder, *Beweisverbote und Beweislast im Strafprozess* (Munich: Herbert Utz Verlag, 2015), 217.

that their cumulative effect undermined his overall defence against the charges [...].[80]

There is also case law on evidence which has not formed any part of the probative evidence. In *Loboda*, the applicant had failed to provide the necessary substantiation for his allegation that the impugned statements were used for his conviction or that they had otherwise affected the verdict.[81] In *Kalēja* "[t]he applicant's statements were not cited as evidence when convicting the applicant. Instead, her conviction was based on the testimony of numerous witnesses and other case material [...]".[82] In *Simeonovi*, it was of decisive importance in the overall fairness analysis that no evidence capable of being used against the applicant was obtained during the time his access to a lawyer was restricted.[83]

It should be noted that the formulation "integral or significant" is not that different from "sole or decisive". Indeed, we will come across the importance of the impugned evidence in other contexts than the privilege against self-incrimination. But there is a crucial difference between those pairs of words. This is because in the contexts of other improperly obtained evidence (Chapter 8) and untested evidence (Chapter 9), corroborating evidence can counterbalance an infringement, whereas in the context of the privilege criterion (g) should be understood as a yardstick for the impact of a violation. This means that additional, corroborative evidence will not counterbalance a violation of the privilege while it may counterbalance other violations.

(h) Whether the assessment of guilt was performed by professional judges or lay jurors, and in the case of the latter the content of any jury directions. In its post-*Ibrahim* case law, the Court has considered the fact that professional judges have assessed the applicant's guilt a factor militating in favour of considering the proceedings against them fair.[84] At the same time, it would seem far-fetched to suggest that a jury trial as such would point towards unfairness. What matters perhaps more is whether the trial judge has given the jury appropriate directions if the guilt is to be decided by one. Let us remember that *Ibrahim* itself was a case concerning a jury trial. There, the Court also assessed in detail the directions given:

> In his summing-up to the jury, [...] the trial judge summarised the prosecution and defence evidence in detail and carefully directed the jury on matters of law [...]. He set out in detail the circumstances of each of the applicants' arrests and interviews, including the contents of the interviews and the applicants' explanations for the lies that they had told. He also summarised the extensive prosecution and defence evidence in the case. He expressly

---

80 Sitnevskiy and Chaykovskiy v. Ukraine, 10.11.2016, § 84.
81 Loboda v. Ukraine, 17.11.2016, § 43.
82 Kalēja v. Latvia, 5.10.2017, § 67.
83 Simeonovi v. Bulgaria [GC], 12.5.2017, § 136.
84 See, for example, Sitnevskiy and Chaykovskiy v. Ukraine, § 79 and Fefilov v. Russia, 17.7.2018, § 64.

instructed the jury to take into account when considering the lies told by the applicants that they had been questioned before having had access to legal advice. He explained that this was a right normally afforded to suspects. He gave examples of advice which might have been given by a lawyer and which might have persuaded the applicants to act differently. He further directed the jury to bear in mind that incorrect cautions had been used [...], explaining that this was potentially confusing for the applicants and might have put inappropriate pressure on them to speak.

He pointed out, however, that they had not in fact been pressured into revealing anything relied on at trial but had lied. He instructed the jury members that unless they were sure that each applicant had deliberately lied, they were to ignore the lies told. If, on the other hand, they were satisfied that the lies were deliberate, they were required to consider why the applicant had lied. The judge explained to them that the mere fact that a defendant had lied was not in itself evidence of guilt, since he might have lied for many, possibly innocent reasons. He reminded them that the applicants had put forward a variety of reasons as to why they had lied and told the jury members that if they were satisfied that there was an innocent explanation for the lies told then no notice should be taken of those lies. The lies could only be used as evidence to support the prosecution cases if the jury was sure that the applicants had not lied for innocent reasons. The judge also emphasised that the jury was not permitted to hold it against the applicants that they had failed to mention in the safety interviews matters on which they relied in court. Again, he reminded them that legal advice had been denied to them before the safety interviews. He further instructed the jury to bear in mind as regards Mr Ibrahim that he had been incorrectly denied legal advice by telephone before his safety interview.[85]

As for the fourth applicant, the Court considered the following directions left too much room for discretion, regardless of both his right to a lawyer and right to notification had been breached:

In his summing-up to the jury, the trial judge drew attention to the irregularities that had occurred in the questioning of the fourth applicant and the taking of the witness statement. He summarised the fourth applicant's challenge to the statement and instructed the jury members that they were obliged to disregard the statement if they considered that it might have been obtained by something said or done which was likely to render it unreliable, even if they thought that it was or might be true [...]. However, it is significant that the jury members were instructed to take the statement into account if they were satisfied that it had been freely given, that the fourth applicant would have said these things even if the correct procedure had been followed and that the statement was true.[86]

---

85 Ibrahim and Others v. the United Kingdom [GC], 13.9.2016, § 292.
86 Ibrahim and Others v. the United Kingdom [GC], 13.9.2016, § 310.

(i) The weight of the public interest in the investigation and punishment of the particular offence in issue. The relationship between the right to a fair trial on the one hand and public interest considerations on the other has already been discussed in general terms. As an *Ibrahim* criterion, domestic courts are allowed to balance the public interest against the rights of an individual when deciding whether to admit or exclude evidence. The more serious the crime, the more reason there would be to admit the evidence, and *vice versa* – but only up to a point. It should be remembered that the right to a fair trial also becomes more important when the accusations are serious.

This criterion is also a part of the "original" *Jalloh* test, introduced in that very judgment. It has already been mentioned that the Court considered the weight of that offence too little in relation to the breach of defence rights. The criterion itself may have emerged because it was a part of the German legal framework concerning the admissibility of evidence – similarly to what was being said of the possible role PACE section 76 in *Ibrahim* and the reliability criterion (d). Indeed, the criterion is sometimes not assessed at all, even in post-*Ibrahim* case law.[87] This would, at the very least, indicate that criterion (i) serves an auxiliary function but cannot be a decisive factor in the overall assessment.

It should come as no surprise that there was a strong public interest at hand in *Ibrahim*. The Court formulated its view as follows:

> Indiscriminate terrorist attacks are, by their very nature, intended to strike fear into the hearts of innocent civilians, to cause chaos and panic and to disrupt the proper functioning of everyday life. In such circumstances, threats to human life, liberty and dignity arise not only from the actions of the terrorists themselves but may also arise from the reaction of the authorities in the face of such threats. [...] These very applications, calling into question aspects of the police response to a terrorist attack, attest to the strain that such attacks place on the normal functioning of a democratic society. The public interest in preventing and punishing terrorist attacks of this magnitude, involving a large-scale conspiracy to murder ordinary citizens going about their daily lives, is of the most compelling nature.[88]

The public interest was deemed "very strong" in *Sitnevskiy and Chaykovskiy*, where the crimes in question were aggravated murders committed by an organised armed gang.[89] The applicant in *Artur Parkhomenko* was charged with an attempted robbery with a firearm. The Court stated that the public interest was strong. Because the composition of the chamber was largely the same, omitting the word "very" would appear intentional to differentiate the crimes by their degree. An

---

87 See, for example, Simeonovi v. Bulgaria [GC], 12.5.2017, where the crimes were an armed robbery and two murders; Kalēja v. Latvia, 5.10.2017, and Ogorodnik v. Ukraine, 5.2.2015.
88 Ibrahim and Others v. the United Kingdom [GC], 13.9.2016, § 293.
89 Sitnevskiy and Chaykovskiy v. Ukraine, 10.11.2016, § 79.

interesting detail is that according to the Court, "the public interest in admitting the applicant's statement made in the absence of his co-defendants was further reinforced by the indications that his co-defendants may have attempted to intimidate him".[90] In the case of *Farrugia*, the applicant was convicted of simulation of an offence. Here, the Court stated that "while it appears that there was no actual victim of the hold up in the present case, the Court nevertheless considers that there was at least some public interest in prosecuting the applicant for the crime at issue".[91]

(j) **Other relevant procedural safeguards afforded by domestic law and practice.** The last criterion makes the list of criteria non-exhaustive and there is some case law to illustrate what these other safeguards might be. This criterion would, in my opinion, easily overlap with criterion (b), because they both have to do with the relevant domestic legislation and practice. Indeed, the safeguards regarding the forceful use of emetics, which were considered procedural safeguards in *Jalloh*, were already discussed under criterion (b). The existence of any relevant safeguards in the procedure is, furthermore, another "original" *Jalloh* criterion.

This is not to say that this criterion would be unimportant, just that drawing the line between the various criteria in Ibrahim is again proving quite difficult. "Safeguards" were actually examined in *John Murray* in the context of drawing inferences from silence, a subject we shall discuss below. The various preconditions for drawing inferences against the applicant were considered (procedural) safeguards.[92] This category might also include the possibility of appellate review. In *Simeonovi*, for example, the Court attached weight to the fact that the applicant's case was examined by three domestic courts and they all gave due consideration to the evidence and the applicant's procedural rights.[93]

One might even argue that criterion (j) is too confined, because there may be relevant circumstances which affect the overall fairness of a trial other than normative ones. For example, the Court noted in *Kalēja* that the applicant was not held in detention during the investigation and was therefore not prevented from getting legal assistance before and after her questioning by the police, if she wished so.[94] It might also be a relevant factor whether the suspect was a first-time offender or whether it could be considered likely that, having experience from police investigations, they would be already aware of their rights even though not properly notified by the authorities. This could be seen as a factor which mitigates the impact of a violation.

5.7 Overall assessment

Regardless of whether the privilege against self-incrimination is being violated by way of improper compulsion, including subterfuge, insufficient notification or

---

90 Artur Parkhomenko v. Ukraine, 16.2.2017, § 89.
91 Farrugia v. Malta, 4.6.2019, § 114.
92 John Murray v. the United Kingdom [GC], 8.2.1996, § 51.
93 Simeonovi v. Bulgaria [GC], 12.5.2017, § 143.
94 Kalēja v. Latvia, 5.10.2017, § 68.

restricting access to a lawyer, the decisive question is always whether the fairness of a trial as a whole has been violated or not. But we have already seen that the *Ibrahim* criteria does little to clarify the relevant factors of the overall assessment. In fact, the factors listed in *Jalloh* would seem quite sufficient for the actual impact assessment. Of course, the list is non-exhaustive, and cherry-picking is allowed ("should, where appropriate, be taken into account").

There are indications of the slow adoption of the *Ibrahim* criteria even by the Court itself. It seems to often bundle the criteria together when making an overall assessment. The only reason I can think for this is how much they overlap. So, while the list definitely clarifies some of the criteria, there is also plenty of redundancy for most cases. Additionally, the list fails to bring a coherent structure to the overall assessment. Such structure must, therefore, be deduced from the Court's case law. *Simeonovi*, a post-Ibrahim grand chamber judgment, provides a good example. But let us begin with *Ibrahim*.

The first three applicants and the fourth applicant's cases were assessed separately. As regards the first three applicants, there were compelling reasons to restrict their right to legal advice. In the overall assessment, the Court does not mention criteria (a) at all. It notes, however, that the domestic law provided for the possibility to restrict access to legal advice and overall, legal framework was complied with (b). The interviews conducted during the delay focused on the relevant public safety issues and not on the applicants' involvement. The applicants had been informed of both their right to silence and legal advice. The applicants were able to oppose the use of their statements and trial court gave a reasoned decision, ruling that they were admissible in evidence (c). The only compulsion they complained of was that an erroneous caution was administered, but this could not have led to any real misunderstandings (d). Then, the Court repeats that the statements were obtained lawfully (e). The statements were modified only after a year later (f). There was a substantial prosecution case against the applicants, including evidence on the material of the bombs (g) and the jury were properly directed (h). Additionally, there was a strong public interest in question (i). There was no violation of Article 6.[95]

The case of the fourth applicant was different and his criminal involvement was limited. Also, the starting point of the *Salduz* test was different in that there were no compelling reasons to restrict his right to legal assistance. Thus, the presumption of unfairness was applied. In the overall assessment, criterion (a) is again omitted. The Court begins by noting that there was no legal basis to continue questioning the fourth applicant as a witness and not caution him (b). Although he was able to oppose the use of his statement (c), the Court were dissatisfied by the fact that the senior police official who had authorised the continuation of the interview. There had been no oppression (d) and the fourth applicant did not seek to retract his statement (f). Here, again, the Court then repeated that continuing the interview was unlawful (e). As already explained, his statement effectively revealed his involvement and was, therefore, considered integral and significant

---

95 Ibrahim and Others v. the United Kingdom [GC], 13.9.2016, §§ 276–294.

(g). The Court also stated that the jury was given too much discretion with regard to the violation of defence rights (h). Although there was an important public interest (i), the cumulative effect of the aforementioned procedural shortcomings rendered the fourth applicant's trial as a whole unfair.[96]

In *Simeonovi*, the Court's first observation was that the starting point for the application of Article 6 was the applicant's arrest. He was suspected of having committed an armed robbery and two murders. After that, the Court examined whether he had waived his right to legal assistance. Because he had not been notified of that right, the Court dismissed the possibility of an implicit waiver and found that his right to a lawyer had been restricted. Next, the Court proceeded to the two stages of the *Salduz* test, finding first that there were no compelling reasons. It then begun the overall assessment, noting that the parties disagreed on whether the applicant had been questioned in the absence of a lawyer or not. There was no evidence to support the applicant's version of the events, which had changed during the proceedings. The decisive finding was that

> no evidence capable of being used against the applicant was obtained and included in the case file. No statement was taken from the applicant. No evidence in the file indicates that the applicant was involved in any other investigative measures over that period, such as an identification parade or biological sampling.[97]

Following this finding, the Court seemingly uses some of the *Ibrahim* criteria but does not mention them in the order of the list. It does point out, however, that the domestic legal framework provided for the exclusion of evidence (b), that only the applicant's voluntary confession, given while receiving and having received legal assistance, was used to convict him with "a whole body of consistent evidence" (g). The applicant had participated actively in the proceedings, retracting his initial statements (f) and contesting the incriminating evidence (c). Finally, his case was examined at three levels of jurisdiction, which apparently was considered as an additional safeguard (j). The restriction to legal assistance had not irretrievably prejudiced the privilege against self-incrimination, although there were no compelling reasons to restrict the access to a lawyer.[98]

In some cases, the Court has adopted a simplified model of reasoning. One example is *Sitnevskiy and Chaykovskiy*, where the Court begun, like it did in *Simeonovi*, by finding that the first applicant had not waived his right to a lawyer. Again, it also considered that there were no compelling reasons for the lack of legal assistance. In the overall assessment, the Court first listed "those factors which tend to argue in favour of considering the proceedings fair: (i) the applicant was not particularly vulnerable; (ii) as to the quality of evidence, there is no evidence before the Court that would indicate that any compulsion was involved

---

96 Ibrahim and Others v. the United Kingdom [GC], 13.9.2016, §§ 295–311.
97 Simeonovi v. Bulgaria [GC], 12.5.2017, §§ 136.
98 Simeonovi v. Bulgaria [GC], 12.5.2017, §§ 132–144.

[…]; (iii) the evidence in the case was assessed by professional judges, and (iv) the public interest in the prosecution of the offences imputed to the applicant – aggravated murders committed by an organised armed gang – was very strong". It then assessed in more detail the factors suggesting the opposite. First, it noted that while legal assistance would have been mandatory for murder suspects under domestic law, it was a common practice already condemned by the Court to classify murders as less serious crimes to circumvent this procedural safeguard (b). His initial statement was used as evidence and some of the other evidence was admitted in violation of the right to cross-examination (g).[99]

In *Beuze*, the Court underlined that it was "the combination of the various above-mentioned factors, and not each one taken separately, which rendered the proceedings unfair as a whole". Its analysis regarding the overall fairness were summarised in a list, which will be cited in full:

a   The restrictions on the applicant's right of access to a lawyer were particularly extensive. He was questioned while in police custody without having been able to consult with a lawyer beforehand or to secure the presence of a lawyer, and in the course of the subsequent judicial investigation no lawyer attended his interviews or other investigative acts.

b   In those circumstances, and without having received sufficiently clear prior information as to his right to remain silent, the applicant gave detailed statements while in police custody. He subsequently presented different versions of the facts and made statements which, even though they were not self-incriminating *stricto sensu*, substantially affected his position as regards, in particular, the charge of the attempted murder of C.L.

c   All of the statements in question were admitted in evidence by the Assize Court without conducting an appropriate examination of the circumstances in which the statements had been given, or of the impact of the absence of a lawyer.

d   While the Court of Cassation examined the admissibility of the prosecution case, also seeking to ascertain whether the right to a fair trial had been respected, it focused on the absence of a lawyer during the period in police custody without assessing the consequences for the applicant's defence rights of the lawyer's absence during his police interviews, examinations by the investigating judge and other acts performed in the course of the subsequent judicial investigation.

e   The statements given by the applicant played an important role in the indictment and, as regards the count of the attempted murder of C.L., constituted an integral part of the evidence on which the applicant's conviction was based.

f   In the trial before the Assize Court, the jurors did not receive any directions or guidance as to how the applicant's statements and their evidential value should be assessed.[100]

99 Sitnevskiy and Chaykovskiy v. Ukraine, 10.11.2016, §§
100 Beuze v. Belgium [GC], 9.11.2018, § 193.

The case law may still develop, of course, but some general outlines can be identified. First, it is rarely one factor or criteria alone which would be decisive. At the same time, some factors have greater weight than others. Particular vulnerability (a), lapses regarding the domestic legal framework (b), ineffective opportunity to challenge the evidence (c), possibly in connection with insufficient directions to the jury (h), extensive limitations or compulsion (d), and extensive use or significance of the impugned evidence (g) are factors which could gain a great weight in favour of finding a violation.

By contrast, adhering to domestic legislative framework of sufficient quality (b), proper assessment and reasoning regarding the reliability and admissibility of the impugned evidence (c) or sufficient jury directions (h), the limited nature of a violation, especially in the light of any warnings administered (d), repeating the impugned statement when being granted legal assistance (f), as well as there being plenty of other, independent prosecution evidence which would have been obtained irrespective of the violation (g) could be factors which tend to argue in favour of considering the proceedings fair. An "extreme" situation for the application of criterion (g) is when no incriminating evidence has been obtained as the result of a violation.

Finally, the lack of particular vulnerability (a), compliance with domestic legal framework (b), lack of compulsion (d), there being no violation of another Convention Article (e), the fact that a statement was not retracted (f), existence of other incriminating evidence (g), the case being decided by a professional judge (h) and there being a considerable public interest (i) are all factors which are not decisive themselves. They need to be accompanied by other relevant factors of the *Ibrahim* criteria. It should always be borne in mind that the question to be answered is whether the factors, when combined, show that a trial has been fair in spite of a violation of potentially irretrievable impact.

5.8 Drawing inferences from silence

Now, let us turn to a special feature of the privilege. First, as already mentioned briefly, the privilege does not prevent courts from drawing inferences from the accused remaining silent under certain circumstances. This might seem inconsistent with the right or to negate its protection, because one might think that the right would remain effective only if invoking it could not lead to any negative consequences. But, as also mentioned, the privilege does not entail a right to secure a particular outcome in the proceedings.

Unlike some aspects of the privilege, the doctrine of adverse inferences has not seen much change since it was first formulated in *John Murray*. Upon his arrest, the applicant was cautioned by the police in the following terms:

> You do not have to say anything unless you wish to do so but I must warn you that if you fail to mention any fact which you rely on in your defence in court, your failure to take this opportunity to mention it may be treated in

court as supporting any relevant evidence against you. If you do wish to say anything, what you say may be given in evidence.

Without much argumentation, the Court found the right to silence was not absolute:

> On the one hand, it is self-evident that it is incompatible with the immunities under consideration to base a conviction solely or mainly on the accused's silence or on a refusal to answer questions or to give evidence himself. On the other hand, the Court deems it equally obvious that these immunities cannot and should not prevent that the accused's silence, in situations which clearly call for an explanation from him, be taken into account in assessing the persuasiveness of the evidence adduced by the prosecution.[101]

This means, of course, that the pivotal question is what are the circumstances under which inferences can be drawn. The Court stated in very general terms that

> [w]hether the drawing of adverse inferences from an accused's silence infringes Article 6 is a matter to be determined in the light of all the circumstances of the case, having particular regard to the **situations** where inferences may be drawn, the **weight** attached to them by the national courts in their assessment of the evidence and the **degree of compulsion** inherent in the situation.[102]

Additionally, the Court did take into account the **procedural safeguards** which were in place to protect the defendant.

The applicant had been convicted of aiding and abetting the unlawful imprisonment of a Mr L., a police informant, in connection with the IRA in Northern Ireland. The police had seen the applicant coming down a flight of stairs upon their entry of a house where Mr L. was kept. Mr L. told in his testimony that the captors had made him confess that he was a traitor. Mr L. also testified that he had seen the applicant in the house, at the stairs, and the applicant had told him that the police were at the door. While having this conversation, the applicant had pulled tape out of a cassette. Real evidence found during a house search, including the tape, corroborated this testimony. The applicant, however, never provided an explanation for his presence in the house.

I shall begin from the last element, the degree of compulsion, as the Court did. It noted, first, that the applicant was able to remain silent throughout the proceedings and was, therefore, not compelled to give evidence against himself. The Court did consider that, given "the weight of the case against him", warning the applicant of the possibility of drawing adverse inferences from silence involved "a certain level of indirect compulsion". However, this was not the

101 John Murray v. the United Kingdom [GC], 8.2.1996, § 47.
102 John Murray v. the United Kingdom [GC], 8.2.1996, § 47.

decisive factor.[103] One might add that if the domestic legislation allowed adverse inferences to be drawn, it would appear unfair not to warn suspects of this possibility.

Next, the Court addressed whether there was a situation where inferences could be drawn. First of all, which would be important under the current Ibrahim criterion (b), the drawing of inferences was explicitly permitted by the domestic legal framework which, furthermore, provided procedural safeguards. The Court also mentioned, although briefly, a factor relevant for criterion (h), that the evidence was evaluated by an experienced judge sitting without a jury. The key requirement, though, was that of a prima facie case against a defendant before any inferences could be drawn.[104]

What this meant, according to the domestic case law, was that

> the prosecutor must first establish a prima facie case against the accused, i.e. a case consisting of direct evidence which, if believed and combined with legitimate inferences based upon it, could lead a properly directed jury to be satisfied beyond reasonable doubt that each of the essential elements of the offence is proved.[105]

This threshold is linked with the domestic law, which provides the possibility of the defence submitting that there is no case to answer after the closure of the prosecution case. Such submissions are then decided by the trial judge, not the jury.

If, on the other hand, there is a sufficiently strong *prima facie* case against a defendant, the trial would be continued with the case for the defence and their evidence. But even this does not automatically allow the drawing on inferences. Instead, only if the evidence against the defendant would call for an explanation which they would be in a position to give that adverse inferences could be drawn. The Court's argumentation in this connection seems to already touch upon the third element, the weight of such inferences, but we shall return to that soon. It was additionally pointed out that the trial judge had discretion whether an inference should be drawn, and it was also subject to appellate review.

As far as the weight of an inference goes, the Court stated as a general principle the "self-evident" starting point that silence could not be "solely or mainly" used as evidence of guilt. To hold otherwise would, of course, completely reverse the presumption of innocence and shift the burden of proof to the defence. While this element resembles *Ibrahim* criterion (g), I think there is a crucial difference as to how the adverse inferences work as evidence. In the case of *John Murray*, there was "formidable" evidence against the applicant, because the testimony of Mr L. was strongly corroborated by other evidence.[106]

---

103 John Murray v. the United Kingdom [GC], 8.2.1996, §§ 48–50.
104 John Murray v. the United Kingdom [GC], 8.2.1996, § 51.
105 A. L-T Choo, *Evidence*, 2nd edn (Oxford: Oxford University Press, 2015), 69–70.
106 John Murray v. the United Kingdom [GC], 8.2.1996, § 52.

Although the Court does not discuss the theory of adverse inferences, Glover has described such inferences as "quasi-corroborative rules", which I find to be a fitting description.[107] That is because the inferences are not, strictly speaking, evidence. Instead, when the prosecution evidence requires an answer, that evidence would be potentially strong enough to convict the defendant. Should they fail to provide an explanation, the common-sense inference would be that there is no alternative hypothesis and no reasonable doubt about the defendant's guilt. That is, the inferences can only corroborate an already strong prosecution case, but not be used as evidence of guilt as such.

In at least Finland and Sweden, there has been some scholarly discussion about what is required of the prosecution case. It has been suggested that if the level is anything less than "beyond reasonable doubt" (i.e. sufficient for conviction), the possibility to draw inferences could be abused to strengthen a prosecution case which would otherwise be too weak. Most writers agree that prosecution evidence should reach this level of certainty before it would be appropriate to draw inferences from silence. On the other hand, it has also been suggested that the mechanism would be futile if there is sufficient evidence anyway.[108]

According to Glover, the establishment of a prima facie case means that the prosecution has discharged their evidential burden, after which the eyes turn to the defence. There is an area of risk for the defendant between the levels of a prima facie case and a conviction.[109] But this risk does not compensate for lack of prosecution evidence. Instead, it represents the possibility that refusal to provide an explanation will work against the defendant and, indirectly, support the prosecution case. In an adversarial trial, it does not seem futile to me to take into account the answer of the defence – or lack of it.

Finally, it has also been discussed whether similar rules apply if it is discovered that a defendant has been lying. I submit the answer is yes. Even if a lie is quite obvious, no adverse inferences should be drawn before the prosecution has discharged its evidential burden and adduced enough evidence against the defendant. A lie, just like silence, cannot be the sole or decisive evidence of someone having committed a crime. This is also the view of one Finnish author, who has suggested that it would have perhaps had a similar effect as silence under the circumstances if John Murray would have claimed to have just delivered a pizza, but no pizza or even a pizza restaurant employing him would have been found.[110]

---

107 R. Glover, *Murphy on Evidence*, 15th edn (Oxford: Oxford University Press, 2017), 281.

108 A. Nordlander, "Förklaringsbördan i brottmål och dess förenlighet med oskyldighetspresumtionen" (2017) *Svensk Juristtidning*, 653, 660–663; L. Schelin, *Bevisvärdering av utsagor i brottmål* (Stockholm: Stockholms Universitet, 2007), 55–56; compare C. Diesen, *Bevisprövning i brottmål*, 2nd edn (Stockholm: Norstedts juridik, 2015), 133–134.

109 Glover 2017, 92–93.

110 M. Fredman, *Puolustajan rooli: Rikoksesta epäillyn ja syytetyn avustajan roolin kehitys Suomessa 1980-luvulta nykypäivään* (Helsinki: Alma Talent, 2018), 83.

5.9 The assessment of irretrievable prejudice

I would not be surprised if the preceding presentation of the various tests has been slightly overwhelming and confusing. Although the Court made an attempt to clarify its approach in *Ibrahim*, it did not entirely succeed. It is important to understand the continuum of the Court's case law as well as the differences of the various mechanisms it has introduced over the years. In this section, I will attempt to present a rule of evidence, keeping in mind the domestic judge. This rule will be derived from not only *Ibrahim* itself but also from case law before and after it. *Simeonovi* provides a good basis for the formulation of the rule.

The first stage would be to determine the **applicability** of Article 6, if it is disputed. As discussed above, when a person is either "officially notified" or "substantially affected", Article 6 will become applicable. This will also trigger the right to notification and the right to a lawyer. Naturally, improper compulsion to obtain evidence would substantially affect a suspect if they have not already been officially notified. In any case, I submit that the first stage of the overall assessment will be determining whether Article 6 applies in the case and, in that connection, whether they were notified of their rights or not. If the impugned evidence is real evidence, the privilege might not be applicable.

If the accused has been notified properly, the second stage would be to determine whether they have validly **waived**, either expressly or tacitly, their right to a lawyer and/or to remain silent. It is at this stage where the first *Ibrahim* criterion, particular vulnerability (a), would often have great importance. The applicable standard of unequivocal waiver and minimum safeguards has been discussed already. One key safeguard is that if a suspect waives their right to legal assistance, it will be incumbent on the authorities to make sure they understand the seriousness of the suspicion as well as their rights, including the right to remain silent. If a waiver has been valid, the right to legal assistance cannot be considered to have been restricted.

The following stage would be to determine the nature and **seriousness** of the violation, whether it is improper compulsion. The conceptual framework of types of improper compulsion or compelling reasons discussed above can be used to make this assessment. I submit that any type of violation discussed above – be it improper compulsion, lack of notification or restriction of legal assistance – would trigger a presumption of unfairness, requiring that the authorities demonstrate convincingly why, exceptionally and in the specific circumstances of the case, the overall fairness of the trial would not have been irretrievably prejudiced by the violation.

Assessing the seriousness of the violation could include applying some of the *Ibrahim* criteria, especially (b) and (e). If the domestic legal framework fails to provide sufficient protection of if it was not complied with, the violation would be more serious. The nature of the unlawfulness would supposedly be more serious if a sanction has been heavy or if someone's bodily integrity has been violated. If another Convention Article was violated, this could lead to another test to be applied instead of the one presented here (see Chapters 6 and 8 for violations of Articles 3 and 8, respectively).

The more serious the violation, the lesser **impact** could be tolerated for the trial to remain fair as a whole. This follows the formula of the SIC framework. As we have seen, the *Ibrahim* criteria seem to be confusing even for the Court itself and they seem incapable of providing the clarity that was probably attempted. Perhaps, then, the *Jalloh* criteria would still offer sufficient general structure for assessing the impact of a breach of defence rights and, in particular, whether the essence of the privilege against self-incrimination has been affected.

That criteria can also be paired up with or interpreted in the light of the *Ibrahim* criteria. The first *Jalloh* criterion, the weight of the public interest in the investigation and punishment of the offence in issue, matches criterion (i). The relevant safeguards in the procedure should include, at the very least, the opportunity to challenge the authenticity of the evidence and oppose its use (c). These opportunities are not efficient unless the trial court, whatever its composition (h), assesses the quality of the evidence and whether the circumstances in which it was obtained cast doubt on its reliability or accuracy (d) and, in the case of a statement, the nature of the statement and whether it was promptly retracted or modified (f).[111]

As the case law shows, the impact of a violation would be greatly reduced if no self-incriminating material is obtained from an accused person or if they give such material voluntary while being aware of their right not to. Excluding the impugned evidence would have a similar effect. On the other hand, it is not enough to conclude that the reliability of the impugned evidence has not suffered as a result of how it was obtained. There is some margin of appreciation in the balancing act between fairness and the public interest. Apparently, it would also serve to mitigate a violation if these assessments were performed by professional judges. I suspect this factor is of rather limited weight.

The final element of the *Jalloh* criteria is the use to which the evidence is put. This means in particular whether the evidence formed an integral or significant part of the probative evidence upon which the conviction was based, and the strength of the other evidence in the case (g). Under this criterion, what matters most is whether the potential violation of the privilege leads to the authorities discovering new "integral or significant" evidence. By contrast, if there is plenty of other evidence already, the impact of a breach would be smaller – perhaps even tolerable. In *O'Halloran and Francis*, it was mentioned as a factor that the identity of the driver at a given time was only one element of the offence.[112]

Judge Bošnjak gives an interesting analysis of the assessment model in his partly dissenting opinion in *Murtazaliyeva*. According to him, various substantive *Ibrahim*

111 In *O'Halloran and Francis* the Court noted that according to the domestic legal framework concerning the duty to disclose the identity of a driver at a given time, no offence would be committed if the keeper of the vehicle shows that he did not know and could not with reasonable diligence have known who the driver of the vehicle was. The relevant safeguards were that the offence was not one of strict liability and the risk of unreliable admissions was negligible (O'Halloran and Francis v. the United Kingdom [GC], 29.6.2007, § 59).

112 O'Halloran and Francis v. the United Kingdom [GC], 29.6.2007, § 60.

criteria such as (d) and (g) "remained in the shadow of a large number of solely procedural elements. This cannot be said for examination of complaints concerning the use of evidence obtained in violation of Convention rights". He concludes that the Court's case law is inconsistent.[113] I would say that it at least seems inconsistent, but perhaps this difference in approaches can be explained by looking at the rationales of the various defence rights.

In the context of the privilege against self-incrimination, the primary rationale is to protect the accused's freedom of choice against any subversions – whether they result from lack of knowledge of their rights or compulsion or something in between. The right is not primarily concerned with the reliability of evidence, which would explain why the "procedural" elements of the *Ibrahim* criteria are usually decisive. In the context of other improperly obtained evidence, the substantive elements have more weight because Article 8 rights, for example, are not protected as such. The key criterion in that context is reliability, which calls for a more substantive approach (see Chapter 8).

---

113 Murtazaliyeva v. Russia [GC], 18.12.2018, § 11 of the opinion.

6 The prohibition of torture and inhuman or degrading treatment

6.1 Introduction

As explained in Chapters 2 and 3, the Court cannot, in principle, introduce any rules of admissibility requiring certain evidence to be excluded. This is simply because such rules do not have a legal foundation in the Convention. The Court's jurisdiction is limited to determining if a right protected by the Convention has been violated. It has also been explained that the admissibility of evidence is generally a matter under Article 6 of the Convention, but there may be situations where evidence is obtained, presented, or even evaluated in violation of some other Article.

In its landmark *Jalloh* judgment the Court referred to Article 15 of the Convention against Torture and Other Cruel, Inhuman or Degrading Treatment or Punishment (UNCAT), which does require exclusion of evidence: "Each State Party shall ensure that any statement which is established to have been made as a result of torture shall not be invoked as evidence in any proceedings, except against a person accused of torture as evidence that the statement was made."[1] Such provisions are not to be found from the Convention, and thus the Court may only assess torture evidence in the context of guaranteeing a fair trial.[2]

Article 3 of the Convention includes a clear and unequivocal prohibition of torture and other ill-treatment: "No one shall be subjected to torture or to inhuman or degrading treatment or punishment." This Article is **absolute** in that it does not allow any exceptions and derogation from it is not permissible even in times of emergency (see Article 15 § 2 of the Convention). The absolute nature of Article 3 is also reflected into how violations against it are assessed in the context of fair trial. According to the Court, "the use of such evidence, secured as a result of a violation of one of the core and absolute rights guaranteed by the Convention, always raises serious issues as to the fairness of the proceedings".[3]

---

1 Jalloh v. Germany [GC], 11.7.2006, § 48.
2 J. D. Jackson and S. J. Summers, *The Internationalisation of Criminal Evidence: Beyond the Common Law and Civil Law Traditions* (Cambridge: Cambridge University Press, 2012), 163.
3 Gäfgen v. Germany [GC], 1.6.2010, § 165 (with further references).

DOI: 10.4324/9781003311416-6

coercing him or a third person, or for any reason based on discrimination of any kind, when such pain or suffering is inflicted by or at the instigation of or with the consent or acquiescence of a public official or other person acting in an official capacity. It does not include pain or suffering arising only from, inherent in or incidental to lawful sanctions.

Macabre though it may sound, we might imagine a scale of ill-treatment beginning from that which fails to attain the minimum level of severity. For example, in its *Raninen* judgment the Court found that handcuffing the applicant, although it was unjustified, had not been proven to have adversely affected the applicant either mentally or physically and did not attain the minimum level of severity. It is worth noting that the applicant had claimed to have been a victim of only degrading treatment (i.e. not torture or inhuman treatment).[25] Also, it seems unnecessary to examine inhuman or degrading *punishment* here, because the gathering of evidence would amount to treatment, not punishment.

In *Stanev*, with references to its case law, the Court explained:

> Treatment has been held by the Court to be "inhuman" because, inter alia, it was premeditated, was applied for hours at a stretch and caused either actual bodily injury or intense physical or mental suffering [...]. Treatment has been considered "degrading" when it was such as to arouse in its victims feelings of fear, anguish and inferiority capable of humiliating and debasing them and possibly breaking their physical or moral resistance or driving them to act against their will or conscience [...].

The Court is also of the opinion that the absence of intent to humiliate does not inevitably lead to a finding that there has been no violation of Article 3.[26]

At the other end of the scale is torture, a term which attaches "a special stigma to deliberate inhuman treatment causing very serious and cruel suffering".[27] Article 3 therefore makes a distinction between torture and *other* ill-treatment, a wording not to be found from the Article itself but, for example, from the very title of UNCAT.[28] Inhuman or degrading treatment is, then, something between the minimum threshold and torture. But should a distinction between these two types of ill-treatment be drawn also in terms of severity or do they only differ in their nature?

Tyrer would seem to suggest there is a difference in severity as well as nature. The Court did not consider that the particular (minimum) level of severity was attained and agreed with the Commission that the penalty imposed on the applicant was not to be considered an inhuman punishment. The Court then continued: "Accordingly, the only question for decision is whether he was subjected

---

25 Raninen v. Finland, 16.12.1997, see especially §§ 52 and 58.
26 Stanev v. Bulgaria [GC], 17.1.2012, § 203.
27 Ireland v. the United Kingdom [plenary], 18.1.1978, § 167.
28 Pattenden 2006, 20–21.

to a 'degrading punishment' contrary to that Article (art. 3)."[29] This statement would seem to suggest that not all degrading treatment is necessarily inhuman and therefore that degrading treatment should be considered the lowest degree of severity.[30]

However, one cannot help noticing that the minimum level should also be attained before it can be established that ill-treatment would be degrading either (as in *Raninen*).[31] Also, neither the wording of Article 3 nor that of *Ireland v. the United Kingdom* suggest that inhuman treatment should be considered more serious than degrading treatment. Even in its recent case law the Court has not drawn such a distinction, but only stated that "[i]ll-treatment must attain a minimum level of severity if it is to fall within the scope of Article 3". In both *Öcalan* and *Jalloh*, for example, this statement is followed by examples of both inhuman and degrading treatment.[32]

Based on the lack of more compelling arguments than what seems to be an *obiter dictum* statement in *Tyrer* suggesting otherwise I am inclined to believe that the Court has not meant to distinguish between the degree but only the nature of inhuman treatment on the one hand and degrading treatment on the other. Indeed, it sometimes does not distinguish between the two.[33] After reaching the minimum level of severity but falling short of torture, ill-treatment could be classified as inhuman or degrading (or both) depending on its nature. A distinction in degree is, furthermore, not especially important for rules of evidence because they must reflect the absolute nature of Article 3.

6.5 The scope of the rule

The rule against torture evidence is clear-cut and, in many ways, universal in scope. Its scope in the German classification (see at the end of Section 3.4) of admissibility rules would be a method of gathering evidence. The type of evidence does not matter; both statements and real evidence obtained through torture should be inadmissible as using such evidence would make the trial automatically unfair in violation of Article 6 of the Convention. One can say that the rule is "type neutral" in this sense. This makes the rule more widely applicable than UNCAT Article 15, which only refers to statements. Naturally, the rule cannot be

---

29 Tyrer v. the United Kingdom, 25.4.1978, § 29.
30 R. Clayton and H. Tomlinson, *The Law of Human Rights*, vol. I (Oxford: Oxford University Press, 2000), 394.
31 Similarly, in the more recent judgment M.S. v. the United Kingdom, 3.5.2012, the applicant submitted that he had been subjected to inhuman and degrading treatment when inappropriately detained in a police cell during a period of acute mental suffering. Without much elaboration the Court only considered whether his treatment was degrading and explained that a minimum level of severity must be reached.
32 Öcalan v. Turkey [GC], 12.5.2005, §§ 180 and 181, Jalloh v. Germany [GC], 11.7.2006, §§ 67 and 68.
33 See, for example, Jalloh v. Germany [GC], 11.7.2006, § 82; Idalov v. Russia [GC], 22.5.2012, § 101; and Simeonovi v. Bulgaria [GC], 12.5.2017, § 90.

bent by, for example, taking statements from other people present during the acts of torture.

In a typical situation under the UNCAT state officials would have tortured a person to get their confession. However, the Court has clarified in *Harutyunyan, Othman* (in the context of flagrant denial of justice) and *Kaçiu and Kotorri* that torture evidence cannot be used against *anyone*, neither the victim nor a third person.[34] What is slightly less clear is whether such evidence could be offered *in favour* of someone (i.e. as proof of someone's innocence). Because of the dangers inherent, both integrity and reliability concerns, even such use should be possible under extremely limited circumstances only.[35]

As far as statements are concerned, a clear rule has also been established by the Court against evidence obtained by way of ill-treatment falling short of torture. Here, the Court has also referred to the inherent unreliability of such evidence as well as the deterrence principle. For example, in *Gäfgen*, with a reference to *Söy-lemez*, the Court stated that the admission of statements obtained as a result of not only torture but also other ill-treatment in breach of Article 3 would automatically render the proceedings unfair.[36] Statements obtained through inhuman and/or degrading treatment should, therefore, not be admitted as evidence.

The Court made clear in its recent *Ćwik* judgment, that the strict rule against admitting statements obtained in violation of Article 3 applies also if the state-ment has been taken by a private individual. This is perfectly in line with the concept of a rule of evidence forbidding a method of obtaining it. Because the rule applies also regardless of whether the ill-treatment can be classified as tor-ture, the Court considered it unnecessary to determine that issue – it was suffi-cient to find that the statement had been obtained through treatment which violated Article 3.[37]

The Court has not indicated whether using real evidence obtained by way of inhuman and/or degrading treatment automatically renders the trial unfair. In *Gäfgen*, as well as in *Jalloh*, the Court had an opportunity to rule on the matter, but it expressly refused to do so, stating in *Jalloh*: "In the present case, the general question whether the use of evidence obtained by an act qualified as inhuman and degrading treatment automatically renders a trial unfair can be left open."[38] Similarly, in *Othman*, after repeating the rule against torture evidence, the Court continued that is "does not exclude that similar considerations may apply in respect of evidence obtained by other forms of ill-treatment which fall short of torture. However, on the facts of the present case [...], it is not necessary to decide this question."[39]

---

34 Harutyunyan v. Armenia, 28.6.2007, §§ 64–66; Othman (Abu Qatada) v. the United Kingdom, 17.1.2012, § 266 and Kaçiu and Kotorri v. Albania, 25.6.2013, § 128.
35 See also Pattenden 2006, 10–12 and 36–37.
36 Gäfgen v. Germany [GC], 1.6.2010, § 166 and Söylemez c. Turquie, 21.9.2006, § 122.
37 Ćwik v. Poland, 5.11.2020, especially §§ 82–84 and 88–89.
38 Jalloh v. Germany [GC], 11.7.2006, § 107.
39 Othman (Abu Qatada) v. the United Kingdom, 17.1.2012, § 267.

We have taken and will take a closer look at *Jalloh* in the contexts of both the privilege against self-incrimination (Chapter 5) and other improperly obtained evidence (Chapter 8). It can be noted here that a breach of Article 3 to obtain real evidence is, irrespective of whether that evidence is used against the subject of such treatment or not, a factor weighing heavily in the scales as a very serious violation. So, although there is a little more leeway in comparison to statements and torture evidence, admitting real evidence obtained by way of inhuman or degrading treatment is far from being free. The phrase "always raises serious issues" could perhaps be interpreted as an assumption of violation, albeit not an automation.

The Court's reluctance to expand the rule to real evidence could be partly explained through the reliability rationale, although this does (at least indirectly) undermine the absolute nature of Article 3. It may also be that UNCAT Article 15 plays a role here – let us remember that it only requires the exclusion of *statements* obtained through *torture*. At the same time, there is nothing preventing the Court to act as a pioneer in protecting the absolute rights of the Convention and expanding the rule against torture evidence in line with the effectiveness principle, for example.

If torture is used to get self-incriminating information or objects, it would seem most appropriate to apply the rule against torture as a *lex specialis* rule forbidding that cruel method. This would mean applying only the inflexible rule even though the use of evidence could also be assessed using the slightly more flexible test applicable to the privilege against self-incrimination. The same also applies to statements obtained through other ill-treatment violating Article 3. When it comes to real evidence obtained through such ill-treatment, it seems that the choice between "tests" should be done based on whether the evidence is self-incriminating or not (i.e. whether it is tendered against the victim of such ill-treatment or a third person).

6.6 Long-range effect

As already quoted, the Court has stated that

> the repression of, and the effective protection of individuals from, the use of investigation methods that breach Article 3 may [...] also require, *as a rule*, the exclusion from use at trial of real evidence which has been obtained as the result of any violation of Article 3, even though that evidence is *more remote* from the breach of Article 3 than evidence extracted *immediately* as a consequence of a violation of that Article.[40]

This would seem to touch upon a subject of heated scholarly debate, namely the so-called fruit of the poisonous tree doctrine.

---

40 Gäfgen v. Germany [GC], 1.6.2010, § 178.

The doctrine is, in principle, simple enough to understand: if a breach of rights leads the authorities to discover new evidence they would not have discovered otherwise, can such "derivative" evidence be used or not? The new pieces of evidence are, naturally, the "fruits" in this analogy. In the United States, there is long-established support for the doctrine. In the landmark judgment *Silverthorne Lumber Co.*, SCOTUS stated that to allow the authorities to use real evidence discovered as a result of an illegal search would reduce the fourth amendment of the U.S. Constitution "to a form of words" – an expression for what the Court might call the need to make sure rights are "practical and effective".[41]

Gäfgen offers several interesting insights to how the Court approaches (rules of) evidence and the possibility of long-range effect. The applicant was suspected of having kidnapped an 11-year-old boy. The police had him under surveillance when he came to pick up the ransom money from a tram station in Frankfurt am Main. Later that day he was arrested at the airport. When questioned by the police, the applicant claimed that others had kidnapped the boy and were holding him in a hut by a lake.

The next day the deputy chief of police had ordered another police officer to question the applicant and to threaten him with considerable physical pain, and, if necessary, to subject him to such pain to make him reveal the boy's whereabouts. The officer followed this order and threatened the applicant. According to the applicant, he had also been threatened with sexual abuse and physically assaulted. After some ten minutes, the applicant revealed the location of the boy's body. Next, the police drove him to a lake and videotaped the applicant pointing out where the body was. Other forensic evidence was also found from the scene, including tyre tracks.

During the return journey from the lake, the applicant confessed to having kidnapped and killed the boy. He then pointed out in various places more real evidence which corroborated his confession. The German lower court ruled that all evidence was admissible, but higher court upon appeal ruled that the applicant's statements were inadmissible. The real evidence was, however, deemed admissible. The applicant confessed to the crime in trial and was convicted of murder and other crimes for life. The Court considered that the confession made in trial was the decisive evidence and was not tainted by ill-treatment. There was no violation of Article 3.

In German jurisprudence, a distinction has been made between two types of "long-range effect": *Fernwirkung*, which means the fruits of the poisonous tree, and *Fortwirkung*, which means a situation where the effects of the breach of someone's rights continue – this might be translated best as "continuation effect" while the former could also be named "discovery effect" for reasons I shall explain shortly.[42] The **continuation effect** is at hand, for example, when a suspect is first

41 Silverthorne Lumber Co. v. United States, 251 U.S. 385 (1920). See also Chavez v. Martinez, 538 U.S. 760 (2003).
42 M. Heghmanns, "Beweisverwertungsverbote und Fernwirkung" (2010) *Zeitschrift für das Juristische Studium*, 98, 99.

questioned illegally and then legally without explaining that their earlier statements are not going to be used against them. A similar effect might come into
play if real evidence has been gathered illegally and the suspect sees no alternative
but to confess. Here, too, one can think that the effect of the initial breach is
continued to receive more evidence.

Discovery effect, by comparison, refers to another type of causal link between
the initial breach and other evidence. *Gäfgen* provides examples of this type of
long-range effect, because the police would not have discovered (at least not as
quickly) the boy's body and other incriminating real evidence without the suspect
having pointed them out as a result of ill-treatment by the police officer. Moreover, the confession he made on the way back from the lake where the body and
tyre tracks were discovered, could be considered a result of the continuation effect
of the ill-treatment. Indeed, the Frankfurt am Main Regional Court ruled *all*
statements made to the police inadmissible to break the causal link of the continuation effect because the applicant had not been informed that the earlier
statements could not be used.[43]

The Court seems to have adopted a theoretically valid but not overly complicated approach to long-range effect, a question still debated in Germany and many
other countries.[44] For the purposes of its assessment, the Court considered it
decisive that there was a *causal link* between the applicant's interrogation in
breach of Article 3 and the real evidence secured by the authorities as a result of
the applicant's indications, including the discovery of the victim's body and the
autopsy report thereon, the tyre tracks left by the applicant's car at the pond, as
well as the victim's backpack, clothes and the applicant's typewriter. This evidence
was secured *as a direct result* of his interrogation that breached Article 3.[45]

There was also real evidence at hand not tainted by the initial interrogation:
The items obtained from the applicant's home as well as all the information the
police had gathered by observing him. The items and traces obtained at the lake
and other hideouts, however, seem more problematic. The German courts allowed
them to be used weighing the seriousness of the violation and the seriousness of
the crime against each other, ruling that it would be disproportionate to exclude
the evidence. It seems that this evidence was given some weight as corroboration
of the applicant's later confession but according to the Court it "was not necessary, and was not used to prove him guilty or to determine his sentence".[46]

The term "discovery effect" would also be especially useful because it would
help understand the various possible **exceptions** to the long-range effect. In the
United States, there are several types of exception, three of which deserve special
attention here: (1) independent source, (2) inevitable discovery, and (3) attenuation.[47] The first type was introduced by SCOTUS in *Silverthorne* already.

---

43 Gäfgen v. Germany [GC], 1.6.2010, §§ 28–30.
44 Jackson and Summers 2012, 191.
45 Gäfgen v. Germany [GC], 1.6.2010, § 171.
46 Gäfgen v. Germany [GC], 1.6.2010, § 180.
47 J. J. Tomkovicz, *Constitutional Exclusion* (Oxford: Oxford University Press, 2011),
    42. There are also exceptions explained only by the deterrence rationale, such as the

Explained shortly, evidence is deemed admissible if it in reality was also obtained from an independent source without resorting to unfair or illegal actions. For example, if the same information or object was also obtained from another witness or lawful search, it would be admissible. This is because the facts themselves do not become "sacred and inaccessible", only the method of obtaining evidence is wrong.[48]

Inevitable discovery differs from independent source in that now it can only be assumed that the evidence would have been inevitably discovered from an independent source, that is, without a causal link to a breach of rights. In such hypothetical situations where the causal link between a violation and evidence is lacking, there is a "clean path" between the two. According to the Court in *Gäfgen*, "factors such as whether the impugned evidence would, in any event, have been found at a later stage, independently of the prohibited method of investigation, may have an influence on the admissibility of such evidence".[49] However, in *Svetina* the Court stated that it "does not draw any conclusion as to the compliance of the 'inevitable discovery doctrine' with the Convention requirements".[50]

In the American case of *Nix v. Williams* SCOTUS stated:

> If the prosecution can establish by a preponderance of the evidence that the information ultimately or inevitably would have been discovered by lawful means [in that case a search by volunteers] then the deterrence rationale has so little basis that the evidence should be received.

Although the Court has not endorsed the deterrence rationale as strongly and unequivocally as SCOTUS, it can also be said that the causal link in such situations is not a "conditio sine qua non" (i.e. the violation is not indispensable condition for the discovery of the evidence). The facts of the case were strongly in favour of the conclusion of inevitable discovery, because the local authorities had organised and directed some 200 volunteers to search for the 10-year-old girl who had gone missing (similarly to *Gäfgen*, the child had been murdered). An agent testified that they would have continued the search in the area where the body was located. He had even obtained a map of that area already.[51]

The third exception, known as attenuation, means a situation where the causal link between the breach and obtaining evidence is weak (i.e. attenuated). The question is "whether, granting establishment of the primary illegality, the evidence

good faith exception, which would not be compatible with the Court's case law. Whether the authorities have acted in good faith might be a factor in other situations (see, for example, Chapter 8), but not in the context of torture evidence.

48 Silverthorne Lumber Co. v. United States, 251 U.S. 385 (1920).
49 Gäfgen v. Germany [GC], 1.6.2010, § 174. See also the South African case referred in Gäfgen, Mthembu v. The State [2008] ZASCA 51, especially the following statement in § 33: "There is no suggestion that the discoveries would have been made in any event. If they had the outcome of this case might have been different."
50 Svetina v. Slovenia, 22.5.2018, § 49 *in fine*.
51 Nix v. Williams, 467 U.S. 431 (1984).

to which instant objection is made has been come at by exploitation of that illegality or instead by means sufficiently distinguishable to be purged of the primary taint". Relevant factors which may attenuate the causal link include passing of time, additional links in the causal chain (such as informing a suspect of their right to remain silent or release from custody prior to confession), and the purpose and flagrancy of the breach. Tomkovicz points out, however, that SCOTUS "has not fleshed out the logic underlying the attenuation exception in any detail".[52]

It seems that the Court has accepted the possibility of a long-range effect, be it one of continuation or discovery. Real evidence "extracted immediately as a consequence of a violation" would seem to refer to situations such as in *Jalloh*, where the violation itself produces the evidence. In *Gäfgen*, the applicant revealed through his own actions the additional real evidence and their discovery was less immediate, definitely not a case of "extracting" evidence from the suspect. What the Court has not been willing to elaborate on is when the possibility of a long-range effect might realise, while it seems to have left the door open to exceptions similar to those accepted by SCOTUS.

One possible solution could be found employing the SIC framework. Because all breaches of Article 3 of the Convention should be deemed very serious, only a minimal impact can be accepted and there is little, if any, room for counterbalancing the breach. Although at some point the causal chain would become so long that factors relevant for attenuation, independent source or inevitable discovery might appear, a rule of thumb might be that the reach of the effect should be proportional to the seriousness of the breach. At least in cases of torture the threshold for accepting a long-range effect should therefore be low, because an obvious causal link would add to the impact of the breach and the use of such evidence would taint the integrity of a trial.[53]

6.7 The rule against torture evidence

First, the rule against torture evidence requires domestic courts to carry out an **effective investigation** into any arguable claim of ill-treatment. The lack of such investigation would lead the Court to conclude that the procedural obligation of Article 3 has been violated. If a claim is wholly improbable, it can be dismissed without such inquiries, but the threshold triggering the duty to investigate is quite low. The key to an effective investigation is that an arguable claim is taken seriously and not dismissed saying, for example, "such things never happen in this country". If that is so, it should not be difficult to obtain evidence to disprove any allegations to the contrary.

---

52 See Wong Sun v. United States, 371 U.S. 471 (1963) and Tomkovicz 2011, 47–49.
53 U. Lundqvist, *Bevisförbud: En undersökning av möjligheterna att avvisa oegentligt åtkommen bevisning i brottmålsrättegång* (Uppsala: Iustus förlag, 1998), 178. See also Jackson and Summers 2012, 193: "[I]t seems likely that use of indirect evidence obtained after recourse to torture would violate the right to a fair trial."

The relevant evidence might be documentation about the detention of a suspect as well as any medical evidence. A domestic court may, if appropriate, fulfil this function by requesting the prosecutor to provide the relevant material and make the necessary investigations. Because ill-treatment would constitute a crime, a trial court might even want to wait for a police investigation to take place. In any case, the trial court has the ultimate responsibility and may have to approach the outcome of a police investigation with some caution, given that it would usually be in the authorities' interests to cover up any ill-treatment.

Should it appear that the accused has been subjected to some questionable treatment, the trial court would then have to interpret the definitions discussed above. This would mean determining, as a preliminary question, if the treatment would attain the minimum level of severity for Article 3 to become applicable. If this is to be answered in the affirmative, the following stage would be to determine whether that treatment should be classified as torture (a term attaching a special stigma to deliberate inhuman treatment causing very serious and cruel suffering) or inhuman and/or degrading treatment. It was submitted above that these two forms of ill-treatment do not differ in degree, while they are lesser violations of Article 3 than torture.

Second, the rule acts as an **exclusionary rule**. On the face of it, the rule against admitting torture evidence is clear-cut. Any statement obtained by way of violating Article 3 must be excluded, irrespective of whether the violation is classified as torture, inhuman or degrading treatment. The rule applies also regardless of whether the torturer is acting in an official capacity or not and whether such evidence is being used against the victim or someone else. The same, strict rule applies to real evidence obtained by way of torture. It is far less clear, however, whether it also applies to real evidence obtained by way of inhuman or degrading treatment.

This distinction is probably not that important in practice. The reader might remember from the previous chapter that in *Jalloh*, the privilege against self-incrimination was exceptionally applicable to real evidence because it was obtained by way of inhuman and degrading treatment (forced administration of emetics). This means that self-incriminating real evidence obtained through such ill-treatment should be presumed inadmissible. On the other hand, the same grand chamber judgment would suggest that if such evidence were used against someone else (i.e. it would not be self-incriminating), ill-treatment violating Article 3 would still be a heavy factor in favour of finding a trial unfair as a whole based on the rule of "other improperly obtained evidence" (see Chapter 8).

7 The prohibition of entrapment

7.1 Introduction

Entrapment or police incitement means an improper influence which leads to a crime being committed. According to the definition in *Ramanauskas*:

> Police incitement occurs where the officers involved – whether members of the security forces or persons acting on their instructions – do not confine themselves to investigating criminal activity in an essentially passive manner, but exert such an influence on the subject as to incite the commission of an offence that would otherwise not have been committed, in order to make it possible to establish the offence, that is, to provide evidence and institute a prosecution.[1]

The definition includes three essential elements. First, the initiative to committing an offence must come from **state authorities**, either directly from undercover policemen or indirectly from people who are acting upon their instructions. The initiator of a crime in entrapment situations is called an *agent provocateur*. Second, the initiator must have exerted an **influence** to commit a crime instead of having stayed in the confines of a passive, investigative role typical to undercover operations. Third, the influence must lead to a **"new" offence** in the sense that it would not have been committed otherwise. Obviously, and as with most definitions discussed in this book, all three elements are closely related.

In its landmark judgment on entrapment, *Teixeira de Castro*, the Court took a careful approach, stating:

> The use of undercover agents must be restricted and safeguards put in place even in cases concerning the fight against drug trafficking. While the rise in organised crime undoubtedly requires that appropriate measures be taken, the right to a fair administration of justice nevertheless holds such a prominent place [...] that it cannot be sacrificed for the sake of expedience. The general requirements of fairness embodied in Article 6 apply to proceedings concerning

---

1 Ramanauskas v. Lithuania [GC], 5.2.2008, § 55.

DOI: 10.4324/9781003311416-7

all types of criminal offence, from the most straightforward to the most complex. The public interest cannot justify the use of evidence obtained as a result of police incitement.[2]

A slightly modified view was expressed in *Ramanauskas*, where the Court at the very outset of its reasoning observed that

> it is aware of the difficulties inherent in the police's task of searching for and gathering evidence for the purpose of detecting and investigating offences. To perform this task, they are increasingly required to make use of undercover agents, informers and covert practices, particularly in tackling organised crime and corruption". It then continued to state expressly that "the use of special investigative methods – in particular, undercover techniques – cannot in itself infringe the right to a fair trial.[3]

The risk of entrapment is inherent in the use of undercover or other similar secret methods of investigation. For example, a police officer who has infiltrated a criminal organisation may encounter situations where they have to choose between a more active participation and blowing their cover, which might mean risking their life. On the other hand, if the police pose as potential buyers of illegal material, they might not know whether the suspect has any of it already. This, in turn, might lead to the suspect being incited to obtain the material simply to fulfil an order placed actually by the police. Many other examples can be imagined.

As with the Article 3 violations discussed in the previous chapter, there is a well-established rule against entrapment. The rule is equally inflexible, too. According to the Court:

> while the use of undercover agents may be tolerated provided that it is subject to clear restrictions and safeguards, the public interest cannot justify the use of evidence obtained as a result of police incitement, as to do so would expose the accused to the risk of being definitively deprived of a fair trial from the outset.[4]

In other words, fairness of a trial cannot be reinstated through counterbalancing measures. The violation is considered so serious that any impact must be removed for the trial to be fair.

7.2 The rationale of the rule

Given the drastic consequences of the rule against entrapment and evidence obtained through such a method, the Court has done rather little to explain why it violates overall fairness so profoundly and irretrievably. Historically and

2 Teixeira de Castro v. Portugal, 9.6.1998, § 36.
3 Ramanauskas v. Lithuania [GC], 5.2.2008, §§ 49 and 51.
4 Ramanauskas v. Lithuania [GC], 5.2.2008, § 54.

comparatively there have been many approaches to entrapment, starting from the view that because it – by definition – requires that the subject commits a crime of their own free will, it should have no effect, and ending with remedies capable of removing its impact altogether. Between these extreme alternatives, some jurisdictions, for example Germany, have concerned it as grounds for mitigating the sentence.[5]

Teixeira, quoted above, only referred to the public interest and did so negatively, underlining that it cannot justify the use of entrapment evidence. It fails to explain what makes entrapment problematic even when weighed against such interests. Indeed, the Court expressed some understanding to the need of adopting special measures in fighting organised crime in the same paragraph.[6] But no express rationale can be read from the judgment. Nor can it be found from *Ramanauskas*, where the Court mainly refers to *Teixeira*. Under the general principles, it explains at some length the assessment criteria which we shall soon examine, but does not elaborate on the rationale of the strict rule against entrapment.

It would seem, however, that the definition of police incitement given in *Ramanauskas* and quoted above provides a hint. Its first element, the involvement of state authorities, becomes clearer when read together with an influential decision from 2005. In *Shannon*, a journalist had acted as *agent provocateur*. Having played the role of a sheikh, the journalist had contacted an actor who had, after a conversation about drugs, stated that he could supply cocaine for the fake sheikh's party. The actor proceeded to actually deliver drugs to the reporter who then wrote a newspaper Article about the events and handed the material over to the police. Later, the actor was convicted.[7]

The Court strongly underlined that the rule developed in *Teixeira* should only be applied in similar factual circumstances:

> The operation which was there being examined constituted a misuse of State power, the police officers having gone beyond their legitimate role as undercover agents obtaining evidence against a suspected offender to incite the commission of the offence itself. The Court considers that the principles set out in the *Teixeira* judgment are to be viewed in this context and to be seen as principally directed to the use in a criminal trial of evidence gained by means of an entrapment operation carried out by or on behalf of the State or its agents.[8]

---

5 For the alternative approaches, see B. Murphy and J. Anderson, "After the Serpent Beguiled Me: Entrapment and Sentencing in Australia and Canada" (2014) 39 *Queen's Law Journal*, 621, 629 and The Law Commission, *Report on Defences of General Application* (Law Com. No. 83, 1977), 45–52. The Court sketched out the relevant German case law in Furcht v. Germany, 23.10.2014, §§ 29–31.
6 Teixeira de Castro v. Portugal, 9.6.1998, § 36.
7 Shannon v. the United Kingdom [dec.], 6.4.2004.
8 In *Vanyan*, a private individual has acted as an undercover agent, but the operation had been organised by the police. Because that individual had incited the offence, there was a violation of Article 6 § 1 (Vanyan v. Russia, 15.12.2005, § 49).

"In the present case the applicant's conversation with G. was secretly recorded without a prior judicial authorisation. This constituted a breach of domestic law and of the Convention, as discussed above under Article 8 of the Convention."[12]

The second and third stages of the test become more understandable when discussed together. My interpretation is that emphasis should be on the effectivity of the opportunity of challenging the authenticity of the evidence and of opposing its use. Indeed, Goss has pointed out that "an accused person is already entitled to these things".[13] However, this entitlement is not effective if the domestic courts fail to assess such claims properly and reject them without sufficient reasoning. The essence of this feature of the test is, in my opinion, not that domestic procedural legislation allows the defence to challenge the evidence in the abstract, but whether the domestic courts take them seriously.[14]

On the other hand, if domestic courts simply dismiss arguable claims about the reliability or admissibility of prosecution evidence, this will clearly put the defence in a disadvantaged position vis-á-vis the prosecution and violate equality of arms which, in turn, would violate the fairness of the trial as a whole. Even worse, it would open the possibility that the verdict is based on inadmissible or unreliable evidence, raising questions about the correctness of the outcome. If the defence seeks to challenge the authenticity of the evidence, it is necessary to take into consideration the quality of the evidence and whether the improper method of obtaining it has affected its reliability. This connects the assessment criteria.

It should also be noted that the defence has the choice as to if and how they wish to challenge prosecution evidence. They can seek to either only challenge the authenticity of the evidence or only oppose its use. They can also do both or neither. Domestic authorities are not responsible if the defendant does not make use of such opportunities if the legislation provides them. It may also be relevant whether the defence has made the same claims throughout the proceedings or whether they seek to challenge evidence with new grounds at later stages.[15]

When the defence seeks to challenge the authenticity and reliability of evidence, it is natural to look at the quality of the evidence as well as the circumstances in which it was obtained. Real evidence may often be less affected by methods of obtaining it, unless the defence claims, for example, that the murder weapon was planted in the defendant's car while it was searched. The seemingly technical rules of procedures to be followed, including various notices, protocols and the use of attesting witnesses, may prove vital in disproving such allegations later. For the judicial control to be effective, domestic courts should investigate and respond to any arguable claims of unreliability.

---

12 Berlizev v. Ukraine, 8.7.2021, § 53.
13 R. Goss, *Criminal Fair Trial Rights: Article 6 of the European Convention on Human Rights* (Oxford: Hart, 2014), 146.
14 See e.g. Horvatić v. Croatia, 17.10.2013, § 84: "By dismissing all requests by the defence and accepting all the prosecution arguments and evidence, the trial court deprived the applicant of any **practical** opportunity to **effectively** challenge the authenticity of the evidence or to oppose its use."
15 See e.g. Berlizev v. Ukraine, 8.7.2021, §§ 53 and 54.

The defence did not have an effective opportunity to challenge the use of prosecution evidence in *Jalloh*, where "any discretion on the part of the national courts to exclude that evidence could not come into play as they considered the administration of emetics to be authorised by domestic law". This statement immediately follows the Court noting that the applicant had challenged the use of the evidence in question.[16] The lack of exclusionary discretion made that option, although available on paper, ineffective for the purposes of guaranteeing a fair trial under the circumstances.

In *Kobiashvili* the applicant claimed to have no knowledge of the drugs allegedly found on his person as the result of a search the police had conducted. The search was not authorised by a judge, but instead by the police, which under domestic law was possible in urgent situations. That decision, however, did not contain anything explaining the suspicion against the applicant or the urgency requiring the bypassing of judicial control prior to searching him. No light was shed on these questions during the domestic proceedings. On the other hand, the decision did contain the applicant's full name and address, although the police officers claimed that they only knew an address.[17]

There was also ambiguity about how and even when the search was conducted. The applicant's friends had witnessed his arrest but argued that no search has been conducted immediately. One of the two attesting witnesses withdrew his statement completely, and the other was, according to the defence, a former police officer whose credibility was questionable. The domestic courts dismissed the first attesting witness's withdrawal as illogical and failed to address the second attesting witness's credibility at all. Thus, the manner in which the investigation was carried out had casted doubt on the reliability and accuracy of the evidence obtained.[18]

By comparison, in *Bašić* the applicant did not contest the authenticity of the recordings and all the defence's doubts as to the accuracy of the recordings were examined and addressed by the trial court. This included questioning the police officers in charge of the operation against the applicant in order to clarify the circumstances. The trial court had provided a reasoned decision setting out its findings as to the manner in which the recordings had been obtained and documented.[19]

Finally, it became clear already from *Schenk* that the domestic courts are, of course, not obliged to declare evidence inadmissible or deprive them of evidentiary value. The applicant in that case had the opportunity of challenging the authenticity of the impugned evidence, a recording, and opposing its use. He had initially agreed that it should be heard. However, the fact that his attempts to challenge the evidence were unsuccessful, made no difference. It was sufficient that he had an effective opportunity to do so.[20]

16 Jalloh v. Germany [GC], 11.7.2006, § 107.
17 Kobiashvili v. Georgia, 14.3.2019, §§ 61 and 62.
18 Kobiashvili v. Georgia, 14.3.2019, §§ 62–65.
19 Bašić v. Croatia, 25.10.2016, §§ 45 and 46.
20 Schenk v. Switzerland [plenary], 12.7.1988, especially § 47. See also Dragojević v. Croatia, 15.1.2015, § 132: "The domestic courts examined his arguments on the merits and provided reasons for their decisions [...]. The fact that the applicant was

Another criterion concerns the quality of the impugned evidence. This criterion is linked with the complaints raised by the defence and the amount of other evidence:

> While no problem of fairness necessarily arises where the evidence obtained was unsupported by other material, it may be noted that where the evidence is very strong and there is no risk of its being unreliable, the need for supporting evidence is correspondingly weaker.[21]

I shall call this the **corroboration** aspect of the rule. The Court has created a sort of adaptable corroboration rule, where the need of corroboration depends upon the reliability of the impugned evidence and whether it has been challenged by the defence.

Additionally, the **importance** of the impugned evidence in relation to the outcome of the criminal procedure is a factor. If it can be said, for example, that "the evidence in question played a limited role in the applicant's conviction",[22] it is not as important as if "the impugned personal search of the applicant was the focal point which triggered the initiation of criminal proceedings against him". In the latter situation, the Court concluded that the search and the use of its results "had an influence on the procedural fairness of the trial in its entirety".[23] We shall soon return to the interplay between corroboration and importance, because they have an important role in the overall fairness assessment.

Let us now take a brief look at the final two criteria, both of which seem to be far from determinative in the overall assessment. It seems unclear whether the weight of the public interest is even an established part of the criteria. Public interest is mentioned already in *Schenk*, but only when referring to the findings of domestic courts.[24] *Bykov* makes no explicit mention of it when reiterating the general principles, but when applying them the Court refers to how this factor was weighed in *Heglas*.[25] The absence of such criterion is noticeable in recent judgments such as *Berlizev*, *Svetina*, and *Dragojević*.[26] Furthermore, although mentioned in *Hambardzumyan* and *Bašić*, it is not actually applied (i.e. the Court makes no mention of the severity of the crime when applying the general principles).[27]

---

unsuccessful at each step does not alter the fact that he had an effective opportunity to challenge the evidence and oppose its use [...]."

21 Bykov v. Russia [GC], 10.3.2009, § 90. In *Kobiashvili*, the Court confirmed that this applies also the other way: "Where doubts arise as to the reliability of a certain source of evidence, the need to corroborate it by evidence from other sources is correspondingly greater" (Kobiashvili v. Georgia, 14.3.2019, § 72).

22 Lysyuk v. Ukraine, 14.10.2021, § 69.

23 Kobiashvili v. Georgia, 14.3.2019, § 60.

24 See Schenk v. Switzerland [plenary], 12.7.1988, § 44.

25 Bykov v. Russia [GC], 10.3.2009, § 100.

26 Berlizev v. Ukraine, 8.7.2021, §§ 51 and 52; Svetina v. Slovenia, 22.5.2018, §§ 42–44; and Dragojević v. Croatia, 15.1.2015, §§ 127–130.

27 Hambardzumyan v. Armenia, 5.12.2019, §§ 76 and 78–81; and Bašić v. Croatia, 25.10.2016, §§ 43–49.

In *Prade*, for example, the Court does explicitly state that "when determining whether the proceedings as a whole have been fair, the weight of the public interest in the investigation and punishment of the particular offence in issue may be taken into consideration and be weighed against the individual interest that the evidence against him be gathered lawfully". According to the applicant, "the public interest in prosecution could not outweigh his right to respect for his home as the offence had been of minor consequence for the public, and the breach of his basic rights severe".[28] Thus, his case was not comparable with *Jalloh*, where the Court took into account that the forceful use of emetics in that case "targeted a street dealer selling drugs on a relatively small scale who was eventually given a six-month suspended prison sentence and probation".[29]

The applicant in *Prade* had had 2.606 consumption units of hashish at his apartment. The drugs were found by accident, because he was actually suspected of copyright piracy by selling fake goods. The domestic courts had, in their decisions, balanced the public interest in prosecuting the crime of drugs possession against the applicant's interest in respect for his home. The Court's key finding with regard to public interest seems to touch upon the opportunity of opposing the use of evidence, because it continued: "[the domestic courts'] conclusion that the public interest outweighed the applicant's basic rights was carefully and thoroughly reasoned and did not disclose any appearance of arbitrariness or disproportionality". Of course, this balancing happened *ex post facto*, after the drugs had already been found.[30]

One might also point out that in *Jalloh* the applicant complained and the Court found violations under not only Article 8 but also Article 6 § 2 (i.e. privilege against self-incrimination). The mention of public interest is, furthermore, not quoted in full in *Prade*. It continues: "However, public interest concerns cannot justify measures which extinguish the very essence of an applicant's defence rights, including the privilege against self-incrimination guaranteed by Article 6 of the Convention." Likewise, in the context of other improperly obtained evidence, public interest concerns cannot be an overriding argument. However, domestic courts are permitted to take them into consideration when balancing the "unlawfulness" against the rights of the defendant.

Lastly, there is nothing to indicate that the list of relevant factors would be exhaustive. *Svetina* provides a seemingly rare mention of "other safeguards", a criterion similar to *Ibrahim* criterion (j). There were two such safeguards. First, notes regarding the impugned examination of the applicant's mobile phone were not admitted to the case file, and second, that court orders were subsequently issued authorising the obtaining of the traffic data relied on by the first-instance court in convicting the applicant.[31] It seems clear from the terminology already that such safeguards are only complementary arguments and not crucial elements

---

28 Prade v. Germany, 3.3.2016, §§ 30 and 35.
29 Jalloh v. Germany [GC], 11.7.2006, § 107 *in fine*.
30 Prade v. Germany, 3.3.2016, § 41.
31 Svetina v. Slovenia, 22.5.2018, § 52.

of the overall assessment. As such, they cannot be found from most judgments concerning other improperly obtained evidence.

8.4 Corroboration and importance

It was already pointed out that the Court seems to assess not only the quality of the impugned evidence as such, but also its importance. The core principle is easy to understand, although perhaps difficult to explain: the more reliable the evidence is, especially in light of the defendant's submissions, the less need there is for other evidence to support its reliability. If the defence agrees that there is no risk of the impugned evidence being unreliable, it could even be unsupported by other material. But, *vice versa*, the less reliable the impugned evidence would prove out to be, the greater the need for corroborating evidence supporting the factual conclusions based on it.

As Redmayne has pointed out:

> there are different evidentiary structures that fall within the broad descriptions "corroboration" and "supporting evidence". We can usefully distinguish three ways in which one piece of evidence may support another. First, two pieces of evidence may be corroborative of the same fact, such as when two witnesses both report seeing the same event ("same fact corroboration"). Secondly, two pieces of evidence may be "convergent", that is, they point in the same broad direction, for instance, towards guilt. Thirdly, one piece of evidence may support the credibility of another, such as when one witness testifies that another witness has a reputation for being truthful ("credibility corroboration").[32]

No such theoretical distinctions have been made in the Court's case law. It would seem that any of the types of corroboration could come into question. However, here we come to what I called the weight dimension of the test. In the first two situations, there are more than one piece of evidence supporting the same factual conclusion. The more pieces of evidence there are "pointing in the same direction", the lesser would be the importance of any single piece evidence. In the third situation, though, there may be only one piece of evidence and other evidence is presented to prove its reliability. Here, the importance of a single piece evidence would be greater.

Put more simply, when the Court uses the term "unsupported" evidence, this could probably refer to any type of corroboration requirement. Situations "where the evidence is very strong and there is no risk of its being unreliable" would seem to refer more to the third type, i.e. credibility corroboration and "the need for supporting evidence is correspondingly weaker" in such situations because the credibility is not questionable. When the impugned evidence is "not the only evidence on which the conviction was based", this seems to me as a reference better

---

32 M. Redmayne, "A Corroboration Approach to Recovered Memories of Sexual Abuse: A Note of Caution" (2000) 116 *Law Quarterly Review*, 147, 150.

fitting the first two types of corroboration, i.e. same fact corroboration or convergence.

The applicant in *Schenk* had been convicted of attempted incitement to murder his wife. The evidence included a secret recording made by the man the applicant had attempted to use as contract killer. The applicant had had the opportunity to both challenge the authenticity of the recording (it was examined by the personnel of a tape-recorder factory) and oppose its use. The Court noted that domestic courts relied on other pieces of evidence in addition to the recording, including witnesses. This other evidence corroborated the inferences of the applicant's guilt based on the recording.[33]

Khan is another particularly important early case about improperly obtained evidence. The impugned evidence, again a secret recording, was in effect the only evidence against the applicant. Unlike in Schenk, though, its authenticity was not in question. Instead, the recording was acknowledged to be very strong evidence, which meant that the need for supporting evidence (of any kind, one might assume) was weaker.[34]

In *Bykov*, the key evidence for the prosecution was the initial statement of the later informant who had reported to the authorities that the applicant had ordered him to kill a person. This statement was made before the impugned recording took place and as a private individual. He repeated this statement during the investigation and also when confronted by the applicant at the pre-trial stage. The incriminating statements were found to be corroborated by circumstantial evidence which revealed a conflict of interests between the applicant and the intended victim. The recording was not the sole basis for the applicant's conviction. Furthermore, it was not even directly relied upon by the domestic courts. Thus, it only "played a limited role in a complex body of evidence assessed by the court".[35]

The central complaint in *Horvatić* was that the police had taken samples of the applicant's hair and nails as well as his clothes in one place but packed them elsewhere without the applicant being present. The government opposed this claim. The case file, however, contained documentation only about the applicant's trousers and t-shirt being taken. There was nothing to verify how the samples were taken and packed, even though domestic legislation would have required documentation. The trial court dismissed the applicant's claims, concluding that the documentation was sufficient. Assessing the extent to which the domestic courts relied on the forensic evidence, the Court concluded that

> there was no other concrete and direct evidence proving that the applicant was the bank robber, and that the witness statements concerning the identity and description of the bank robber were inconclusive [...]. Therefore, the only evidence actually linking the applicant with the bank robbery were the fibres from his clothes and the strands of his hair found on the clothes worn by the bank robber [...].

33 Schenk v. Switzerland [plenary], 12.7.1988, §§ 47 and 48.
34 Khan v. the United Kingdom, 12.5.2000, § 37.
35 Bykov v. Russia [GC], 10.3.2009, §§ 96–97 and 103.

Even in the absence of an explicit statement, it seems obvious that the potentially unreliable forensic evidence had played a decisive role in the trial.[36]

It seems that the more important the impugned evidence is for the outcome of the case, the greater the need would be for corroboration. The impugned evidence is not decisive if, for example, it only corroborates other, more important evidence, such as the recording in *Bykov*. In such situations, the impugned evidence forms only one part within a larger body of evidence against the defendant. For some reason, the Court does not explicitly mention the importance of the evidence as a factor under the general principles, but is seems to assess it very consistently, although it was stated in *Khan* that "this element was not the determining factor in the Court's conclusion" in *Schenk*.[37]

The mechanism and effect of a corroboration requirement is rather difficult to explain even if it is not relative to the importance of evidence. It seems to have characteristics of at least three types: an admissibility rule, a rule regarding the evaluation of evidence, and a rule relating to the standard of proof. Wigmore explains that such a rule seems not to be truly an admissibility rule, but it has the effect of making admissibility conditional. In *Carmell*, SCOTUS determined that lack of legally required corroboration made the prosecution case "legally insufficient", which meant that the defendant was "entitled to a judgment of acquittal" if there was no corroboration.[38]

Both the minority and majority in that case discussed whether a corroboration rule should best be seen as a rule addressing the trustworthiness of evidence. According to the dissenting opinion, the purpose of the corroboration rule in question was "to rein in the admissibility of testimony the legislature has deemed insufficiently credible standing alone". In *Kilbourne*, Lord Reid famously stated:

> There is nothing technical in the idea of corroboration. When in the ordinary affairs of life one is doubtful whether or not to believe a particular statement one naturally looks to see whether it fits in with other statements or circumstances relating to the particular matter; the better it fits in, the more one is inclined to believe it.[39]

Here, we are dealing with the reliability aspect of the corroboration rule.

Although the majority in *Carmell* stated that "[t]he issue of the admissibility of evidence is simply different from the question whether the properly admitted evidence is sufficient to convict the defendant", this statement concerns a jury system. If a single judge or panel are triers of both fact and law, it would seem a natural third aspect to also understand corroboration rules as rules which modify the burden and standard of proof. In other words, their essence from this point of view would be that prosecution cannot discharge that burden and prove a

36 Horvatić v. Croatia, 17.10.2013, §§ 80–86.
37 Khan v. the United Kingdom, 12.5.2000, § 37 *in fine*.
38 Carmell v. Texas, 529 U.S. 513 (2000).
39 DPP v. Kilbourne [1973] 2 W.L.R. 254.

defendant's guilt beyond reasonable doubt without corroborative evidence. Perhaps corroboration rules can have all three characters depending on the situation and point of view.

To conclude this section, I would like to point out a key difference between the assessment model discussed here and that applied in complaints concerning the privilege against self-incrimination: the fact that the impugned evidence provides the authorities with "the framework around which they subsequently built their case and the focus for their search for other corroborating evidence" does *not*, in itself, suggest that evidence would be unfair. On the contrary, they should attempt to discover other evidence to properly control the reliability of the impugned evidence and thereby counterbalance any unlawfulness.

For example, one key aspect in support of finding a violation in the fourth applicant's case in *Ibrahim* was the fact that his self-incriminating statement provided the authorities with a narrative of the events. The evidence was considered important in the context of criterion (g) discussed above in Section 5.6. It could be said that the recorded statements in *Khan* and *Bykov* were of similar importance since they provided a first-hand account of the events. However, because of sufficient reliability in *Khan* and other evidence in *Bykov*, using them as evidence did not violate Article 6. So in the context of other improperly obtained evidence, discovery of further incriminating evidence is a factor in favour of overall fairness, not against it.

8.5 Overall assessment

Let us now attempt to bring the various criteria together and see how they interact. My interpretation of the relationship of these factors, using the SIC framework, is the following. The **seriousness** of the potential violation of right to a fair trial depends, first, on the "unlawfulness" in question. Violations of Article 8 or domestic legislation do not render a trial automatically unfair as a whole, but the seriousness of such violations should be assessed as part of the overall fairness approach. Obviously, the more serious the violation is, the greater would be the need to limit its impact and counterbalance it.

It has already been pointed out that the Court's attitude towards real evidence obtained through inhuman or degrading treatment is somewhat unclear, although the seriousness of the violation is a factor weighing heavily in the overall assessment. The rigid rule against torture evidence does not cover such situations, although it does apply to statements obtained by way of inhuman or degrading treatment. In *Jalloh*, the Court also attached weight to other factors than the "unlawfulness" in question. It also deliberately left open "whether the use of evidence obtained by an act qualified as inhuman and degrading treatment automatically renders a trial unfair".[40]

The test obliges domestic courts to examine thoroughly any arguable claims about unreliability or inadmissibility of improperly obtained evidence and give

---

40 Jalloh v. Germany [GC], 11.7.2006, §§ 106 and 107.

sufficient reasons if they are rejected. Any failures in this regard would increase the **impact** of the "unlawfulness". If the claims are rejected following a proper examination, there has been an effective opportunity to challenge the evidence even if the defence is unsuccessful at each step. This requirement is primarily procedural in nature and related to the duty to give reasoned decisions, explained by the Court in the recent *Budak* judgment:

> The extent to which this duty to give reasons applies may vary according to the nature of the decision and must be determined in the light of the circumstances of the case [...]. Without requiring a detailed answer to every argument advanced by the complainant, this obligation presupposes that parties to judicial proceedings can expect to receive a specific and explicit reply to the arguments which are decisive for the outcome of those proceedings [...]. Moreover, in cases relating to interference with rights secured under the Convention, the Court seeks to establish whether the reasons provided for decisions given by the domestic courts are automatic or stereotypical [...]. In view of the principle that the Convention is intended to guarantee not rights that are theoretical or illusory but rights that are practical and effective, the right to a fair trial cannot be seen as effective unless the requests and observations of the parties are truly "heard", that is to say, properly examined by the tribunal [...]. In examining the fairness of criminal proceedings, the Court has also held in particular that by ignoring a specific, pertinent and important point made by the accused, the domestic courts fall short of their obligations under Article 6 § 1 of the Convention [...].[41]

Additionally, the impact assessment has a substantial dimension, where the importance of the impugned evidence as well as its quality and the circumstances under which it was obtained are key criteria. The more important that evidence is, the greater the impact of any violation would be. The impact would also be greater, if the circumstances in which it was obtained cast doubt on its reliability or accuracy. Naturally, if these two factors are combined, the impact would be even greater. If, on the other hand, domestic courts reject evidence as inadmissible or lacking evidentiary value, any impact would be removed or at least greatly diminished.

Finally, the impact of other improperly obtained evidence upon the right to a fair trial can sometimes be **counterbalanced**, especially if the violation is not of a particular severity. The counterbalancing "weight" should be proportionate with the seriousness and impact of a violation. If the defence has opposed the use of improperly obtained evidence, domestic courts should address the admissibility and provide a reasoned decision where they balance the defendant's rights against other interest, including the public interest of punishing. It is also an important counterbalance that domestic courts have exclusionary discretion.

41 Budak v. Turkey, 16.2.2021, §§ 72 and 73.

Let us continue using *Jalloh* as an example. In addition to the serious "unlaw-fulness", the use of a method violating Article 3, the impugned evidence was the decisive element in securing the applicant's conviction. Thus, the violation had a great impact. As already noted, the applicant had not enjoyed an effective oppor-tunity to challenge its use, because the domestic courts considered the method lawful. The Court also pointed out that the public interest in securing the appli-cant's conviction was not of "such weight as to warrant allowing that evidence to be used at the trial" – the applicant was given a six-month suspended prison sen-tence and probation.

By comparison, if defence challenges the reliability of the impugned evidence, the most important counterbalance is the existence of corroborating evidence. Domestic courts must assess the reliability and authenticity of the impugned evi-dence and take into consideration the circumstances in which it was obtained as well as any arguable claims of the defence regarding its reliability. If those claims can be rejected and if there is sufficient corroborating evidence supporting the reliability of the evidence, given its importance, the impugned evidence may even be of decisive importance for conviction.

It would follow from the mechanism of the SIC framework that unreliable evi-dence should not be accepted simply because it would be less important. This is because if a potential violation of sufficient severity has any impact, that should be counterbalanced. Such a reasoning would also diminish the effectiveness of the requirement of proper assessment of evidence. Another interpretation would, in principle, allow unreliable evidence if there was a lot of it. Perhaps this is why the Court underlined in *Khan*, as cited above, that lesser importance of the impugned evidence is not a decisive factor in the overall assessment.

8.6 The rule against other improperly obtained evidence

This chapter has dealt with other violations than those covered in Chapters 5–7. Typically, complaints about other improperly obtained evidence arise when the domestic legal framework governing the pre-trial proceedings has not been com-plied with and/or evidence has been obtained by way of violating Article 8 of the Convention. The right to respect for private and family life can be violated through, for example, illegal house searches and placement of covert listening devices. Obtaining real evidence through inhuman or degrading treatment is another possible violation to be assessed using the test discussed here.

Any of the above-mentioned violations do not, on their own, lead to the con-clusion that the fairness of a trial has been irretrievably prejudiced. The reasons for this are varied. As far as unlawful evidence is concerned, the principle of sub-sidiarity would give domestic actors a relatively wide margin of appreciation and it will be left for them to determine, in the abstract, whether unlawful evidence can be admitted or not. I am not aware of legislation requiring that all unlawfully obtained evidence should always be automatically excluded. Usually, this would be left to the domestic courts' discretion on case-by-case basis, with the possible exception of testimonial privileges.

The Court has not really explained why the use of recordings at trial is not necessarily contrary to the requirements of Article 6 § 1 notwithstanding that they were obtained by violating Article 8. This could be because the limitation clause of Article 8 § 2 expressly allows interferences for the purposes of criminal investigation among other important competing interests. That being so, it could be considered that the existence of a legitimate aim, even in the lack of a legal basis or necessity in a democratic society, would suffice to make an infringement of privacy more tolerable in the context of an otherwise fair trial.

Be that as it may, Article 6 would require that an accused enjoys an effective opportunity to challenge the reliability of evidence and oppose its use. If reliability of the impugned evidence is challenged, it should be examined whether the circumstances in which it was obtained cast doubt on its reliability or accuracy, and there should be sufficient corroborating evidence. If admissibility of the impugned evidence is challenged, domestic courts should have discretion to exclude unfair evidence, but may balance the defendant's rights against inter alia the public interest of investigating and punishing crimes.

The accused may choose to challenge only the reliability or only the admissibility of evidence. Additionally, the domestic courts should provide sufficient reasoning for rejecting such claims, especially in relation to the arguments of the accused. It follows from the principle of adversarial proceedings and equality of arms that such arguments are taken seriously by domestic courts. The admissibility and reliability of prosecution evidence are decisive questions for the accused. There is also a more general interest that evidence is gathered lawfully. Such an interest is not only individual but, in a state governed by the rule of law, also a public interest to be balanced against the public interest of fighting crime.

Lastly, although real evidence obtained by way of ill-treatment need not be automatically excluded according to the Court's case law, any violation of Article 3 should weigh heavily in the overall assessment. It can only be speculated what the outcome in *Jalloh* would have been if the applicant had been suspected of murder and gone through a proper medical examination prior to the forceful use of emetics. At the very least it can be said that only under the most exceptional and compelling circumstances would it be permissible to afford such brutality the cloak of law by admitting the evidence. Therefore, similarly to the *Salduz* test, I submit that a strong presumption of unfairness should be triggered by such a serious unlawfulness.

9 The right to cross-examine prosecution witnesses

9.1 Introduction

In this final chapter we are going to address a rule of evidence which has seen several developments and is theoretically quite interesting. According to Article 6 § 3 (d) everyone charged with a criminal offence has the right to examine or have examined witnesses against him and to obtain the attendance and examination of witnesses on his behalf under the same conditions as witnesses against him. We have already briefly discussed the latter element of this provision, the right to obtain the attendance of a witness for the defence, in Section 4.3. Now, we shall focus on the first element, also known as the right to cross-examination.

To begin with,

> Article 6 does not grant the accused an unlimited right to secure the appearance of witnesses in court. It is normally for the domestic courts to decide whether it is necessary or advisable to hear a witness [...]. Furthermore, evidence must normally be produced at a public hearing, in the presence of the accused, with a view to adversarial argument. There are exceptions to this principle, but they must not infringe the rights of the defence; as a general rule, paragraphs 1 and 3 (d) of Article 6 require that the defendant be given an adequate and proper opportunity to challenge and question a witness against him, either when he makes his statements or at a later stage [...].[1]

Rather like the right to adduce evidence, the right to cross-examine is clearly an active right. It is an important feature of the adversarial principle and equality of arms. Maffei has identified six elements of fair collection of testimonial evidence, which he calls the *confrontational paradigm*: a witness, whose real identity is known to the accused, should give evidence in open court, facing both the accused and the trier of fact, under an obligation to tell the truth and the accused should be given an opportunity to cross-examine them.[2] Similarly, the Court has

---

1 Krasniki v. the Czech Republic, 28.2.2006, § 75.
2 S. Maffei, *The European Right to Confrontation in Criminal Proceedings: Absent, Anonymous and Vulnerable Witnesses* (Groningen: Europa Law Publishing, 2006), 23.

DOI: 10.4324/9781003311416-9

ruled that "all the evidence must in principle be produced in the presence of the accused at a public hearing with a view to adversarial argument".[3]

Although our interest will focus mainly on the first and last element of the paradigm, a brief overlook of the other four will be useful to describe the "normal" course of examining witnesses. That a hearing should be public follows already from the wording of Article 6 § 1. Additionally, it may help guarantee the truthfulness of the testimony, through a certain social pressure. This effect should not be exaggerated, though. Sometimes publicity must be restricted to protect other interests, such as the rights of the victim or the witness. But restricting publicity will not restrict the admissibility or use of evidence and is not, therefore, a relevant concern here.[4]

Even if the public's access to a trial is restricted, a hearing would normally take place in the presence of the parties and the judge. This would allow all of them to make observations simultaneously, whether the witness is giving their statement or being questioned.[5] Exceptionally, the presence of the parties – typically the defendant – during the hearing can also be restricted. But even this will not usually affect the admissibility of evidence. Neither will restricting the duty to give an oath. It should be kept in mind that the victims and co-accused are to be considered witnesses in the Court's case law because the concept of witness is an autonomous one.

Being aware of the real identity of a witness is a prerequisite for effective cross-examination, because otherwise the accused would not be able to question their credibility. But even this facet of the confrontational paradigm is not absolute.[6] Some legal systems allow a witness to give their statement without revealing their identity. Such *anonymous witnesses* can sometimes be heard in open court and otherwise as normal witnesses. They can also be cross-examined by the defence. Because of the challenges anonymity poses on the effectiveness of cross-examination, the Court has treated it much like evidence which does not permit cross-examination at all:

> While the problems raised by anonymous and absent witnesses are not identical, the two situations are not different in principle, since, as was acknowledged by the Supreme Court, each results in a potential disadvantage for the defendant. The underlying principle is that the defendant in a criminal trial should have an effective opportunity to challenge the evidence against him. This principle requires not merely that a defendant should know the identity of his accusers so that he is in a position to challenge their probity and credibility but that he should be able to test the truthfulness and reliability of their evidence, by having them orally examined

---

3 Barberà, Messegué and Jabardo v. Spain [plenary], 6.12.1988, § 78 *in fine*.
4 Maffei 2006, 23–24.
5 Maffei 2006, 24–26.
6 Maffei 2006, 27–28.

in his presence, either at the time the witness was making the statement or at some later stage of the proceedings.[7]

The Court stated in *Kostovski*:

> The Convention does not preclude reliance, at the investigation stage of criminal proceedings, on sources such as anonymous informants. However, the subsequent use of anonymous statements as sufficient evidence to found a conviction, as in the present case, is a different matter. It involved limitations on the rights of the defence which were irreconcilable with the guarantees contained in Article 6.

With regard to the applicant's situation, it noted: "If the defence is unaware of the identity of the person it seeks to question, it may be deprived of the very particulars enabling it to demonstrate that he or she is prejudiced, hostile or unreliable."[8]

If a written or otherwise recorded statement is presented as evidence instead of hearing a witness in person, cross-examination would not take place immediately in front of the trier of fact, which would also mean a departure from the confrontational paradigm and potentially violate Article 6 § 3 (d). It should not come as a surprise to the reader that even this specific aspect of the right to cross-examination is not absolute and, indeed, the use of recorded witness statements as evidence is not, by itself, unfair.[9] However, the Court has set certain conditions for the use of such recordings as evidence. Those conditions form a rule of evidence.

Maffei's theory fits very well with the SIC framework. According to him, a departure from each of the six elements of the confrontational paradigm, as well as a combination of such departures, has a specific impact. However, "the effects of departures may sometimes be compensated for by counterbalances favourable to the accused". What is more, those counterbalanced should be proportionate to the impact of a departure (i.e. "[t]he more profound the departure, the more effective the compensation for the accused").[10] The confrontational paradigm and its elements will help us analyse and understand the seriousness, impact, and counterbalancing of a departure from the right to cross-examine.

9.2 The rationale and development of the "sole or decisive rule"

The sole or decisive rule was first introduced in *Unterpertinger*, where two witnesses refused to give evidence as they were entitled to do according to domestic law as family members. The Court approved such legislation in principle, pointing

---

7 Al-Khawaja and Tahery v. the United Kingdom [GC], 15.12.2011, § 127.
8 Kostovski v. the Netherlands [plenary], 20.11.1989, §§ 42 and 44.
9 See, for example, Schatschaschwili v. Germany [GC], 15.12.2015, § 105.
10 Maffei 2006, 31–32.

out that such privilege "is calculated to protect such a witness by avoiding his being put in a moral dilemma". Their refusals resulted in reading out of their previous statements, which was not regarded as being inconsistent with Article 6 §§ 1 and 3 (d) in itself. But the use of such statements as evidence had to comply with the rights of the defence. This would be especially so if there has not been an opportunity to cross-examine witnesses at any stage in the earlier proceedings.[11]

By refusing to give evidence, the witnesses prevented the applicant from examining them or having them examined in open court. He was able to comment on their written statements but was not allowed to admit the evidence he sought to adduce in order to put the witnesses' credibility to doubt. Additionally, he had not been present when they gave evidence in the pre-trial investigation. The Court noted that the written statements "were not the only evidence before the courts", but the applicant's conviction was mainly based on them. Although it was for the domestic courts to assess the evidence, the applicant's conviction was based on "'testimony' in respect of which his defence rights were appreciably restricted".[12]

Unterpertinger was interpreted in *Kostovski*:

> As a rule, [the rights of the defence] require that an accused should be given an adequate and proper opportunity to challenge and question a witness against him, either at the time the witness was making his statement or at some later stage of the proceedings.

Neither judgment addresses explicitly the rationale for such a rule. However, *Kostovski* also includes the following statement:

> Testimony or other declarations inculpating an accused may well be designedly untruthful or simply erroneous and the defence will scarcely be able to bring this to light if it lacks the information permitting it to test the author's reliability or cast doubt on his credibility. The dangers inherent in such a situation are obvious.[13]

That cross-examination is intended to promote the reliability of oral evidence is well-established. Wigmore, in the context of the confrontation clause found in the sixth amendment of the United States constitution, has famously put this as follows:

> The main and essential purpose of confrontation is to secure for the opponent the opportunity of cross-examination. The opponent demands confrontation, not for the idle purpose of gazing upon the witness, or of being gazed upon by him, but for the purpose of cross-examination, which cannot be had except

11 Unterpertinger v. Austria, 24.11.1986, §§ 30 and 31.
12 Unterpertinger v. Austria, 24.11.1986, §§ 32 and 33.
13 Kostovski v. the Netherlands [plenary], 20.11.1989, §§ 41 and 42.

by the direct and personal putting of questions and obtaining of immediate answers.[14]

According to the confrontation clause, "in all criminal prosecutions, the accused shall enjoy the right to be confronted with the witnesses against him". SCOTUS discussed the rationale of the clause in *Crawford*:

> To be sure, the Clause's ultimate goal is to ensure reliability of evidence, but it is a **procedural** rather than a substantive guarantee. It commands, not that evidence be reliable, but that reliability be assessed in a particular manner: by testing in the crucible of cross-examination. The Clause thus reflects a judgment, not only about the desirability of reliable evidence (a point on which there could be little dissent), but about how reliability can best be determined.[15]

In its earlier case law, SCOTUS had given greater weight to the reliability aspect. In *Ohio v. Roberts*, for example, an explicitly **substantive** approach was taken. Referring to its earlier case law, SCOTUS summarised:

> [W]hen a hearsay declarant is not present for cross-examination at trial, the Confrontation Clause normally requires a showing that he is unavailable. Even then, his statement is admissible only if it bears adequate "indicia of reliability". Reliability can be inferred without more in a case where the evidence falls within a firmly rooted hearsay exception. In other cases, the evidence must be excluded, at least absent a showing of particularized guarantees of trustworthiness.[16]

In 1996, the Court ruled for the first time in *Doorson* that "even when 'counterbalancing' procedures are found to compensate sufficiently the handicaps under which the defence labours, a conviction should not be based either solely or to a decisive extent on anonymous statements".[17] This was also applied to other untested evidence:

> [W]here a conviction is based solely or to a decisive degree on depositions that have been made by a person whom the accused has had no opportunity to examine or to have examined, whether during the investigation or at the trial, the rights of the defence are restricted to an extent that is incompatible with the guarantees provided by Article 6 [...].[18]

---

14 J. H. Wigmore, *A Treatise on the Anglo-American System of Evidence in Trials at Common Law*, vol. III, 2nd edn (Boston, MA: Little, Brown and Company, 1923), 94.
15 Crawford v. Washington, 541 U.S. 36 (2004).
16 Ohio v. Roberts, 448 U.S. 56 (1980).
17 Doorson v. the Netherlands, 26.3.1996, § 76.
18 Lucà v. Italy, 27.2.2001, § 40.

The interpretation meant that the importance of the untested evidence was the decisive factor within the overall assessment, which made the test quite rigid. It also reflected an essentially procedural approach that "[e]ven where the evidence of an absent witness has not been sole or decisive, the Court has still found a violation of Article 6 §§ 1 and 3 (d) when no good reason has been shown for the failure to have the witness examined [...]".[19] In *Lüdi*, for example, the Court considered that a confrontation between the applicant and an undercover agent could have been arranged in a manner which would have preserved the agent's anonymity. It found a violation of Article 6 although the evidence only "played a part" in the applicant's conviction.[20]

The Supreme Court of the United Kingdom contested this formalistic or procedural approach, pointing out in *Horncastle* that there is no "discussion of the principle underlying it or full consideration of whether there was justification for imposing the rule as an overriding principle applicable equally to the continental and common-law jurisdictions".[21] Although the exchange of ideas between the two courts has been called, among other things, a "saga", it is also an example of a fruitful dialogue between domestic judiciary and the Court.[22] It resulted in fundamental changes to the application of the rule and the Court accepting much of the domestic criticism as well as agreeing to explain the rationale of the rule.

According to the Court, there were two reasons underpinning the sole or decisive rule. First, it referred to the passage from *Kostovski* already cited above (i.e. that "inculpatory evidence against an accused may well be 'designedly untruthful or simply erroneous'"). It was added that it might be seductively easy to believe evidence which has not been subjected to cross-examination. Additionally, "[t]he dangers inherent in allowing untested hearsay evidence to be adduced are all the greater if that evidence is the sole or decisive evidence against the defendant".[23] This confirms that *at least* securing the reliability of the statements is a rationale of the rule.

The second reason was that

> the defendant must not be placed in the position where he is effectively deprived of a real chance of defending himself by being unable to challenge the case against him. Trial proceedings must ensure that a defendant's Article 6 rights are not unacceptably restricted and that he or she remains able to participate effectively in the proceedings [...]. The Court's assessment of whether a criminal trial has been fair cannot depend solely on whether the evidence against the accused appears prima facie to be reliable, if there are no means of challenging that evidence once it is admitted.[24]

---

19 Al-Khawaja and Tahery v. the United Kingdom [GC], 15.12.2011, § 127.
20 Lüdi v. Switzerland, 15.6.1992, §§ 47–50.
21 R v Horncastle and others [2009] UKSC 14.
22 J.-P. Loof, "Is Judicial Dialogue the Answer to the Challenges the ECHR is Facing?" (2015) 40 *Nederlands Tijdschrift voor de Mensenrechten*, 463, 465.
23 Al-Khawaja and Tahery v. the United Kingdom [GC], 15.12.2011, § 142.
24 Al-Khawaja and Tahery v. the United Kingdom [GC], 15.12.2011, § 142.

This rationale seems to be linked with reliability as well, but it also emphasises the rights of the defence.

Although the Court attempted very hard to fade that out, it effectively changed its interpretation of the rule. This was expressly admitted four years later in *Schatschaschwili*, where the Court explained that "the rationale underlying its judgment in *Al-Khawaja and Tahery*, in which it departed from the so-called 'sole or decisive rule', was to abandon an indiscriminate rule and to have regard, in the traditional way, to the fairness of the proceedings as a whole [...]".[25] Indeed, the Court also underlined the importance of the overall fairness assessment: "It would not be correct, when reviewing questions of fairness, to apply this rule in an inflexible manner."[26]

This can also be read from one simple change to a passage which, for example in *Lucà*, read as follows:

> [W]here a conviction is based solely or to a decisive degree on depositions that have been made by a person whom the accused has had no opportunity to examine or to have examined, whether during the investigation or at the trial, the rights of the defence **are restricted** to an extent that is incompatible with the guarantees provided by Article 6.[27]

Only the words "are restricted" were changed in *Al-Khawaja* to "may be restricted", while the passage has otherwise remained exactly the same.[28]

Compared to the SCOTUS case law, it seems that the Court's case law has developed the other way around: from a rule of more procedural nature into a substantive direction. Initially, decisive weight was put on more formalistic features of the right to a cross-examination, either the importance of the evidence as in *Doorson* or whether every reasonable effort was made to avoid the use of untested evidence as in *Lüdi*. Although these factors remain elements of the sole or decisive test, they are not necessarily decisive anymore. Instead, a more substantial approach has now emerged, where the reliability of evidence plays an important role.

9.3 The *Al-Khawaja and Tahery* test

The Court concluded in *Al-Khawaja and Tahery* that

> where a hearsay statement is the sole or decisive evidence against a defendant, its admission as evidence will not automatically result in a breach of Article 6 § 1. At the same time, where a conviction is based solely or decisively on the evidence of absent witnesses, the Court must subject the proceedings to the

---

25 Schatschaschwili v. Germany [GC], 15.12.2015, § 112.
26 Al-Khawaja and Tahery v. the United Kingdom [GC], 15.12.2011, § 146.
27 Lucà v. Italy, 27.2.2001, § 40.
28 Al-Khawaja and Tahery v. the United Kingdom [GC], 15.12.2011, § 119.

most searching scrutiny. Because of the dangers of the admission of such evidence, it would constitute a very important factor to balance in the scales, [...] and one which would require sufficient counterbalancing factors, including the existence of strong procedural safeguards.[29]

The Court continued:

> The question in each case is whether there are sufficient counterbalancing factors in place, including measures that permit a fair and proper assessment of the reliability of that evidence to take place. This would permit a conviction to be based on such evidence only if it is sufficiently reliable given its importance in the case.[30]

The new, more substantial formulation of the rule links the importance and reliability of the impugned evidence similarly to the rule against other improperly obtained evidence discussed in the previous chapter. It also resembles the older SCOTUS case law discussed above.

The point of this is that it changes the rule applicable to decisive evidence. Unlike before, untested evidence *can* be accepted as the sole or decisive evidence of guilt, provided that there are sufficient counterbalancing measures in place. Of greatest importance are counterbalances which allow the reliability of the untested evidence to be controlled. Such evidence should not be considered prima facie reliable. Instead, the accused must have an effective opportunity to challenge its reliability and there must be sufficient mechanisms for controlling the reliability in place. Otherwise, the trier of fact cannot address the question of reliability in an effective manner as the right to a fair trial requires.

The importance of the evidence determines how strong the counterbalances must be: the more important the untested evidence is, the more important it is that its reliability is being controlled. This means that there is a correlation between the importance and counterbalancing, just as the SIC framework suggests. We shall take a closer look at these elements soon. The earlier case law seems to have implied that a violation could not have been counterbalanced if it reached the critical level of impact (i.e. "sole or decisive"). In that respect, the earlier interpretation very much resembled the rule applicable to the privilege against self-incrimination and often decisive *Ibrahim* criterion (g).

On the other hand, the Court also expressed the following view in *Al-Khawaja and Tahery*, prior to discussing the sole or decisive test:

> The requirement that there be **a good reason** for admitting the evidence of an absent witness is a preliminary question which must be examined before any consideration is given as to whether that evidence was sole or decisive. [...] As a general rule, witnesses should give evidence during the trial and all

29 Al-Khawaja and Tahery v. the United Kingdom [GC], 15.12.2011, § 147.
30 Al-Khawaja and Tahery v. the United Kingdom [GC], 15.12.2011, § 147.

reasonable efforts will be made to secure their attendance. Thus, when witnesses do not attend to give live evidence, there is a duty to enquire whether that absence is justified.[31]

So although the inflexible application of the sole or decisive rule instead of an overall approach "would transform the rule into a blunt and indiscriminate instrument that runs counter to the traditional way in which the Court approaches the issue of the overall fairness of the proceedings, namely to weigh in the balance the competing interests of the defence, the victim, and witnesses, and the public interest in the effective administration of justice",[32] the Court seemed to have elevated another element to a higher status. This would have meant that the lack of a good reason, a procedural factor, would still have automatically rendered a trial unfair.

In the following landmark judgment, *Schatschaschwili*, the Court noted that its own case law had been ambivalent about this, because

> in a number of cases following the delivery of the judgment in *Al-Khawaja and Tahery* it took an overall approach to the examination of the fairness of the trial, having regard to all three steps of the *Al-Khawaja and Tahery* test [...]. However, in other cases, the lack of a good reason for a prosecution witness's absence alone was considered sufficient to find a breach of Article 6 §§ 1 and 3 (d) [...]. In yet other cases a differentiated approach was taken: the lack of good reason for a prosecution witness's absence was considered conclusive of the unfairness of the trial unless the witness testimony was manifestly irrelevant for the outcome of the case [...].[33]

The Court pointed out that one of the very aims of *Al-Khawaja*

> was to abandon an indiscriminate rule and to have regard, in the traditional way, to the fairness of the proceedings as a whole [...]. However, it would amount to the creation of a new indiscriminate rule if a trial were considered to be unfair for lack of a good reason for a witness's non-attendance alone, even if the untested evidence was neither sole nor decisive and was possibly even irrelevant for the outcome of the case.

Thus, it considered that "the absence of good reason for the non-attendance of a witness cannot of itself be conclusive of the unfairness of a trial".[34]

In that connection, the Court also stated that if a defendant or someone acting on their behalf has threatened a witness, this should not benefit the defendant. In such a situation, a witness need not

---

31 Al-Khawaja and Tahery v. the United Kingdom [GC], 15.12.2011, § 120.
32 Al-Khawaja and Tahery v. the United Kingdom [GC], 15.12.2011, § 146.
33 Schatschaschwili v. Germany [GC], 15.12.2015, § 113.
34 Schatschaschwili v. Germany [GC], 15.12.2015, §§ 112 and 113.

give live evidence or be examined by the defendant or his representatives – even if such evidence was the sole or decisive evidence against the defendant. [...] Consequently, a defendant who has acted in this manner must be taken to have waived his rights to question such witnesses under Article 6 § 3 (d).[35]

Of course, an unequivocal waiver can also be made expressly. However, the Court seems to have applied the test even though it has found that an applicant has waived their right to cross-examination.[36]

While the Court did not introduce any presumption mechanism similar to the *Salduz* test, it did add that "the lack of a good reason for a prosecution witness's absence is a very important factor to be weighed in the balance when assessing the overall fairness of a trial, and one which may tip the balance in favour of finding a breach of Article 6 §§ 1 and 3 (d)". Furthermore, while the Court also confirmed that the order of the test is flexible, it maintained that *Al-Khawaja and Tahery* had expressed a sort of default order. Deviating from it would be appropriate in particular it one of the three steps should prove particularly conclusive for the overall fairness.[37]

Additionally, the grand chamber wanted to clarify whether sufficient counter-balancing factors are still necessary if the untested witness evidence was neither sole nor decisive. The answer raises perhaps more questions. According to the Court, the existence of sufficient counterbalancing factors must be reviewed not only when the "sole or decisive" threshold has been met but "also in those cases where, following its assessment of the domestic courts' evaluation of the weight of the evidence [...], it finds it unclear whether the evidence in question was the sole or decisive basis but is nevertheless satisfied that it **carried significant weight** and that its admission may have handicapped the defence".[38]

This passage is a clear reference to the principle of subsidiarity and, indeed, the Court later mentions the fourth instance doctrine, according to which the "starting-point for deciding whether an applicant's conviction was based solely or to a decisive extent on the depositions of an absent witness is the judgments of the domestic courts [...]".[39] A domestic ruling on the importance of evidence should only be overridden if it is unacceptable or arbitrary. Of course, the Court would also make its own assessment if the domestic court fails to state with sufficient clarity its position on the weight of the untested evidence.

It remains slightly unclear whether the counterbalancing measures should still be assessed if the evidence is not sole, decisive or even carrying significant weight. Moreover, the concept of "significant weight" lacks clarity. It seems likely that the Court (probably through another grand chamber judgment) will have to make yet another attempt at explaining the test and its mechanism. I submit that when

---

35 Al-Khawaja and Tahery v. the United Kingdom [GC], 15.12.2011, § 123.
36 See, for example, Poletan and Azirovik v. the former Yugoslav Republic of Macedonia, 12.5.2016, § 87; and Bátěk and Others v. the Czech Republic, 12.1.2017, § 57.
37 Schatschaschwili v. Germany [GC], 15.12.2015, §§ 113 and 117–118.
38 Schatschaschwili v. Germany [GC], 15.12.2015, § 116.
39 Schatschaschwili v. Germany [GC], 15.12.2015, § 124.

assessing the right to a fair trial one cannot easily condone an arbitrary assessment of the reliability of even less meaningful untested evidence. A flexible overall assessment would therefore normally require going through all three steps in every situation, although it might differ which of them is decisive.

Be that as it may, according to *Schatschaschwili*, the entire test should be applied in a flexible manner. This means essentially that the procedural elements of the test, the reason for non-attendance and the weight of the evidence, are not necessarily decisive. If there are substantive counterbalancing factors allowing the reliability of the untested evidence to be sufficiently controlled in the absence of cross-examination, the trial can be considered fair as a whole. This is quite logical, because cross-examination is a tool for such control as well as effective participation. We shall now examine more closely the three steps of the test:

i   [W]hether there was **a good reason** for the non-attendance of the witness and, consequently, for the admission of the absent witness's untested statements as evidence [...];

ii whether the evidence of the absent witness was the **sole or decisive** basis for the defendant's conviction [...]; and

iii whether there were sufficient **counterbalancing factors**, including strong procedural safeguards, to compensate for the handicaps caused to the defence as a result of the admission of the untested evidence and to ensure that the trial, judged as a whole, was fair [...].[40]

Before moving on, one last remark. We have seen that one increasingly common feature for the Court's judgments is to attempt to make its tests more understandable by listing typical situations it has assessed in previous case law. Thus, it observed in *Gani* that the question of compliance with Article 6 §§ 1 and 3 (d) has arisen mainly in three contexts: anonymous witnesses, absent witnesses, and witnesses who invoke their privilege against self-incrimination.[41] An additional fourth group, vulnerable witnesses, could be added to the list. Indeed, the witness in *Gani* was the victim of a sexual crime. It should be reminded that although much of what will be said about the test will be based on absence, there are other types of untested evidence as well.

9.4 A good reason

As a general principle, the Court stated in *Schatschaschwili*:

> Good reason for the absence of a witness must exist from the trial court's perspective, that is, the court must have had **good factual or legal grounds** not to secure the witness's attendance at the trial. If there was a good reason

40 Schatschaschwili v. Germany [GC], 15.12.2015, § 107.
41 Gani v. Spain, 19.2.2013, § 40.

for the witness's non-attendance in that sense, it follows that there was a good reason, or justification, for the trial court to admit the untested statements of the absent witness as evidence. There are a number of reasons why a witness may not attend a trial, such as absence owing to death or fear [...], absence on health grounds [...] or the witness's unreachability.[42]

It would appear that the existence of good factual and legal grounds can be assessed based on the classification in *Gani*. Anonymity, absence and vulnerability can be classified as primarily factual grounds, although they are often linked with legislation. By this I mean that there would normally be legal provisions for granting a witness anonymity, compelling witnesses to appear or allowing the use of their recorded statements, and the use of techniques for obtaining statements from children or otherwise vulnerable witnesses. Legal grounds, on the other hand, can cover a range of privileges allowing one not to testify – not only the privilege against self-incrimination but also various family and professional privileges.

Let us begin with perhaps the simplest category, **absent witnesses**. The quote from *Schatschaschwili* provides yet another list of examples based on case law. Absent witnesses can also be classified into two subcategories based on whether the trial court is aware of whether they are able to give a statement or not. For example, if a death certificate or medical statement is submitted, it can be proven that a witness cannot be heard. It is obvious that death prevents cross-examination, and so may a serious illness, although sometimes measures can be taken to hear a witness from a hospital or other facility.[43]

The Court discussed at some length in *Al-Khawaja and Tahery* when absence owing to fear could justified. It begun by distinguishing two types of fear: "fear which is attributable to threats or other actions of the defendant or those acting on his or her behalf and fear which is attributable to a more general fear of what will happen if the witness gives evidence at trial". The first situation would, as already mentioned, constitute an unequivocal waiver of the right to cross-examine witnesses, allowing a court to use a statement even as the sole or decisive evidence of guilt. But such situations were considered rare:

> The Court's own case-law shows that it is more common for witnesses to have a general fear of testifying without that fear being directly attributable to threats made by the defendant or his agents. For instance, in many cases, the fear has been attributable to the notoriety of a defendant or his associates [...].[44]

The Court then clarified that even a more general fear not directly attributable to threats made by the defendant or someone acting on their behalf, can excuse a witness from giving evidence in a normal fashion. It even created yet another rule

42 Schatschaschwili v. Germany [GC], 15.12.2015, § 119.
43 See Maffei 2006, 43–46.
44 Al-Khawaja and Tahery v. the United Kingdom [GC], 15.12.2011, §§ 122–124.

of evidence in the form of an assessment model: "The trial court must conduct appropriate enquiries to determine, firstly, whether or not there are **objective grounds** for that fear, and, secondly, whether those objective grounds are **supported by evidence** [...]". The objective grounds may be "fear of death or injury of another person or of financial loss", but "any subjective fear of the witness" will not suffice.[45]

When a witness is unreachable, it may well be that they are in perfect health and would be capable of being examined. The factual problem in such situations is that either the domestic authorities are unaware of their whereabouts or although aware of them, unable to compel them to attend a trial. Before it could be said that every reasonable effort has been made from a trial court's perspective, "they must have actively searched for the witness with the help of the domestic authorities, including the police [...] and must, as a rule, have resorted to international legal assistance where a witness resided abroad and such mechanisms were available [...]".[46]

The Court found a sort of systemic violation in *Mild and Virtanen*, where the domestic legislation did not provide efficient means to compel the witnesses to appear. In fact, it stated in the abstract that "the law was inadequate on this point". Their evidence was considered important, and the Court found a violation of Article 6 §§ 1 and 3 (d) taken together.[47] In *Yevgeniy Ivanov*, the trial court had ordered bailiffs to ensure the appearance of three witnesses. The bailiffs visited the former address of the first witness five times in spite of having been told every time by the new occupants that the witness no longer lived there. The second witness's apartment at a university campus was visited once and because he was not at home, a summons was left to the campus guard without making any further attempts to reach him. The third witness was on a business trip and the bailiffs made no attempts to get any further information from his employer. These attempts and the trial court's control were considered inadequate.[48]

These examples show that the trial court bears the ultimate responsibility and should make sure that every reasonable effort has been made to secure the attendance of witnesses, given the circumstances and the reason for unreachability. Sometimes this may require reviewing the efforts of the domestic authorities. Referring to *Yevgeniy Ivanov* and another case, the Court reminded in *Schatschaschwili* that

> [t]he need for all reasonable efforts on the part of the authorities to secure the witness's attendance at the trial further implies careful scrutiny by the domestic courts of the reasons given for the witness's inability to attend trial, having regard to the specific situation of each witness [...].[49]

45 Al-Khawaja and Tahery v. the United Kingdom [GC], 15.12.2011, § 124.
46 Schatschaschwili v. Germany [GC], 15.12.2015, § 121.
47 Mild and Virtanen v. Finland, 26.7.2005, §§ 45–48.
48 Yevgeniy Ivanov v. Russia, 25.4.2013, §§ 46 and 47.
49 Schatschaschwili v. Germany [GC], 15.12.2015, § 122.

For our purposes, witnesses who refuse to give evidence without any privilege could be identified with absent witnesses. It is relatively common for a witness to claim, for example, that they have forgotten the events. Usually, this would result in the reading of their previous statements. The Court noted in *Pichugin* that "as a result of the refusal by a prosecution witness to answer questions put by the defendant, the essence of his right to challenge and question that witness may be undermined". Contrary to domestic legislation which would have allowed the witness to be compelled to give evidence, the presiding judge simply allowed this refusal, which the Court found "peculiar".[50]

Now, let us turn to the other contexts in which departures from the right to cross-examination has often been assessed. A common feature between all of them is that they involve the right to cross-examine being balanced against the rights and interests of the witness. This fundamental feature makes them different from the context of absent witnesses, where the question is whether the witness's absence is imputable to the domestic authorities or not. Here, the question is rather more complex. The general principle was introduced in *Doorson*, where it was formulated as follows:

> It is true that Article 6 (art. 6) does not explicitly require the interests of witnesses in general, and those of victims called upon to testify in particular, to be taken into consideration. However, their life, liberty or security of person may be at stake, as may interests coming generally within the ambit of Article 8 of the Convention. Such interests of witnesses and victims are in principle protected by other, substantive provisions of the Convention, which imply that Contracting States should organise their criminal proceedings in such a way that those interests are not unjustifiably imperilled. Against this background, principles of fair trial also require that in appropriate cases the interests of the defence are balanced against those of witnesses or victims called upon to testify.[51]

We begin with **anonymous witnesses**. In *Al-Khawaja and Tahery*, the Court expressed a preference for anonymity:

> [W]hen a witness has not been examined at any prior stage of the proceedings, allowing the admission of a witness statement in lieu of live evidence at trial must be a measure of last resort. Before a witness can be excused from testifying on grounds of fear, the trial court must be satisfied that all available alternatives, such as witness anonymity and other special measures, would be inappropriate or impracticable.[52]

50 Pichugin v. Russia, 23.10.2012, §§ 201 and 204.
51 Doorson v. the Netherlands, 26.3.1996, § 70.
52 Al-Khawaja and Tahery v. the United Kingdom [GC], 15.12.2011, § 125.

On the other hand, the types listed in *Gani* are not mutually exclusive because a witness may be, for example, both anonymous and absent.[53]

This does not mean that the threshold for allowing anonymity would be low. Although the use of anonymous informants might be unproblematic during the investigative stage to obtain other evidence, maintaining the anonymity of prosecution witnesses would mean that the defence faces "unusual difficulties", the nature of which has already been discussed above. The question of the existence of a good reason takes the form of whether "the interest of the witness in remaining anonymous could justify limiting the rights of the defence".[54] It is crucial that the domestic courts provide sufficient reasons to justify anonymity. Because "any measures restricting the rights of the defence should be strictly necessary", the least restrictive measures should be used.[55]

The Court accepted the domestic courts' decision to maintain the anonymity of two witnesses in *Doorson*. One of them stated that "he had in the past suffered injuries at the hands of another drug dealer after he had 'talked' and feared similar reprisals from the applicant", while the other stated that "he had in the past been threatened by drug dealers if he were to talk". The applicant pointed out that there was nothing to suggest that he had threatened either witness. The Court, however, endorsed the reasoning of the domestic courts that "drug dealers frequently resorted to threats or actual violence against persons who gave evidence against them".[56]

An anonymous witness in *Krasniki*

> stated before the investigating officer that she was giving evidence as an anonymous witness because she owed money for drugs, and that a "Yugoslav" to whom she had owed money for drugs had beaten her up and that there had been similar incidents [...]. Interviewed on the same day, [another anonymous witness] stated that the "Yugoslavs" were temperamental people, that they had threatened him when he wanted to buy narcotics from someone else and that he had been concerned about the safety of his family. However, he said that he had never been threatened by the man in photograph number five, whom he recognised as the applicant.

Under circumstances which bear striking resemblance to those in *Doorson*, the Court found that anonymity was not justified. One important difference was that the "reasonableness of the personal fear of the witnesses, vis-à-vis the applicant" was not assessed by domestic authorities.[57]

An even higher threshold seems to apply to police officers, who can only be examined anonymously in exceptional circumstances because unlike disinterested

---

53 Gani v. Spain, 19.2.2013, § 40.
54 Krasniki v. the Czech Republic, 28.2.2006, §§ 76 and 83.
55 Van Mechelen and Others v. the Netherlands, 23.4.1997, § 58.
56 Doorson v. the Netherlands, 26.3.1996, §§ 28 and 71.
57 Krasniki v. the Czech Republic, 28.2.2006, §§ 80–82.

witnesses or victims "[t]hey owe a general duty of obedience to the State's executive authorities and usually have links with the prosecution". Additionally, their duties may include giving evidence. However, "it may be legitimate for the police authorities to wish to preserve the anonymity of an agent deployed in undercover activities, for his own or his family's protection and so as not to impair his usefulness for future operations".[58]

In *Van Mechelen* it was stated very briefly that "[i]n the absence of any further information, the Court cannot find that the operational needs of the police provide sufficient justification".[59] But in a more recent case of *Bátěk*, the Court accepted that protecting the usefulness of an undercover agent in future operations was sufficient justification. It is important to note that two domestic courts gave this as the reason to hearing her as an anonymous witness.[60]

It might be easier for the reader to proceed with **vulnerable witnesses** before moving on to legal grounds for non-attendance. This category could be seen as a subcategory of absent witnesses, but because of some special features it is more appropriate to address it separately. Vulnerable witnesses could, in principle, be compelled to appear in open court, but doing so would risk their well-being. Maffei has distinguished three groups of typically vulnerable witnesses: children, victims of sexual offences, and adults with learning disabilities.[61] The list is non-exhaustive, and it may be added that these categories can also overlap, for example if a child is the victim of a sexual offence.

In the often-quoted *S.N. v. Sweden* the Court noted that it

> has had regard to the special features of criminal proceedings concerning sexual offences. Such proceedings are often conceived of as an ordeal by the victim, in particular when the latter is unwillingly confronted with the defendant. These features are even more prominent in a case involving a minor. In the assessment of the question whether or not in such proceedings an accused received a fair trial, account must be taken of the right to respect for the private life of the perceived victim. Therefore, the Court accepts that in criminal proceedings concerning sexual abuse certain measures may be taken for the purpose of protecting the victim, provided that such measures can be reconciled with an adequate and effective exercise of the rights of the defence [...].[62]

The untested evidence in *Gani* was the pre-trial statement of the victim who was present at the trial. She had already once attempted to give evidence, but as a result of post-traumatic stress symptoms, the first hearing was adjourned. The domestic authorities provided the witness with psychological assistance both

---

58 Van Mechelen and Others v. the Netherlands, 23.4.1997, §§ 56 and 57.
59 Van Mechelen and Others v. the Netherlands, 23.4.1997, § 60.
60 Bátěk and Others v. the Czech Republic, 12.1.2017, § 47.
61 Maffei 2006, 52–56.
62 S.N. v. Sweden, 2.7.2002, § 47.

before and during the second hearing. She was also examined prior to it and declared fit to testify. In the second hearing, after having begun to answer the questions of the prosecution, she broke down again. Her symptoms were medically confirmed after the hearing. Having taken into account that the witness would not be available for cross-examination within a reasonable time – a conclusion that was preceded by "countless unsuccessful efforts, including medical support, had been made to enable [her] to continue with her statement" – and that the applicant was in prison on remand, the trial court allowed the use of her previous statements. The domestic court could not "be accused of lack of diligence in its efforts to provide the defendant with an opportunity to examine the witness".[63]

Finally, let us take a quick look at the **legal privileges** which may prevent an effective cross-examination.[64] Notice that there can only be a problem in this regard if a witness has given a statement at some stage before the trial but then refuses to give evidence in open court. The privilege against self-incrimination, discussed in Chapter 5, is perhaps the most obvious example as it is also protected under Article 6. Note also that while the problem may arise between co-defendants, this is not necessarily so because the privilege protects everyone who cannot exclude the possibility that answering a question could lead to them being prosecuted of a crime.

The Court explained in *Vidgen* that

> evidence on which the applicant was convicted included statements made by M. to a German police officer. However, invoking his privilege against self-incrimination, M. refused to allow these statements to be tested or challenged by or on behalf of the applicant. The respondent Party cannot be criticised for allowing M. to make use of rights which, as a criminal suspect, he enjoyed under Article 6 of the Convention [...].[65]

Additionally, there can be little doubt that domestic legislation may include various other privileges which are allowed. For example, the Court has referred to *Unterpertinger*, summarising that

> provisions granting family members of the accused the right not to testify as witnesses in court with a view to avoiding their being put in a moral dilemma can be found in the domestic law of several member States of the Council of Europe and are, as such, not incompatible with Article 6 §§ 1 and 3 (d) of the Convention [...].[66]

Case law on the effects of a witness invoking a privilege is somewhat ambiguous. The case of *Peltonen* was declared manifestly ill-founded because the applicant's

---

63 Gani v. Spain, 19.2.2013, § 45.
64 See Maffei 2006, 44–45.
65 Vidgen v. the Netherlands, 10.7.2012, § 42.
66 Hümmer v. Germany, 19.7.2012, § 41.

counsel had not put any further questions to a witness who refused to answer questions, although there were many opportunities to do so. The Court stated that although the witness's

> "persistence to remain silent may have made further questioning futile, in the circumstances of the present case this neither discloses lack of equality of arms nor justifies the conclusion that the judicial authorities denied the applicant the possibility of examining witnesses in conformity with Article 6 §§ 1 and 3 (d) of the Convention".[67]

In both *Cabral* and *Kaste and Mathisen*, the Court found violations of those same provisions. In *Cabral*, the witness's "persistence to remain silent made such questioning futile" but, unlike in *Peltonen*, the applicant or his counsel never had an opportunity to challenge his statement which, moreover, was decisive evidence of the applicant's guilt.[68] In *Kaste and Mathisen*, the Court stated that in addition to the appearance of a witness, which the authorities should secure, "there must also be a proper and adequate opportunity to question the witness" (i.e. they must answer the questions of the defence). In that case, the Court did not consider the opportunity effective because the domestic court had not allowed questions to be put to a co-defendant after he had refused to give evidence – even in part.[69]

9.5 The weight of the untested statement

The second stage of the *Al-Khawaja and Tahery* test is, effectively, the old sole or decisive test. The Court has not indicated any change in the (autonomous) interpretation of "sole or decisive" evidence, although this threshold was explained in *Al-Khawaja and Tahery* as a response to criticism from the judiciary of the United Kingdom. Of course, it is the word "decisive" which requires more explaining – it is rather evident that the word "sole" should be understood as the only evidence against the accused.[70] Such was the situation in *Saïdi*, where the court noted that "in convicting the applicant the two courts which tried him referred to no evidence other than the statements obtained prior to the trial".[71]

The Court may have referred to an older case quite deliberately in this context. *Saïdi*, after all, precedes even the landmark *Doorson* judgment. At least this would suggest that the Court did not intend to overrule or revise any of its older judgments in this regard (i.e. it did not set to give a new meaning to the concept of "sole or decisive" in *Al-Khawaja and Tahery*, only to clarify its assessment). I therefore conclude that the pre-*Al-Khawaja* case law can still be used to interpret the importance

---

67 Peltonen v. Finland [dec.], 11.5.1999.
68 Cabral v. the Netherlands, 28.8.2018 §§ 36 and 37.
69 Kaste and Mathisen v. Norway, 9.11.2006, §§ 47, 50 and 51.
70 Al-Khawaja and Tahery v. the United Kingdom [GC], 15.12.2011, § 131.
71 Saïdi v. France, 20.9.1993, § 44.

of evidence. Of course, it should be remembered that this reference was made in the context of "sole evidence".

The Court then continued to explain the word "decisive". It should be understood as something more than "probative" or that "without the evidence, the chances of a conviction would recede and the chances of an acquittal advance". Both these interpretations would, in fact, cover all relevant evidence in any given case:

> Instead, the word "decisive" should be narrowly understood as indicating evidence of such significance or importance as is **likely to be determinative** of the outcome of the case. Where the untested evidence of a witness is supported by other corroborative evidence, the assessment of whether it is decisive will depend on the strength of the supportive evidence; the stronger the corroborative evidence, the less likely that the evidence of the absent witness will be treated as decisive.[72]

So here, too, we meet the concept of corroboration. As it was explained in Section 8.4 above, three types of corroborative evidence can be distinguished. It seems to me that the ending of the quote would refer to same fact corroboration, a situation where several independent pieces of evidence are proof of the same fact. By contrast, credibility corroboration would seem less likely to diminish the importance of a statement, because such evidence is only offered to prove its reliability. The supported evidence, in such a situation, would remain the only proof of the facts in issue and should probably for that reason alone be treated as decisive.

Like the rule against other improperly obtained evidence, the *Al-Khawaja and Tahery* test can be seen at least partially as a corroboration rule. As the quote suggests, corroborative evidence will limit the **impact** of a potential violation. As with other improperly obtained evidence, an untested statement may well be the "silver bullet" and provide the authorities "with the framework around which they subsequently built their case and the focus for their search for other corroborating evidence". This will not, contrary to Ibrahim criterion (g) in the context of the privilege against self-incrimination, increase the impact, but decreases it. In other words, any derivative evidence will not be treated as "fruits of the poisonous tree".

Finding the applicant in *Doorson* guilty of a drug crime the domestic court based its judgment on a large body of evidence. They included the evidence of two drug addicts who had identified the applicant from a photo and stated that he had sold drugs. Similar statements were obtained from two anonymous witnesses who were questioned in the presence of the applicant's counsel. Prior to this, there was already a suspicion against the applicant and his photo was added to a collection for the purposes of identification. The applicant also recognised himself from a photo. Interestingly, though, one of the witnesses heard in open court retracted their statement and the other was not cross-examined. Nonetheless, the Court concluded it was sufficiently clear that the applicant's conviction was not "solely or to a decisive extent" based on the anonymous statements.[73] It could perhaps be

---

72 Al-Khawaja and Tahery v. the United Kingdom [GC], 15.12.2011, § 131.
73 Doorson v. the Netherlands, 26.3.1996, §§ 10, 34 and 76.

said that the anonymous statements were treated as corroborative evidence, which usually would not make evidence decisive.[74]

Artner is another example of early case law about non-decisive evidence. The applicant had been convicted on two counts of usury among other crimes. The statement of a victim was read, but there was also plenty of other evidence, including

> the documents concerning the loan agreement, and notably [the applicant's] letter demanding that [the witness] pay him the sum of 2,350 schillings following their first unsuccessful discussions, or again the undertaking which he had made her sign to reimburse with effect from March 1984 the monthly instalments payable [...]. There were in addition the applicant's criminal record and his conviction against which he did not appeal [...] – in the other case of usury on similar facts. Although this evidence did not provide a precise indication as to the amount of commission received, it could nevertheless, in the victim's absence, help the judges to form their opinion.[75]

In the case of *Al-Khawaja*, an untested statement of a witness who died before the trial was considered decisive because it was the only direct evidence of what had happened in a doctor's consultation room between the parties. The Court based its finding, in accordance with the principle of subsidiarity, on that of the domestic court.[76] The untested evidence in the case of *Tahery* was also decisive because it was the statement of the only witness who had seen the alleged crime and the only one implicating the applicant.[77] There is plenty of other case law where an eyewitness statement or similar direct evidence (in the absence of other evidence) has been considered decisive.[78] In *Zadumov*, the untested evidence was also "critical to the domestic courts for resolving the conflict between the testimony of the two co-accused", and deemed decisive.[79]

My interpretation of *Schatschaschwili* is that the Court did not intend to create another threshold of importance when it introduced the "carried significant weight" standard mentioned above. According to it, examining "significant weight" would *only* be triggered if the domestic courts were silent on the weight of the untested evidence. In other words, if a domestic court has considered a piece of untested evidence as a small part of the total evidence, and this finding is not unacceptable or arbitrary, the "significant weight" criterion would not come into operation at all. However, the intents of the grand chamber may have been

---

74 See Bátěk and Others v. the Czech Republic, 12.1.2017, § 52.
75 Artner v. Austria, 28.8.1992, especially §§ 23 and 24.
76 Al-Khawaja and Tahery v. the United Kingdom [GC], 15.12.2011, §§ 13 and 154.
77 Al-Khawaja and Tahery v. the United Kingdom [GC], 15.12.2011, §§ 13 and 160.
78 See e.g. Van Mechelen and Others v. the Netherlands, 23.4.1997, § 63; S.N. v. Sweden, 2.7.2002, § 46; Hümmer v. Germany, 19.7.2012, § 44; Gani v. Spain, 19.2.2013, § 43; Yevgeniy Ivanov v. Russia, 25.4.2013, § 48; Lučić v. Croatia, 27.2.2014, § 81, Schatschaschwili v. Germany [GC], 15.12.2015, § 144; Cabral v. the Netherlands, 28.8.2018 §§ 35 and 36.
79 Zadumov v. Russia, 12.12.2017, §§ 59–61. See also Şandru v. Romania, 15.10.2013, § 62.

understood differently in the Court's subsequent case law, for example the *Seton* judgment:

> [G]iven that its concern was to ascertain whether the proceedings as a whole were fair, the Court should not only review the existence of sufficient coun-terbalancing factors in cases where the evidence of the absent witness was the sole or the decisive basis for the applicant's conviction, but also in cases where it found it unclear whether the evidence in question was sole or decisive but nevertheless was satisfied that it carried significant weight and its admission might have handicapped the defence.

In that case, the Court made its own assessment of the importance of the evidence although the domestic courts had stated that the evidence against the applicant had been "overwhelming" and that "quite apart from [the untested evidence], we had no doubt as to the safety of the conviction of [the applicant]".[80] I see no ambiguity in these statements, and yet the Court seems to overstep its own mark, acting effectively as a fourth instance when it would have been enough to either approve the domestic assessment or at least explain what made it unclear.

Referring to *Seton*, the Court seems to have completely bypassed the domestic constitutional court's opinion on the weight of the anonymous witness's statement in *Báték*. That court had explicitly stated that "the testimony in question was not decisive evidence and there was a large body of other circumstantial evidence". The Strasbourg Court, acting again as a fourth instance, failed to indicate whether this conclusion was in some way arbitrary or unclear. Instead, *accepting* that the evidence was not decisive, it still declared that it carried significant weight and proceeded with the third stage of the test.[81] In light of *Schatschaschwili*, this should have been unnecessary.

By comparison, a more "correct" approach, in my opinion, has been taken in *Poletan and Azirovik*, *Zadumov*, and *Tău*. In all of them, the Court begun by examining the domestic approach on the importance of the impugned evidence (or lack of it). This was strongly underlined in *Zadumov*:

> [W]hile maintaining its firmly established position that the national courts are in principle better placed to assess the evidence presented to them, the Court considers that in the present case the manner in which the Russian courts construed their judgments made the evidence of the absent witness "deci-sive", that is, determinative of the applicant's conviction.[82]

In both of the other judgments the Court stated that "[s]ince the domestic courts did not indicate their position on this issue, it must make its own assessment of the

---

80 Seton v. the United Kingdom, 31.3.2016, §§ 38 and 59.

81 Báték and Others v. the Czech Republic, 12.1.2017, §§ 24, 49 and 50.

82 Zadumov v. Russia, 12.6.2017, § 61.

weight of the evidence given by these witnesses having regard to the strength of the additional incriminating evidence available [...]".[83]

This new threshold seems to be making its way as an established criterion under the radar so to say. In a very recent inadmissibility decision, for example, the second stage of the test was effectively expanded by stating that it includes the examination of "whether the evidence given by the anonymous witness was the sole or decisive basis for the applicants' conviction or carried significant weight in that regard".[84] Note that no mention is made of the principle of subsidiarity in that passage. Furthermore, the Court has yet to define this new threshold in the abstract. What is clear, though, is that it is quite low – perhaps even approaching the level of "probative" evidence.

The applicant in *Seton* had been convicted of a murder. His defence was based on the claim that another person, a Mr Pearson, had committed the crime. The untested evidence was a telephone call Mr Pearson had made from prison, telling his son that he had never heard of the applicant and knew nothing of the murder. He refused to give evidence at any stage. There was, however, exceptionally compelling circumstantial evidence against the applicant. This included, inter alia, evidence that the applicant and victim were known to each other and were both involved in drug dealing on a substantial scale, telephone records revealing they had been in contact shortly before the murder, evidence that a car linked with the murder had belonged to the applicant, the applicant's mobile telephone having been in the vicinity of the murder at the relevant time, several eyewitness descriptions of the gunman matching the applicant and not matching Mr Pearson. Given the volume of evidence, I think that the phone call of Mr Pearson was close to being insignificant for the outcome of the case. Yet, the domestic courts had described it "important" and so did the Court, although it sort of agreed with the domestic courts in that it was not sole nor decisive.[85]

In *Sitnevskiy and Chaykovskiy* the Court compiled a separate appendix showing the various offences of which the applicants were convicted. Episodes 6 and 7 provide some guidance to the interpretation of significant weight. Episode 6 consisted of two armed robberies. There were untested statements from two victims, who could only describe the events, namely that they had been stopped by individuals dressed as traffic police. According to the Court:

the main source of information about the applicants' role in the attacks on them and two other shoe sellers were the statements of the co-defendants. Nothing in the statements of the absent witnesses, and indeed no material in the case file, indicates that the victims had any contact with the applicants or any knowledge of their role in the crime [...]. Therefore, the Court is satisfied

---

83 Poletan and Azirovik v. the former Yugoslav Republic of Macedonia, 12.5.2016, § 88; Tău v. Romania, 23.7.2019, § 58.
84 Çongar and Kala v. Turkey [dec.], 18.1.2022, § 10.
85 Seton v. the United Kingdom, 31.3.2016, §§ 22–32 and 63–64.

that the statements [...] were neither decisive for the applicants' conviction nor carried such significant weight that they may have handicapped the defence.[86]

Episode 7 consisted of a robbery, attempted murder, and a murder. The owner of a currency exchange business and his bodyguard were attacked. The owner was shot in the leg and chest while the bodyguard was killed. The attackers arrived and fled on a motorcycle. Because the owner was the only surviving eyewitness of the attack, his untested statement against the second applicant carried at least significant weight although there was also circumstantial evidence. However, the first applicant was not directly involved and had only helped prepare the offence. Because the victim was unaware of his role and his statement did not implicate the first applicant, the statement "was neither decisive for the first applicant's conviction nor carried such significant weight that it may have handicapped his defence".[87]

9.6 Counterbalancing factors

The Court distinguished between three types of counterbalances in *Schatschasch-wiliSchatschaschwili*. The first of them is **the trial court's approach to the untested evidence**: "The courts must have shown that they were aware that the statements of the absent witness carried less weight [...]." Second, **the availability and strength of further incriminating evidence** should be assessed:

> The Court has taken into account, in that context, whether the domestic courts provided detailed reasoning as to why they considered that evidence to be reliable, while having regard also to the other evidence available [...]. It likewise has regard to any directions given to a jury by the trial judge as to the approach to be taken to absent witnesses' evidence [...].[88]

The first two counterbalances seem to be "measures that permit a fair and proper assessment of the reliability of the evidence to take place" as it was put in *Al-Khawaja and Tahery*. Thus, they focus on the trial court and the evaluation of evidence. The Court added in *Schatschaschwili* that

> [a]n additional safeguard in that context may be to show, at the trial hearing, a video-recording of the absent witness's questioning at the investigation stage in order to allow the court, prosecution and defence to observe the witness's demeanour under questioning and to form their own impression of his or her reliability [...].[89]

---

86 Sitnevskiy and Chaykovskiy v. Ukraine, 10.11.2016, § 120.
87 Sitnevskiy and Chaykovskiy v. Ukraine, 10.11.2016, §§ 121–122.
88 Schatschaschwili v. Germany [GC], 15.12.2015, § 126.
89 Schatschaschwili v. Germany [GC], 15.12.2015, § 127.

This would also suggest that the point of view is not exclusively that of the accused, but the absence of the factfinder should also be counterbalanced.

I submit, however, that a careful approach to the untested evidence does not require "diminuition of the probative value" of an untested statement, as Maffei has suggested.[90] The domestic courts should evaluate the probative with exceptional care because the means to ensure the reliability of such a statement are limited and ineffective. As a result, the probative value need not be diminished, instead it simply *is* lower than that of a statement given in open court. The risk arising from free evaluation is that a factfinder could easily overestimate the probative value of an untested statement, which calls for a cautious approach.

Thirdly, there should be **procedural measures aimed at compensating for the lack of opportunity to directly cross-examine the witnesses** at the trial. These measures, by contrast, focus more on the accused and effective defence participation. Such measures may include "corroborative evidence supporting the untested witness statement", "the possibility offered to the defence to put its own questions to the witness indirectly", or "an opportunity to question the witness during the investigation stage". "The defendant must further be afforded the opportunity to give his own version of the events and to cast doubt on the credibility of the absent witness, pointing out any incoherence or inconsistency with the statements of other witnesses [...]."[91]

Again, it seems that corroborative evidence can take any of the three forms discussed in Section 8.4 (i.e. same fact corroboration, convergence, or credibility corroboration). It should, however, be distinguished from the assessment of other incriminating evidence. The possibility to put questions to the witness indirectly has often been a relevant counterbalance in the contexts of sexual crimes, especially when hearing a child victim. The Court has stated that

> the following minimum guarantees must be in place: the suspected person shall be informed of the hearing of the child, he or she shall be given an opportunity to observe that hearing, either as it is being conducted or later from an audiovisual recording, and to have questions put to the child, either directly or indirectly, in the course of the first hearing or on a later occasion.[92]

Naturally, a suspect may waive their right to observe a hearing or have questions put to the witness. For an opportunity to observe a hearing to be effective, there should in particular be an opportunity of observing the demeanour of the witness under direct questioning. On the other hand, such an opportunity is not sufficient on its own. The Court has also ruled that although a videotape would allow the trial court and the defendant make observations of the witness's demeanour, "it cannot alone be regarded as sufficiently safeguarding the rights of the defence

90 Maffei 2006, 47.
91 Schatschaschwili v. Germany [GC], 15.12.2015, § 128–131.
92 A.S. v. Finland, 28.9.2010, § 56.

where no real opportunity to put questions to a person giving the account has been afforded by the authorities".[93]

The corroborative evidence was the main counterbalancing measure in the case of *Al-Khawaja*:

> S.T. [whose statement was read] had made her complaint to two friends, B.F. and S.H., promptly after the events in question, and that there were only minor inconsistencies between her statement and the account given by her to the two friends, who both gave evidence at the trial. Most importantly, there were strong similarities between S.T.'s description of the alleged assault and that of the other complainant, V.U., with whom there was no evidence of any collusion. In a case of indecent assault by a doctor on his patient, which took place during a private consultation where only he and the victim were present, it would be difficult to conceive of stronger corroborative evidence, especially when each of the other witnesses was called to give evidence at trial and their reliability was tested by cross-examination.[94]

If defence has had an opportunity to question a witness during the investigation stage, one might think that it means "an adequate and proper opportunity to challenge and question a witness against him [...] when he makes his statements [...]" and fulfil the requirements of Article 6. This, however, is not the case. It should be borne in mind that "evidence must normally be produced at a public hearing, in the presence of the accused, with a view to adversarial argument".[95] That is why such an opportunity does not automatically remedy a restriction of the right but may be an important counterbalancing measure.[96] Moreover, it would be a departure from the confrontational paradigm because of the absence of the trier of fact.

It is especially important to provide an opportunity for cross-examination in the pre-trial stage if the investigating authorities assume that a witness cannot be heard at a trial. Under such circumstances, it would also be pertinent to videotape the hearing and the confrontation for later use as evidence. So, if it becomes known that the witness is, for example, a foreign national about to return to their home country, a confrontation should be arranged at the investigative stage, regardless of whether it could be said later that there is a good reason for the later non-attendance of that witness from the trial court's perspective.

A defendant must always "be afforded the opportunity to give his own version of the events and to cast doubt on the credibility of the absent witness, pointing out any incoherence or inconsistency with the statements of other witnesses", which has led some to point out that such a measure would do little to counterbalance a

---

93 A.L. v. Finland, 27.1.2009, § 41 and similarly D. v. Finland, 7.7.2009, § 50.
94 Al-Khawaja and Tahery v. the United Kingdom [GC], 15.12.2011, § 156.
95 Krasniki v. the Czech Republic, 28.2.2006, § 75.
96 See for example Gani v. Spain, 19.2.2013, § 44; and Isgrò v. Italy, 19.2.1991, § 36.

restriction the defence is facing.[97] However, as with the opportunity to challenge the authenticity of the evidence and of oppose its use, discussed earlier in Sections 5.6 and 8.3, what matters most is the effectiveness of such an opportunity.

The Court mentioned in *Schatschaschwili*, referring to other case law, that

> [w]here the identity of the witness is known to the defence, the latter is able to identify and investigate any motives the witness may have for lying, and can therefore contest effectively the witness's credibility, albeit to a lesser extent than in a direct confrontation [...].[98]

Conversely, if the witness is anonymous, this will restrict the effective opportunity to cast doubt on the witness's credibility. Another important aspect of effectivity is that domestic courts should address the version given by the defendant as well as any doubts that have been raised with regard to the credibility of a witness whose statement is used as evidence.[99]

Schatschaschwili itself provides perhaps the best example of the counterbalance assessment. First, the domestic court had approached the untested evidence with caution, noting expressly the need for particular diligence because "neither the defence nor the court had been able to question and observe the demeanour of the witnesses at the trial". Second, there was "some additional incriminating hearsay and circumstantial evidence supporting the witness statements". Moving on to the procedural measures, the only counterbalance was that the applicant

> had the opportunity to give his own version of the events [...] – an opportunity of which he availed himself – and also to cast doubt on the credibility of the witnesses, whose identity had been known to him, by cross-examining the other witnesses giving hearsay evidence at his trial.[100]

On the other hand, several factors did not provide any counterbalance. First, "the applicant did not have the possibility of putting questions to [the witnesses] indirectly, for instance in writing. Moreover, neither the applicant himself nor his lawyer was given the opportunity at the investigation stage to question these witnesses". Second, no lawyer was appointed for the applicant, although that would have been possible and the lawyer "would have had the right to be present at the witness hearing before the investigating judge and, as a rule, would have had to be notified thereof". Third, the applicant was not granted an opportunity to have the witnesses questioned at the investigation stage by his lawyer although the authorities had doubted whether they could be heard at a trial. The Court concluded: "By proceeding in that manner, they took the foreseeable risk, which subsequently

---

97 S. Trechsel, *Human Rights in Criminal Proceedings* (Oxford: Oxford University Press, 2005), 313 and R. Goss, *Criminal Fair Trial Rights: Article 6 of the European Convention on Human Rights* (Oxford: Hart, 2014), 141.
98 Schatschaschwili v. Germany [GC], 15.12.2015, § 131.
99 Compare Dimović v. Serbia, 28.6.2016, § 46.
100 Schatschaschwili v. Germany [GC], 15.12.2015, §§ 146–152.

materialised, that neither the accused nor his counsel would be able to question [the witnesses] at any stage of the proceedings [...]."[101]

Apparently, the fact that a suspect cannot benefit from a lawyer during a pre-trial confrontation does not constitute a violation as such. The Court stated in *Isgrò* that "the purpose of the confrontation did not render the presence of [the applicant's] lawyer indispensable". Furthermore, the public prosecutor was likewise absent from that confrontation.[102] The United Nations Human Rights Committee has ruled in *Brown v. Jamaica*, for example, that "it is axiomatic that legal assistance be available at all stages of criminal proceedings, particularly in capital cases" and that because a witness was heard without allowing the defendant an opportunity to ensure the presence of his counsel, there had been a violation of Article 14 § 3 (d) of the ICCPR, providing the right to legal assistance similarly to Article 6 § 3 (c) of the Convention.[103]

9.7 Overall assessment

We began this chapter by comparing the Court's approach to that of SCOTUS. The preceding presentation should suffice to prove that the current *Al-Khawaja and Tahery* test is very similar to the requirements of the pre-*Crawford* case law in the United States. Let it be reminded that according to it, dispensing with confrontation required, "normally", that a witness is unavailable. This requirement is parallel to the requirement of a good reason for non-attendance. Second, if no exception to the hearsay rule applied, untested evidence was to be excluded unless there were "particularized guarantees of trustworthiness".

Of course, there are also important differences. The Court's case law has developed from the early "sole or decisive rule" epitomised in *Doorson* as well as the stringent requirement of a good reason to a more substantive model, where the importance of the untested evidence sets the bar for the counterbalancing measures. Still, the Court has reminded that the lack of a good reason and the importance of the evidence may prove decisive factors in the overall analysis. The Court seems to have adopted a kind of hybrid model of assessment, combining both procedural and substantial elements.

In the case of *Al-Khawaja*, there was a good reason for non-attendance (death) and although the untested statement was decisive evidence of guilt, there were also sufficient counterbalancing factors in place. The Court focused especially on the corroborative evidence (statements of other witnesses who were heard in open court and cross-examined), a substantive element of the test, and concluded that there was no violation. With regard to the other applicant, *Tahery*, a violation was found. Although there was a good reason (a genuine fear), the counterbalancing

---

101 Schatschaschwili v. Germany [GC], 15.12.2015, §§ 153–160.
102 Isgrò v. Italy, 19.2.1991, § 36.
103 Brown v. Jamaica, 23.3.1999, § 6.6. See also J. D. Jackson and S. J. Summers, *The Internationalisation of Criminal Evidence: Beyond the Common Law and Civil Law Traditions* (Cambridge: Cambridge University Press, 2012), 347–348.

measures (the possibility to rebut the statement and a warning to the jury) were not sufficient because of the importance of the statement.[104]

Also, in *Schatschaschwili* there was a good reason for non-attendance (unreachability in spite of all reasonable efforts). As the only eyewitness statements, the untested evidence was decisive. But the counterbalancing measures were not sufficient even though the trial court had examined the credibility of the absent witnesses carefully and there was some additional incriminating evidence. What proved decisive was that, as discussed above, the domestic investigative authorities failed to arrange legal assistance and an opportunity to cross-examine the eyewitnesses before they returned to their home country, a fact that the authorities were aware of.[105]

This judgment, by comparison, seems to have been based more on the procedural aspects of the right to cross-examination, as the following conclusion suggests:

> In the Court's view, affording the defendant the opportunity to have a key prosecution witness questioned at least during the pre-trial stage and via his counsel constitutes an important procedural safeguard securing the accused's defence rights, the absence of which weighs heavily in the balance in the examination of the overall fairness of the proceedings under Article 6 §§ 1 and 3 (d).[106]

It might be noted, though, that it is difficult to see what the trial court could have done otherwise, given that the mistake was made in the pre-trial investigation. Given that it found the evidence sufficiently reliable, there was little reason to exclude it.

The Court had to make parallel assessments of both absent witnesses and an anonymous witness in *Bátěk*, a case concerning customs officers accepting bribes from truck drivers. An undercover police officer had infiltrated their team. She was heard as the anonymous witness, whereas 20 truck drivers from various countries. There was no good reason for non-attendance (domestic courts did not resort to international legal assistance), but there was for anonymity (usefulness for future operations). The truck drivers' testimonies carried significant weight (they had described the customs officials' general practice of accepting bribes) as did that of the agent (considering the extent and weight of other evidence). The counterbalances regarding the absent witnesses included a rigorous assessment of all the evidence, the existence of other incriminating evidence, the lawfulness and judicial supervision of how the statements were obtained, that their identities were known.[107]

---

104 Al-Khawaja and Tahery v. the United Kingdom [GC], 15.12.2011, §§ 153–165.
105 Schatschaschwili v. Germany [GC], 15.12.2015, §§ 132–165.
106 Schatschaschwili v. Germany [GC], 15.12.2015, § 162.
107 Bátěk and Others v. the Czech Republic, 12.1.2017, §§ 43–54.

The anonymous witness was heard in accordance with domestic law, her identity was known to the judge conducting the hearing, the defendants were able to put questions directly to her although unable to observe her demeanour, the fact that the defendants knew her by her physical appearance. Adding in its overall assessment that there was no arbitrariness in the way the domestic courts approached the evidence and, interestingly, referring to the public interest in seeing the crime of corruption properly prosecuted, the Court concluded that "the lawfully administered procedural safeguards were, in the circumstances of the present case, capable of counterbalancing certain handicaps under which the defence laboured". There were no violations.[108]

The basic mechanism of the *Al-Khawaja and Tahery* test is relatively simple and consists of three factors: the reason(s) for using untested evidence in trial instead of hearing a witness in open court, the significance of that evidence and the existence of counterbalances which must be sufficient in relation to the significance. Each of these factors will assume their own weight in a specific situation, in favour of either fairness or unfairness. The counterbalances should be assessed cumulatively. But I fear the Court will have to revisit some aspects of that test to provide more guidance to how it should be applied.

I have already outlined my criticism at how the Court has applied the "carried significant weight" standard, bypassing statements of domestic courts. In *Sitnevskiy and Chaykovskiy* the Court ruled that when untested statements did not even carry significant weight, it was not necessary to review the existence of counterbalancing factors at all. However, the statements in question did not – at least directly – incriminate the applicants because the witnesses were unaware of their identities. As noted above, the standard seems to approach the level of "probative" evidence. That, of course, was explicitly dismissed in *Al-Khawaja and Tahery* where the Court underlined a narrow interpretation of the "sole or decisive" standard.

In *Seton*, the Court referred to *Schatschaschwili* and explained that "the assessment of 'counterbalancing factors' is a relative one: the extent of the counterbalancing factors necessary in order for a trial to be considered fair depends on the importance of the absent-witness evidence".[109] One potential reason for the Court's willingness to expand the counterbalance assessment is that it wants to keep the test flexible and require, in effect, that the counterbalances – many of which are hallmarks of a fair trial anyway – should be examined even when the untested evidence carries less than decisive weight. Of course, if this is indeed the case, it would be better to do so more openly.

So, by applying the lower threshold the Court can achieve a more flexible overall assessment model. Let us also remember that it has been eager to assess the counterbalances even after finding that an applicant has effectively waived their right to cross-examination. I see this as another indication of its willingness to incorporate the counterbalances as an indispensable part of the *Al-Khawaja and*

108 Bátěk and Others v. the Czech Republic, 12.1.2017, §§ 55–63.
109 Seton v. the United Kingdom, 31.3.2016, § 68.

Tahery test, only to be left out if the interference with the right to cross-examination is negligible. In other words, it would always be safest to examine the counterbalancing measures, even when that evidence is not sole nor decisive.

The Court adopted an interesting model of reasoning in *Rastoder*, where the domestic courts had admitted the statements of two absent witnesses, anonymised as I.B. and Še.A. There was no good reason for their non-attendance. I.B.'s statement was found irrelevant for the applicant's conviction, whereas Še.A.'s statement was used to established certain facts amongst a body of other evidence. That evidence was not considered "sole or decisive" for the applicant's conviction. Furthermore, the Court found it "unnecessary to determine whether the evidence nevertheless carried significant weight because, even if it did, there existed sufficient factors counterbalancing any handicaps that its admission might have entailed for the defence", as it then proceeded to below. They included an opportunity to cross-examination during the investigative stage, that the applicant had not requested the use of videoconference or a similar measure, as well as the opportunity to challenge their reliability, which he failed to do. Lastly, the domestic court had examined the evidence carefully and referred to Še.A.'s statement only as supportive evidence.[110]

9.8 The rule against untested evidence

Many countries allow the use of untested statements either when a witness cannot be reached or refuses to give answers when examined. Previous statements might also be used as material for comparison if a witness changes their story between investigation and trial. The Court has not, as far as I know, applied the *Al-Khawaja and Tahery* test in such situations which actually do not limit the cross-examination in any significant way. However, the test would become applicable if a witness refuses to answer clearly relevant questions. The lack of an effective opportunity to cross-examine such a witness would call for a careful examination of the credibility of their previous statements, if they are used instead.

At the same time, it should be noted that "cross-examination should not be used as a means of intimidating or humiliating witnesses", as the Court stated in *Y. v. Slovenia*. In that case, a defendant was allowed to ask questions of a distinctly personal nature, sometimes repetitively. Some of the questions included suggestions which "were not aimed only at attacking the applicant's credibility, but were also meant to denigrate her character". Although this was not the only issue, the Court's final conclusion was that the domestic authorities had failed in finding an appropriate balance between the rights of the witness and the right of the defendant. It found a violation of Article 8.[111]

Any departure from the confrontational paradigm (i.e. that witness statements must normally be produced at a public hearing, in the presence of the accused, with a view to adversarial argument) could violate the defence rights and must be

110 Rastoder v. Slovenia, 28.11.2017, §§ 57–65.
111 Y. v. Slovenia, 28.5.2015, §§ 101–116.

174 The right to cross-examine prosecution witnesses

strictly necessary to be justifiable. Moreover, if a less restrictive measure can suffice, then that measure should be applied. The other side of this principle is that the onus will be on the trial court to ensure that there are sufficient factual or legal grounds for a restriction, and that every reasonable effort has been made to reach the witnesses and secure the accused an effective opportunity to cross-examine them.

There is no reason to question the various domestic legal frameworks as long as they provide the tools to secure the attendance of witnesses. More often the problem has been that attempts to reach a witness have been ineffective and judicial control superficial before allowing the use of statements which should be a measure of last resort. The requirement of a good reason means, from the domestic viewpoint, that strict scrutiny must precede a decision to allow untested or anonymous evidence against the accused. This must also become apparent from the trial court's reasoning.

Of course, due consideration should be given to the specifics of the situation. For example, if the defendant is on remand, the attempts to reach a witness cannot take a very long time. On the other hand, the mere fact that a witness resides abroad is not, in itself, a valid reason to dispense with hearing them. Instead, attempts should be made to reach them through international legal aid. As a rule, the defence should have an opportunity to have key witnesses questioned at least during the pre-trial stage. Sometimes, "a good reason" to use statements might be quite obvious, such as the witness's death or invoking a legal privilege.

Domestic courts should also clearly indicate their view on the importance of untested evidence. This would be important for determining the impact of a restriction. If there is plenty of other evidence and the untested statement is used as a corroborating piece of evidence or otherwise to a limited extent, this would, on its own, counterbalance a restriction. Secondly, a domestic court's view on whether the impugned evidence is "sole or decisive" should also be the starting point if the case reaches the Court. Finally, the weight of the evidence determines how much counterbalancing is required for a trial to remain fair as a whole.

The counterbalancing measures include both substantive and procedural elements. The former include the trial court's approach to the untested evidence, which must be critical, and the requirement that there is corroborative evidence. The more procedural elements include effective alternative measures to substitute the lack of cross-examination, such as a video-recorded confrontation during pre-trial investigation, a possibility to have questions put to the witness indirectly, and an effective opportunity to challenge the credibility of a witness at the trial.

Because of the increased flexibility of the *Al-Khawaja and Tahery* test, it seems that all three steps discussed above should be addressed before convicting a defendant. This can probably to some extent take place as part of the evaluation of evidence. At least if the trial court finds that the reliability of an untested evidence cannot be controlled to a sufficient degree, it should normally dismiss the charge. A domestic court of appeal would, in turn, be in a good position to review a judgment and apply the test. I suspect, however, that the bar for dismissing charges on mostly procedural grounds would be quite high in many countries.

Lastly, I would say that while the Court has not used a mechanism of presumption in this context either, it could be a rule of thumb that when there is no good reason for the non-attendance of a key witness, this would create a presumption of unfairness. If, on the other hand, there is a good reason and/or the evidence is less important, a more holistic approach should be taken, and the counterbalances need not be as heavy as if the evidence is decisive. As I see it, the test is mainly intended to protect the right to cross-examine important witnesses, which should not be too much to ask, given the dangers in admitting untested statements.

10 Conclusion

I set out to prove that Article 6 of the Convention, protecting the right to a fair trial, can give rise to rules of evidence. First, the Court itself creates rules of evidence by developing assessment models with various criteria to determine whether a trial has been fair as a whole. Nowadays this happens often through grand chamber judgments where the Court makes an overview of its previous case law and attempts to explain or clarify it. Even if a grand chamber judgment effectively modifies a rule of evidence, the Court sometimes attempts to disguise this, leaving domestic actors asking for transparency.

That being said, the Court is not facing an easy task. It has to balance between an increased caseload, several legal traditions, and the political situations of 46 Member States. Statistics from 2020 reveal that almost the Court's judgments that year concerned only three Member States: Russia, Turkey, and Ukraine.[1] Needless to say, this would indicate that the convention system has not been working in these countries as intended, encouraging effective diffusion and filtering effects. Decreased compliance seems to be the price that has to be paid for increased participation, although this does create the obvious paradox: why participate if you won't comply?

My main objective has been to make compliance easier by offering the interpretations of one domestic judge on the Court's case law in one specific area: evidence law. In Finland, the relevant legislation has been amended recently to better reflect the rules of evidence the Court has developed. Additionally, the domestic supreme court often refers to the Court's case law, acting both as a diffuser and a filter. The task of translating the Court's rules of evidence into domestic ones should, of course, be left to the domestic authorities who are best placed to bring together the human rights perspective and the domestic legal tradition and framework.

To help understand how the Court's rules of evidence work, I have developed a simple theoretical framework abbreviated as SIC. I hope to have shown that the possible mechanical components of such rules are seriousness, impact and counterbalancing of an infringement. Some violations are considered so serious that no counterbalancing can take place. That is why the Court has required that torture evidence and entrapment evidence must be excluded altogether, or a similar

---

1 *The European Court of Human Rights in Facts and Figures* (European Court of Human Rights/Public Relations Unit, 2021), 3.

DOI: 10.4324/9781003311416-10

consequence apply. In other words, any impact of these violations must be purged. The third component has no room in the mechanism of these rigid rules of evidence.

The privilege against self-incrimination, by comparison, is not equally absolute. Although protected under Article 6, only violations which destroy the very essence of the privilege are considered unfair. This reflects the slightly less serious nature of the violation. It is noteworthy that the Court has been reluctant to find any counterbalancing measures as being able to alleviate violations. In my opinion, this is because the primary rationale of the privilege is to protect the will of the accused and it would be difficult to counterbalance a violation once it has happened. The fact that the impugned evidence might prove reliable, for example, does not relate to the primary rationale of the rule.

The rest of the rules of evidence discussed above include also the third component, counterbalancing. The general idea is simple: if the seriousness of the infringement is not excessive and if its impact can be counterbalanced, some measures can suffice to restore the overall fairness of a trial. Whether this is possible and what counterbalances could be used depends on the nature of an infringement and its impact which, in turn, reflect the rationale of the rule. The weight needed to counterbalance a restriction of defence rights depends on both the seriousness and impact of the restriction.

The difference is that the other rules of evidence give greater weight – at least under certain circumstances – to whether a restriction has affected the reliability of evidence or not. This is why a violation of a procedural nature is not necessarily determinative in the contexts of other improperly obtained evidence or untested evidence, as long as the evaluation of evidence has been done properly. It should be stressed that the right to a fair trial is, above all, a procedural right and cannot be reduced into a corroboration rule in those contexts either. But the properly controlled reliability of the impugned evidence may act as a counterbalance of some procedural violations.

I hope to have kept my promise of trying to understand rather than criticise the Court. This has not prevented me from pointing out some inconsistencies in the case law. But the emergence of some gaps is probably unavoidable, given that the Court is confined to deciding individual complaints. In doing so, it sometimes adopts handy shortcuts known to any domestic judge. These include placing burdens on the parties or making conclusion based on that a party, either an applicant or the respondent government, do not expressly dispute some claims made by their opponent.

Finally, I have attempted to summarise the Court's approach at the end of each chapter and to provide the reader with at least some idea of what effects any single rule of evidence might have for the domestic law of evidence. These remarks have been quite crude and should be approached with a healthy criticism as well as keeping in mind that I have no knowledge of evidence law in most of the 46 Member States. Still, at least my observations might offer some food for thought. It remains to be seen how the Court's case law will develop and whether the remarks made here will stand the test of time.

Bibliography

A. Aarnio, *Mitä lainoppi on?* (Helsinki: Tammi, 1978)

R. Alexy, *A Theory of Constitutional Rights* (Oxford: Oxford University Press, 2002)

J. Baggini, *A Short History of Truth. Consolations for a Post-Truth World* (London: Quercus, 2017)

M. D. Bayles, *Principles of Law: A Normative Analysis* (Dordrecht: D. Reidel Publishing Company, 1987)

J. Bentham, *A Treatise on Judicial Evidence* (London: J. W. Paget, 1825)

J. Bentham, "An Introductory View of the Rationale of Evidence" in J. Bowring (ed.), *The Works of Jeremy Bentham*, vol. VI (Edinburgh: William Tait, 1843)

F. Bex and B. Verheij, "Legal Stories and the Process of Proof" (2013) 21 *Artificial Intelligence and Law*, 253

D. T. Björgvinsson, "The Effect of the Judgments of the ECtHR before the National Courts – A Nordic Approach?" (2016) 85 *Nordic Journal of International Law*, 303

R. Clayton and H. Tomlinson, *The Law of Human Rights*, vol. I (Oxford: Oxford University Press, 2000)

A. L-T. Choo, *Evidence*, 2nd edn (Oxford: Oxford University Press, 2015)

M. Dahlberg, *Do You Know It When You See It? A Study on the Judicial Legitimacy of the European Court of Human Rights* (Joensuu: University of Eastern Finland, 2015)

C. Diesen, *Bevisprövning i brottmål*, 2nd edn (Stockholm: Norstedts juridik, 2015)

R. Dworkin, *Taking Rights Seriously* (Cambridge, MA: Harvard University Press, 1978)

F. Eder, *Beweisverbote und Beweislast im Strafprozess* (Munich: Herbert Utz Verlag, 2015)

M. Fredman, *Puolustajan rooli: Rikoksesta epäillyn ja syytetyn avustajan roolin kehitys Suomessa 1980-luvulta nykypäivään* (Helsinki: Alma Talent, 2018)

R. Glover, *Murphy on Evidence*, 15th edn (Oxford: Oxford University Press, 2017)

A. I. Goldman, *Epistemology and Cognition* (Cambridge, MA: Harvard University Press, 1986)

R. Goss, *Criminal Fair Trial Rights: Article 6 of the European Convention on Human Rights* (Oxford: Hart, 2014)

M. G. Haselton, D. Nettle, and P. W. Andrews, "The Evolution of Cognitive Bias" in D. M. Buss (ed.), *Handbook of Evolutionary Psychology* (Hoboken, NJ: Wiley, 2005)

M. Heghmanns, "Beweisverwertungsverbote und Fernwirkung" (2010) 2010 *Zeitschrift für das Juristische Studium*, 98

L. R. Helfer, "Nonconsensual International Lawmaking" (2008) 2008 *University of Illinois Law Review*, 71

J. D. Jackson and S. J. Summers, *The Internationalisation of Criminal Evidence: Beyond the Common Law and Civil Law Traditions* (Cambridge: Cambridge University Press, 2012)

D. Kosař, J. Petrov, K. Šipulová, H. Smekal, L. Vyhnánek, and J. Janovský, *Domestic Judicial Treatment of European Court of Human Rights Case Law: Beyond Compliance* (Abingdon: Routledge, 2020)

G. Letsas, *A Theory of Interpretation of the European Convention on Human Rights* (Oxford: Oxford University Press, 2007)

R. L. Lippke, *Taming the Presumption of Innocence* (Oxford: Oxford University Press, 2016)

J.-P. Loof, "Is Judicial Dialogue the Answer to the Challenges the ECHR is Facing?" (2015) 40 *Nederlands Tijdschrift voor de Mensenrechten*, 463

U. Lundqvist, *Bevisförbud: En undersökning av möjligheterna att avvisa oegentligt åtkommen bevisning i brottmålsrättegång* (Uppsala: Iustus förlag, 1998)

Y. Lupu and E. Voeten, "The Role of Precedent at the European Court of Human Rights: A Network Analysis of Case Citations" (2010) Paper 12 (http://opensiuc.lib.siu.edu/pnconfs_2010/12)

M. Madden, "A Model Rule for Excluding Improperly or Unconstitutionally Obtained Evidence" (2015) 33 *Berkeley Journal of International Law*, 442

S. Maffei, *The European Right to Confrontation in Criminal Proceedings: Absent, Anonymous and Vulnerable Witnesses* (Groningen: Europa Law Publishing, 2006)

P. McNamara, "The Canons of Evidence – Rules of Exclusion or Rules of Use?" (1986) 10 *The Adelaide Law Review*, 341

P. Mirfield, *Silence, Confessions and Improperly Obtained Evidence* (Oxford: Clarendon Press, 1997)

A. Mowbray, "An Examination of the European Court of Human Rights' Approach to Overruling Its Previous Case Law" (2009) 9 *Human Rights Law Review*, 179

B. Murphy and J. Anderson, "After the Serpent Beguiled Me: Entrapment and Sentencing in Australia and Canada" (2014) 39 *Queen's Law Journal*, 621

A. Nordlander, "Förklaringsbördan i brottmål och dess förenlighet med oskyldighetspresumtionen" (2017) 2017 *Svensk Juristtidning*, 653

M. S. Pardo, "The Field of Evidence and the Field of Knowledge" (2005) 24 *Law and Philosophy*, 321

R. Pattenden, "Admissibility in Criminal Proceedings of Third Party and Real Evidence Obtained by Methods Prohibited by UNCAT" (2006) 10 *International Journal of Evidence & Proof*, 1

N. Pennington and R. Hastie, "A Cognitive Theory of Juror Decision Making: The Story Model" (1991) 13 *Cardozo Law Review*, 519

B. Rainey, E. Wicks, and C. Ovey, *Jacobs, White and Ovey: The European Convention on Human Rights*, 7th edn (Oxford: Oxford University Press, 2017)

J. Rawls, *A theory of justice*, rev. edn (Cambridge, MA: Harvard University Press, 1999)

M. Redmayne, "A Corroboration Approach to Recovered Memories of Sexual Abuse: A Note of Caution" (2000) 116 *Law Quarterly Review*, 147

A. Ross, *On law and justice* (Berkeley, CA: University of California Press, 1959)

D. K. Rossmo and J. M. Pollock, "Confirmation Bias and Other Systemic Causes of Wrongful Convictions: A Sentinel Events Perspective" (2019) 11 *Northeastern University Law Review*, 970

L. Schelin, *Bevisvärdering av utsagor i brottmål* (Stockholm: Stockholms Universitet, 2007)

A. Stone Sweet, "Constitutional Politics in France and Germany", in M. Shapiro and A. Stone Sweet, *On Law, Politics, & Judicialization* (Oxford: Oxford University Press, 2002)

A. Stone Sweet, "Judicialization and the Construction of Governance", in M. Shapiro and A. Stone Sweet, *On Law, Politics, & Judicialization* (Oxford: Oxford University Press, 2002)

J. Thibaut, L. Walker, S. LaTour, and P. Houlden, "Procedural Justice as Fairness" (1974) 26 *Stanford Law Review*, 1271

J. J. Tomkovicz, *Constitutional Exclusion* (Oxford: Oxford University Press, 2011)

S. Trechsel, *Human Rights in Criminal Proceedings* (Oxford: Oxford University Press, 2005)

L. H. Tribe, *American constitutional law*, 2nd edn (New York: The Foundation Press, 1988)

J. I. Turner, "The Exclusionary Rule as a Symbol of the Rule of Law" (2014) 67 *SMU Law Review*, 821

A. Tversky and D. Kahneman, "Judgment under Uncertainty: Heuristics and Biases" (1974) 185 *Science*, 1124

J. H. Wigmore, *A Treatise on the Anglo-American System of Evidence in Trials at Common Law*, 2nd edn (Boston, MA: Little, Brown and Company, 1923)

A. A. S. Zuckerman, *The Principles of Criminal Evidence* (Oxford: Clarendon Press, 1989)

Official materials

Crown Court Compendium. Part I: Jury and Trial Management and Summing Up (Judicial College, 2021)

The European Court of Human Rights in Facts and Figures (The European Court of Human Rights/Public Relations Unit, 2021)

Guide on Article 6 of the European Convention on Human Rights: Right to a fair trial (criminal limb), The European Court of Human Rights, 1 February 2022, 31 December 2021.

Hallituksen esitys eduskunnalle oikeudenkäymiskaaren 17 luvun ja siihen liittyvän todistelua yleisissä tuomioistuimissa koskevan lainsäädännön uudistamiseksi (HE 46/2014 vp)

The Law Commission, Report on defences of general application (*Law Com.* No. 83, 1977)

Rules of Court, The European Court of Human Rights, 1 February 2022.

Index